Race Politics in Britain and France

Ideas and Policymaking since the 1960s

Since the 1960s, Britain and France have developed substantially different policies to manage racial tensions, in spite of having similar numbers of postwar ethnic minority immigrants. This book provides the first detailed historical exploration of race policy development in these two countries, tracing the sources of Britain's race relations structures and France's antiracism approach. In this path-breaking work, Erik Bleich argues against common wisdom that attributes policy outcomes to the role of powerful interest groups or to the constraints of existing institutions, instead emphasizing the importance of frames – widely held ideas that propelled policymaking in different directions. British policymakers' framing of race and racism principally in North American terms of color discrimination encouraged them to import many policies from across the Atlantic. For decades after World War II, by contrast, French policy leaders' race frames revolved around anti-Semitism, hate speech, and race blindness, guiding French policies down a significantly different path from that taken in Britain.

Erik Bleich is Assistant Professor of Political Science at Middlebury College, where he was appointed Director of European Studies in 2001. He has written on issues of multiculturalism, race, and the role of ideas in policymaking for journals such as *Comparative Politics, Comparative Political Studies,* and *French Politics, Culture and Society*, as well as for popular media such as the British newspaper *The Guardian.*

Race Politics in Britain and France

Ideas and Policymaking since the 1960s

ERIK BLEICH
Middlebury College

CAMBRIDGE UNIVERSITY PRESS
Cambridge, New York, Melbourne, Madrid, Cape Town,
Singapore, São Paulo, Delhi, Mexico City

Cambridge University Press
32 Avenue of the Americas, New York, NY 10013-2473, USA

www.cambridge.org
Information on this title: www.cambridge.org/9780521009539

First published 2003
Reprinted 2012

A catalog record for this publication is available from the British Library.

Library of Congress Cataloging in Publication Data

Bleich, Erik.
Race politics in Britain and France : ideas and policymaking since the 1960s / Erik Bleich.
p. cm.
Includes bibliographical references and index.
ISBN 0-521-81101-5 – ISBN 0-521-00953-7 (pbk.)
1. Great Britain – Race relations – History – 20th century. 2. Great Britain – Race relations – Government policy. 3. France – Race relations – History – 20th century. 4. Blacks – Great Britain – History – 20th century. 5. Blacks – Great Britain – Politics and government. 6. France – Race relations – Government policy. 7. Blacks – France – History – 20th century. 8. Blacks – France – Politics and government. I. Title.
DA125.A1 B595 2003
305.8′00941′09045–dc21 2002031362

ISBN 978-0-521-81101-9 Hardback
ISBN 978-0-521-00953-9 Paperback

Contents

Preface and Acknowledgments

Writing on race is no easy task because the term has no clear meaning. What are, for example, the boundaries that distinguish one "race" from another? Given that there are no biological bases for deciding whether there is such a thing as the "Irish race," the "Jewish race," or the "black race," perhaps it is better to avoid such a loaded term altogether. And if the word is so ambiguous, controversial, or counterproductive, what purpose is served by devoting a book to the subject of "race politics" and "race policies"?

The topic of race arrived brusquely on my agenda when I was wrongfully arrested in December 1995 in Brixton, South London, during what was characterized by some as a race riot. My one phone call after a long night in jail was to a friend who, instead of recommending a lawyer, put me in touch with a journalist. Very early in our discussion, the reporter said that she hated to ask this, but was I by any chance black? One year later, while conducting interviews in Paris, a learned scholar stopped me short upon entering her office: What ethnicity was I, that I was writing a book on race?

Race is certainly an ambiguous word. It is a problematic concept that must be investigated rather than simply accepted. Yet, it remains incredibly meaningful. The term is used – or consciously avoided – because of its power to describe, to stigmatize, or to imply things about the world in which we live. "Race politics" and "race policy" are therefore employed in this book to describe the politics and policies surrounding issues of "race" as the term is widely understood by the general public. The goal is to shed light on how ideas about race, racism, and antiracism translate into politics and policymaking in two important European states.

Although they have managed these issues in substantially different ways, Britain and France have developed strategies for dealing with race that affect their millions of citizens and that serve as potential models for countries around the world. For this reason alone, not only is it possible to write about race, it is imperative.

Over the course of this book's seven-year trajectory, I have accumulated far more debts than I can acknowledge or repay. Financially, I have drawn sustenance from the National Science Foundation, the Social Science and Humanities Research Council of Canada, the Krupp Foundation, and the Mellon Foundation. I have also benefited from the institutional support of the Department of Government, the Graduate Student Council and the Center for European Studies at Harvard University, and Middlebury College. I owe particular thanks to the Center for European Studies at Harvard University and to Middlebury College, institutional homes that enabled me to develop my ideas and to complete my writing. I also gratefully acknowledge the journals *Comparative Political Studies* and *French Politics, Culture and Society* for allowing me to use materials published in their pages in portions of the Introduction and in parts of Chapters 1, 5, 6, and 7 of this book.

More than to any institution, however, I am thankful to certain individuals. I had the privilege of working with five mentors, each of whom nurtured my curiosity and helped me translate it into this book. Stanley Hoffmann's wisdom and wit inspired me to pursue the study of politics when I was an undergraduate, and his vast knowledge and skeptical eye tempered my occasional tendency to reach conclusions where further reflection was required. Daniel Goldhagen pressed me always to think about the bigger picture; and his sage advice led me away from studying narrow subject matter and ultimately toward issues of race and ethnicity. Paul Pierson offered friendly yet pinpoint feedback on how to deal with the thorny problems of studying policymaking from a theoretical angle. Patrick Weil has supported my interests in politics since we first met in his classroom at the Institut d'Etudes Politiques in the fall of 1989; in Paris during 1996 and 1997 he provided me with an intellectual home in the Centre d'Etude des Politiques d'Immigration, d'Intégration et de Citoyenneté (CEPIC) as well as with contacts in the world of the French policy elite. Finally, no young scholar could hope for a better mentor than Peter Hall, who read countless drafts of this book and examined, questioned, and criticized virtually every thought within it. Although none of these individuals is responsible for the content of this book, it would not exist today were it not for them.

Numerous other scholars have also had an immeasurable impact on this book through their careful readings and thoughtful comments. For taking the time to read and comment on the entire manuscript, I would especially like to thank Sheri Berman, Gary Freeman, Randall Hansen, James Hollifield, Ira Katznelson, Anthony Messina, and Abigail Saguy. For discussing portions of the project in its various incarnations and for influencing my thinking, I am also grateful to Karen Alter, Jeff Checkel, Pepper Culpepper, Matthew Dickinson, Adrian Favell, Andrew Geddes, Virginie Guiraudon, Brian Hanson, Stephen Hanson, Lauren Kiefer, Desmond King, Michèle Lamont, Judith Layzer, Robert Lieberman, Jill Parsons, Robert Pekkanen, Saadia Pekkanen, Shamit Saggar, Ted Sasson, Martin Schain, John Skrentny, Yasemin Soysal, Allison Stanger, Pierre-André Taguieff, Steven Teles, Elaine Thomas, Emmanuel Todd, Michèle Tribalat, Gunnar Trumbull, Maurits van der Veen, and Michel Wieviorka. Many thanks in addition to all those I interviewed in Britain and France and to the librarians and archivists who enabled me to access documents that proved crucial to forming my arguments in this book.

Finally, to my family – my large, far-flung, multinational family – and to my friends. You have helped to make me the person I am today. Without your love, this book would not have been possible. And to my wife, Jennifer Oster Bleich. Thank you for reading every word of this book (twice), for inspiring me to song, and for bringing me bundles of joy. You make it all worthwhile.

Abbreviations and Acronyms

ACE	Archives of the French Council of State (Conseil d'Etat)
AN	Assemblée Nationale (French National Assembly), followed by the number of the legislature (of the French Fifth Republic, unless otherwise noted) and the document reference and page number(s), or by the date of publication of the parliamentary debate in the Journal Officiel and page number(s)
ANF	Archives Nationales, Fontainbleau
APM	Archives of the Prime Minister's Office (Matignon), France
CARD	Campaign Against Racial Discrimination
CFDT	Confédération Française Démocratique du Travail
CGT	Confédération Générale du Travail
CIAC	Commonwealth Immigrants Advisory Council
CNCDH	Commission Nationale Consultative des Droits de l'Homme
CRIF	Conseil Représentatif des Juifs de France
EEOC	Equal Employment Opportunity Commission
FAS	Fonds d'Action Sociale (pour les Travailleurs Immigrés et leurs Familles)
Hansard	British Parliamentary Debates (House of Commons unless otherwise noted), followed by the volume number and the column number(s)
ICERD	International Convention on the Elimination of All Forms of Racial Discrimination, United Nations

JODP	Journal Officiel (de la République Française) Débats Parlementaires
JOLD	Journal Officiel (de la République Française: Edition des) Lois et Décrets, followed by the date of publication and the number of the law
LICA	Ligue Internationale Contre l'Antisémitisme. Became LICRA in 1979
LICRA	Ligue Internationale Contre le Racisme et l'Antisémitisme
LPA	Labour Party Archives
MJA I	Ministry of Justice Archives (France). No. 1513-1-A Tome I: Ministère de la Justice; Service Legislatif; Discriminations Raciales, Projet de loi et Prop de loi. Located in the ANF
MJA II	Ministry of Justice Archives (France). No. 1513-1-A Tome II: Ministère de la Justice; Service Legislatif; Discriminations Raciales, Props de loi. Located in the ANF
MJA III	Ministry of Justice Archives (France). No. 1513-1-A Tome III: Racisme; Ministère de la Justice; Direction des affaires criminelles et des grâces; sous-direction de la législation criminelle; Loi du 1er juillet 1972 relative à la lutte contre le racisme. Located in the Ministry of Justice
MRAP	Mouvement contre le Racisme et pour l'Amitié entre les Peuples, 1977–present; Mouvement contre le Racisme, l'Antisémitisme et pour la Paix, 1949–77
MRP	Mouvement Républicain Populaire
NCCI	National Committee for Commonwealth Immigrants
PCF	Parti Communiste Française
PRO	Public Record Office, UK
PS	Parti Socialiste
RPR	Rassemblement Pour la République
S	Senate of the French Fifth Republic, followed by the session number, year, document number and page number(s), or by the date of publication of the parliamentary debate in the Journal Officiel and page number(s)
UDF	Union pour la Démocratie Française
UDR	Union pour la Défense de la République
UNR	Union pour la Nouvelle République

Introduction

We live in an age of diversity. Relatively porous borders and inexpensive international transportation have promoted ethnic mixing on every continent. Post-World War II migration has unfurled to the tremendous benefit of hundreds of millions of people. It has generated economic prosperity, provided new cultural repertoires, and enhanced understanding of different values and worldviews. Diversity is celebrated in the media, in schools and universities, and in the workplace as the essence of the contemporary world.

At the same time as diversity brings indisputable advantages, however, it also generates challenges. Fears related to economic well-being, social status, or national identity can make people suspicious of difference and can heighten tension across what anthropologist Clifford Geertz (1973) refers to as primordial lines – those of race, ethnicity, language, region, and religion.[1] In particular, racism in its many guises has singled out individuals and groups for differential treatment. It has inspired quotidian injustices, structural disadvantages, and passionate hatreds. In its extreme forms, racism has resulted in violence, murder, and genocide. Coping with racism is therefore a crucial challenge for enlightened societies that seek to reap the rewards of diversity while minimizing its dangers.

Throughout most of the second half of the twentieth century, people concerned with race and racism have focused primarily on places like the Jim Crow United States or apartheid South Africa, and on the civil rights and anticolonial movements that have fought racial domination around

[1] Geertz (1973: 261–3) identifies the following primordial attachments: assumed blood ties, race, language, region, religion, and custom.

TABLE 1. *Foreign Population in Selected European Countries (Absolute and Percent of Total Population)*

	1960		1976		1990		1998	
	Absolute	%	Absolute	%	Absolute	%	Absolute	%
France	–	4.7	3,442	6.6	3,608	6.4	3,697	6.3
Germany	686	1.2	3,948	6.4	5,242	8.2	7,320	8.9
Great Britain	–	–	1,542	2.9	1,875	3.3	2,208	3.8
Netherlands	118	1.0	351	2.6	692	4.6	662	4.2

Sources: Soysal (1994: 23) for 1960, 1976, and 1990; SOPEMI (2000) for 1998 foreign population, except France; INSEE (1999) for 1998 French foreign population (http://www.recensement.insee.fr/); United Nations (1998) for 1998 total populations.

the world.[2] Almost one hundred years ago W. E. B. Du Bois famously proclaimed that "the problem of the twentieth century is the problem of the color line," defined as "the relation of the darker to the lighter races of men in Asia and Africa, in America and in the islands of the sea" (Du Bois 1989 [1903]: 10). As perceptive as Du Bois and other scholars have been, they have typically overlooked one troubled region now faced with similar tensions – Western Europe.

In recent decades, European countries have been forced to confront racism, largely due to the influx of millions of "nonwhite" immigrants since World War II.[3] Of course, in comparison to the United States, South Africa, or Brazil, Europe does not appear to be highly ethnically diverse. Nonetheless, it is incorrect to perceive Britain, France, Germany, the Netherlands, and most other West European countries as racially homogeneous. Over the past half-century, the percentage of ethnic minorities in these states has climbed significantly, as Table 1 suggests. Foreigners comprise between 3 and 10 percent of many European countries, and although not all of those foreigners are nonwhite, many nonwhites are not captured in statistics on foreigners because they are full citizens of these states. It is difficult to trace precisely the color line across the European continent, but as Tables 1 and 3 illustrate for Britain and France, ethnic minorities make up considerable percentages of national

[2] For one of the best of the recent comparative books in this vein, see Marx (1998). For a clarion call for decolonization, see Fanon (1966 [1961]).

[3] It is difficult to find neutral, accurate terms to describe populations in a book on this topic. With full knowledge of the drawbacks of terms such as nonwhite and ethnic minority, I use them here – synonymously and usually without quotation marks – for the sake of simplicity and because they convey to most readers a common-sense understanding of the population to which I refer.

TABLE 2. *Population in Britain by Ethnic Group, 1991 (Absolute and Percent of Total Population)*

	Absolute	%
Black	890,700	1.6
Chinese and others	644,700	1.2
South Asian	1,497,600	2.7
Total ethnic minorities	3,015,100	5.5

Source: NEMDA Key data on minority and ethnic groups in Great Britain (http://www.warwick.ac.uk/~errac/keyinf.htm).

TABLE 3. *French Residents Born outside of France by Region, 1999 (Absolute and Percent of Total Population)*

	Absolute	%
Born in the EU	1,839,606	3.1
Born outside the EU	4,028,636	6.9
Total born outside France	5,868,242	10.0

Source: INSEE (1999) (http://www.recensement.insee.fr/).

populations. Moreover, because of their concentration in metropolitan areas, they have become an extremely visible and integral part of life in most major European cities.

European countries were not always quick to recognize or to embrace their multiculturalism. By the last two decades of the twentieth century, however, the issues associated with diversity began to rise to the fore of political agendas across the continent. Most frequently, this manifested itself as a concern about immigration and immigrant integration. Because much of the present ethnic diversity in Europe owes its origin to large-scale postwar immigration, the topic of racism must in part be seen as linked to issues of immigrant integration. Consequently, any exploration of race in Europe must orient itself within (and draw inspiration from) the field of integration studies, defined broadly to include scholarship on issues of civil, social, and political rights; citizenship acquisition; and overviews of policies toward immigrants in one or more countries.

Numerous works have demonstrated that countries faced with similar challenges of integration are capable of dramatically different responses, a conclusion that also holds for the domain of race policies examined in this book. Cross-national divergence in the sphere of European immigration policies was highlighted as early as the late 1970s by Gary Freeman, who noted the more economic approach of the French as contrasted with the more racial approach of the British (1979: 309). Rogers Brubaker's (1992) landmark study of the distinction between Germany's ethnic and France's civic conceptions of citizenship helped to draw renewed attention to integration policies across European countries in the 1990s. More recent research has underlined the different national approaches to incorporation (Soysal 1994), citizenship (Thomas 1998), identity negotiation (Kastoryano 1996), managing immigrant political activity (Ireland 1994, Soysal 1994), and integration broadly defined (Favell 1998, Joppke 1999, Lapeyronnie 1993, Schnapper 1992, Todd 1994).[4] To the extent that works on integration of immigrants have treated issues of race and racism, however, they have done so only partially. The way a country fights racism is typically analyzed in passing, with much more attention devoted to the rights accorded to immigrants or to the nation's citizenship policies.

One major goal of this book is to turn the spotlight of inquiry squarely on race policies. Race policies are those that seek to manage the issues that arise from racial and ethnic diversity, the most prominent of which is racism itself. Although concerns about race and racism cannot be wholly divorced from issues of immigrant integration (as is often done in North America), they must be seen as semi-autonomous, because race policies are not simply targeted at immigrants. Moreover, as growing percentages of ethnic minorities within Europe become citizens through birth or naturalization, race and racism will stake out increasing independence from concerns about immigration and integration. In short, sorting through the complex relationship between immigration, integration, and race in Europe does indeed demonstrate that there are interactions between the spheres, but it also draws attention to the importance of race policies as objects of inquiry in their own right.

[4] Equally important as background for this study and for my thinking are works that investigate immigration policies per se, highlighting similarities and differences across European countries (Guiraudon 2000, Hollifield 1992, Money 1999), cross-national studies of race relations that compare a European country to the United States (Glazer and Young 1983, Katznelson 1976, Lamont 2000, Lieberman 2001), and individual country studies of integration in Britain and France (Feldblum 1999, Hansen 2000, Hargreaves 1995, Layton-Henry 1992, Modood and Berthoud 1997, Paul 1997, Silverman 1992, Tribalat 1995, Weil 1991). In addition to the book-length treatments, there have been a number of shorter explorations of comparative aspects of integration that also serve as orientation points for this study (Crowley 1993, Lloyd 1991, Weil and Crowley 1994, Weir 1995).

Even a cursory glance reveals that racism is a critical issue in Europe, deserving of much more attention than it has traditionally garnered.Fourteen percent of respondents in a 2000 European Union (EU) survey were categorized by their opinions as openly intolerant because they "display strong negative attitudes towards minority groups. They feel disturbed by people from different minority groups and see minorities as having no positive effects on the enrichment of society" (SORA 2001: 24). Extrapolating from this information implies that there are tens of millions of EU citizens that feel this way. Beyond the hard core of intolerant Europeans lies a soft core of residents who are skeptical of the value of ethnic pluralism. When asked if their country's diversity in terms of race, religion, and culture added to its strengths, 37 percent of respondents tended to disagree (SORA 2001: 45). Although it would be wrong to conclude from this data that racism is rampant in Europe, it is clear that there are many millions of people in the EU who are openly dubious about diversity, and among them, potentially millions who are actively racist in one form or another.

Such racism manifests itself in myriad ways. Far right political parties have elbowed their way to notoriety in a number of countries in recent decades, capitalizing on anti-immigrant sentiment and feelings of economic and personal insecurity to capture millions of votes in local and national elections.[5] France's National Front (FN) leader Jean-Marie Le Pen has drawn both fire and publicity for statements about the gas chambers of the Holocaust being a mere "detail of history" and for his open declaration about the "inequality of the races."[6] Jörg Haider's Freedom Party won 27 percent of the vote in the 1999 Austrian elections, catapulting his party into a share of power and instigating a European Union crisis as Austria's EU counterparts ostracized a government it suspected of taking a turn toward fascism.[7]

The statements of politicians and the support of their voters are not the only troubling turns of events. The quotidian injustices of discrimination and the effects of racial harassment and violence are also widely felt. Local antidiscrimination bureaus in the Netherlands have registered

[5] For accounts of the success of far right parties in Europe see especially Kitschelt (1995), Betz (1994) and the contributions in Betz and Immerfall (1998) and Schain, Zolberg, and Hossay (in press).

[6] *Le Monde*, September 15, 1987; *Le Monde*, September 2, 1996.

[7] *International Herald Tribune*, June 23, 2000.

an average of 3,000 complaints per year over the past few years,[8] and a hotline set up by the French government to assist victims of discrimination was overwhelmed by 13,933 phone calls in its first five months (Commission Nationale Consultative des Droits de l'Homme 2001: 131). The British police recorded 47,814 racial incidents in 1999/2000,[9] of which 21,750 were categorized as "racially aggravated offences," such as assault, criminal damage, harassment and wounding.[10] In Germany, the Federal Criminal Office reported 10,037 proven or suspected right wing crimes in 1999, a figure that rose almost 40 percent in 2000.[11] A particularly brutal instance of racially motivated violence occurred on June 11, 2000 in Dessau, Germany. Three skinheads attacked Alberto Adriano, a black immigrant married to a German woman and father to their child, Gabriel. They threw him down, kicked him in the head until they dislodged an eye, and then trampled his body, leaving him dead. In a final act of contempt, they stripped him of his pants and hung them from a bush.[12]

Given such a grim accounting, it is surprising that racism has been so little noticed for so long. As the following chapters of this book demonstrate, states began paying attention to this issue in the 1960s and 1970s.[13] Yet it has really been only in the past decade that the problems of diversity associated with race have generated substantial government and scholarly interest across the continent. These issues have steadily climbed up the political agenda in a number of countries since the 1990s and remain salient today. In addition to state-sponsored efforts, the European Union has begun to address racism at the multi-national level. 1997 was an

[8] U.S. Department of State, Bureau of Democracy, Human Rights, and Labor, Releases, Human Rights Report, 2000, Europe and the New Independent States, Country Report, The Netherlands. Available at http://www.state.gov/g/drl/rls/hrrpt/2000/eur/index.cfm?docid=872.

[9] Defined as "any incident which is perceived to be racist by the victim or any other person."

[10] Statistics on Race and the Criminal Justice System (2000: 49, 52), available at http://www.homeoffice.gov.uk/rds/pdfs/s95race00.pdf.

[11] U.S. Department of State, Bureau of Democracy, Human Rights, and Labor, Releases, Human Rights Report, 2000, Europe and the New Independent States, Country Report, Germany. Available at http://www.state.gov/g/drl/rls/hrrpt/2000/eur/index.cfm?docid=765.

[12] *The New York Times*, August 21, 2000.

[13] During those decades, the United Nations also became active in the field. In 1965 it passed the International Convention on the Elimination of All Forms of Racial Discrimination (ICERD) and it designated 1971 as the International Year for Action to Combat Racism and Racial Discrimination. For an introduction to the UN's antiracism efforts, see Banton (1996).

especially pivotal year, as it saw the establishment of the European Monitoring Center on Racism and Xenophobia and the passage of a provision into the Treaty of Amsterdam that permitted the EU to combat discrimination based on racial or ethnic origin – all this in the officially designated European Year Against Racism. As racism becomes the subject of political scrutiny and action, it is necessary to understand how the issue rose to prominence and what tools have been used to manage this particular challenge.

This book seeks to illuminate European race policies by undertaking a detailed case study of their development in Britain and France. Before retracing the history of policymaking in these countries, it is important to define race policies precisely, and to explain why Britain and France are fruitful locations for an examination of this topic. Race policies are policies aimed at managing the challenges of racism and race relations in diverse societies.[14] Promoting intergroup harmony and vitiating racism can be done in a wide variety of ways. Grass-roots initiatives by civil society groups, conscious efforts by private industries to achieve racial equality, the teaching tolerance in schools, and of international gatherings of experts can all make progress toward these goals. National policies and laws designed to fight racism and to influence interactions across racial or ethnic boundaries, however, are among the most important tools a society has at its disposal. These race policies respond to actual episodes of racism, particularly those that shock us as a nation or terrorize their victims. They set a public tone for what will or will not be tolerated, sending signals to potential perpetrators as well as to society as a whole. Race policies are certainly not the only forces affecting racism or race relations. However, a close examination of national race policies offers crucial insights into these pressing concerns.

Britain and France are particularly important countries to consider in the European context. Among European nations, they have been at the forefront of the field of race policies, having developed their laws and administrative structures in the 1960s and 1970s. Each country's elite proudly asserts that its system is the most advanced available; and each country stands out as a potential exemplar for other continental nations and for the European Union as a whole. Yet the two states diverge substantially in the types of institutions they have established. While France maintains a strict color-blind code, Britain has accepted a number of

[14] By race relations, I refer to the interactions of people across boundaries commonly thought of as racial or ethnic.

race-conscious policies. Whereas France has traditionally preferred to use the criminal law to fight racism, Britain relies heavily on the civil law for punishing discrimination. Britain has erected a quasigovernmental organization to encourage good race relations, in contrast to the pride of place granted to non-governmental associations in France's antiracist structures.

Why these differences? Factors that at first blush might seem to account for such policy divergence do not offer satisfactory explanations. Britain and France share more similarities than differences in their economies and democratic political systems; both were leading colonial powers and experienced decolonization at approximately the same time; and both received large and comparable quantities of ethnic minority immigrants in the decades following World War II (see Hansen 2000, Rose 1969, Weil 1995).[15] Moreover, Britain and France – in contrast to other large European countries such as Germany – have turned their minority populations into citizens at a relatively rapid rate (Brubaker 1992; Hansen 2000).[16] Although Britain's percentage of ethnic minority citizens is greater than France's, this has by no means dictated the different outcomes in the two countries. Britain and France are not perfectly parallel societies; nevertheless, it is difficult to find two countries that share more in common along so many critical dimensions. Policy variation in light of such economic and demographic similarities demands further inquiry.

The goal of this book is to describe, analyze, and explain the differences between the British "race relations" model and the French "antiracism"

[15] By 1966, England and Wales combined were estimated to have just over 900,000 "coloured" residents (Rose 1969: Appendix table III.v.). In 1968, the French census enumerated just under 700,000 foreign residents of African or Asian origin (Weil 1995: Appendix VI), a count that did not include ethnic minority citizens (for which France keeps no statistics).

[16] As of the 1991 census, 1.42 of the 3.02 million total ethnic minority population in Britain were native born and therefore UK citizens (Salt 1996: 132). Combined New Commonwealth and non-European alien naturalization in the UK averaged 56,400 per year between 1983 and 1994 inclusive (Hansen 1997: 341). Foreign nationals of African or Asian origin in France totaled 2,069,890 in 1990. Nationality acquisitions in France averaged 50,242 per year from 1980–9 and rose to a 1990–3 average of 70,487 per year. These figures include acquisitions of nationality from all immigrant groups, of which Africans and Asians together comprised 57.4 percent in 1990 (Weil 1995: Appendices VI and VII). In contrast, annual acquisitions of citizenship for the combined group of Turks, Yugoslavs, Italians, Greeks, and Spanish (the core immigrant groups) in Germany from 1981–8 averaged 4,500 (Brubaker 1992: 83).

approach. Doing so illuminates not only the cases at hand, but also proves relevant at a broader geographic level. Both in Europe and North America, scholars, activists and policymakers are searching for solutions to problems of racism. Britain and France have over three decades of experience with their antidiscrimination institutions. Examining and understanding how these policies came into being, how and why they differ, and what effects they have had in their settings will hopefully enrich intellectual and policy debates in all advanced industrialized countries struggling with this challenge of diversity.

Race Relations Versus Antiracism: The British and French Approaches Compared

What are the principal differences between the British race relations approach and the French antiracism model? British and French race policies diverge along a variety of major and minor dimensions.[17] While many of the smaller differences are revealed in the following chapters, this project focuses its attention on the most significant differences between the two nations. In order to identify the critical policies, I look to the passage of legislation that has defined race policies in each country. British race relations legislation, established through three major rounds in 1965, 1968, and 1976, has formed the core of Britain's race institutions, setting out most of the general rules and founding many of the official organizations devoted to race issues. France passed its cornerstone antiracism law in 1972, and then passed two subsequent laws in 1978 and 1990 that reinforce its institutions.[18]

Before looking to race policy differences, it is helpful to distinguish among access, expressive, and physical racism. Access racism involves discrimination in employment, housing, and provision of goods and services; expressive racism is manifested through inflammatory statements or written expressions made against individuals or groups; and physical racism relates to attacks against persons or destruction of property

[17] See also Lloyd (1991), Crowley (1993).

[18] Each country has other sources of race policies, such as those that emanate from the cabinet or bureaucracies. These policies will be described in passing, although no attempt is made to cover them exhaustively since the primary race institutions in each country have their origins in the passage of antiracist legislation. Each country is also in the process of adding new elements to its race structures. Because these are ongoing developments, they cannot be analyzed as exhaustively as previous laws. They are, however, treated in the concluding chapter.

motivated by racial hatred.[19] At first blush, policies in Britain and France appear to be quite similar, as each country has outlawed essentially the same gamut of racist crimes, penalizing especially access and expressive racism, while resisting new laws to counter physical racism. Moreover, in contrast to the United States, each country has rejected "hard" affirmative action.[20] But these surface similarities mask important differences between the countries. Five central factors distinguish the two countries:

1. The legal procedures used to punish certain types of racist infractions
2. The actors responsible for spearheading the fight against discrimination
3. The existence (or absence) of punishment for denying the Holocaust
4. The existence (or absence) of penalties depriving convicted racists of their civil rights
5. The existence (or absence) of race-conscious policies covering indirect discrimination, positive action, and ethnic monitoring.

Access racism is punished in a significantly different manner on either side of the English Channel. Britain uses the civil law to penalize acts of discrimination in employment, housing, and provision of goods and services. French laws have favored the punishment of these kinds of racist acts by the criminal law.[21] The use of criminal versus civil law has significant implications. In 1991, for example, British civil procedures led to 1,471 cases of employment-related discrimination. By contrast, in 1991 employment-related convictions in France totaled four (Banton 1994: 485). These figures reflect the fact that getting convictions for access racism is extremely difficult when using criminal standards of proof (Costa-Lascoux 1994: 26, Vourc'h, de Rudder, and Tripier 1996: 159).[22]

[19] This typology is intended to facilitate discussion. It is akin to the distinction between discrimination, hate speech, and hate crimes, although it differs from this distinction based upon how Britain and France categorize certain offenses.

[20] Hard affirmative action involves hiring goals required of government contractors, accepted by consent decrees or ordered by courts, and often involves a deliberate adjustment of standards in employment and education (Teles 1998: 1004).

[21] In the past few years, France has turned its attention to the potential for punishing access racism through the civil law, a move discussed in the concluding chapter.

[22] These figures are not perfectly comparable, however, since not all British cases resulted in convictions and since the number of French convictions is higher than officially enumerated, given that, as Costa-Lascoux (1994: 376) notes, the statistics only contain the primary offense for which the guilty party was convicted. Nevertheless, the cross-national differences in cases brought to court and convictions obtained remains substantial.

TABLE 4. *Race Policies in Great Britain and France*

Race Policies	Britain	France
Criminal or civil law predominant for access racism?	Civil	Criminal
Help to victims from:	Administrative agency	Non-governmental groups
Provision against Holocaust denial?	No	Yes
Provisions depriving racists of civil rights?	No	Yes
Race-conscious policies:		
• positive action?	Yes	No
• provisions against indirect discrimination?	Yes	No/Yes*
• ethnic monitoring?	Yes	No

Note: *No for the majority of the postwar years; yes as of law 2001–1066 of November 16, 2001.

The second central dimension along which policy in the two countries can be contrasted is in the locus of responsibility for combating racism. In France, official responsibility is shared by both the state and civil society. Because France uses the criminal law to punish acts of racism, the state (the police and the courts) has, in theory, pride of place in dealing with race problems. French laws, however, also allow nongovernmental antiracist groups to instigate criminal proceedings for racist crimes, even without the state's approval. Approximately 50 percent of racism cases are brought into the courts – or at least to the public prosecutor's attention – by the antiracist associations, which gives them substantial influence in this policy domain (Costa-Lascoux 1994: 376).

Britain, by contrast, established a quasigovernmental organization that takes the lead in dealing with race relations. The Commission for Racial Equality (CRE) has a budget of some £15 million per year and a staff of over one hundred full-time workers. It undertakes national campaigns against discrimination, collects and analyzes statistics on discrimination, publishes an annual report on racism in Britain, funds local bodies that fight racism, helps individual victims of racism with legal advice, and, most important, it undertakes audits of industries or government departments it suspects are acting in a discriminatory manner. Although the CRE is by no measure a powerful national institution, it has more leverage and authority than its French counterparts to combat racism and do so in a wider variety of spheres.[23]

Third, the French antiracism law of 1990 rendered it illegal to contest the existence of crimes against humanity committed during World War II. No such provision exists in Britain. The French law aims to punish revisionist historians who promote anti-Semitic views through denial of the Holocaust. Yet, to the dismay of many, it has also created an "official" interpretation of history, dissent from which can result in fines or imprisonment – a highly controversial step in an open democracy. Fourth, the same French law of 1990 provided for sanctions depriving convicted racists (at the judge's discretion) of certain civil rights. Although the right to vote cannot be withdrawn,[24] the right to stand for public office can be denied to an individual if he or she has been found guilty of racism. To some, this may seem a reasonable and perhaps necessary provision against demagoguery; to others, however, this is a dangerous affront to freedom of speech which risks being put to highly political uses.

Finally, Britain has developed a series of race-conscious policies that France has eschewed. Certain British policies focus on categorizing, protecting, and aiding minorities defined by group rather than by individual characteristics. Indirect discrimination, for example, concerns acts of racism that affect groups of individuals defined by race, rather than those perpetrated against a particular individual. Classic examples, drawn from 1960s America, are literacy tests or educational requirements that had a disparate negative impact on blacks trying to vote or find a job.[25] Indirect discrimination has been outlawed for over twenty-five years in Britain. By contrast, in France the concept has only entered into public and elite consciousness in recent years. Positive action – "soft" forms of affirmative action such as actively recruiting minority job applicants and targeting training resources at minorities – is permitted in Britain to aid disadvantaged racial groups, but is strictly forbidden in France. Britain has also begun to collect extensive ethnic statistics, even incorporating an ethnic question into its 1991 census; France, on the other hand, passed a law

[23] France has three government-sponsored organizations that have issues of racism within their bailiwick: the National Consultative Commission on Human Rights (CNCDH), the recently formed Group for the Study and Fight against Discrimination (GELD), and the recently renamed Fund for Action and Support for Integration and the Struggle against Discriminations (FASILD). None is as influential as Britain's CRE.

[24] This possibility was initially considered.

[25] See the U.S. Supreme Court case Griggs v. Duke Power, 401 U.S. 424 (1971).

in 1978 that virtually prohibits collection of ethnic data. Although the effects of color-blind versus race-conscious policies on immigrant and minority integration are contested and uncertain, the difference in approach between Britain and France is likely to affect both the degree of ethnic self-identification and the strength of minority mobilization in each country.[26]

How can such differences be explained?

Frames and Race Policy Outcomes

To understand why Britain and France have chosen different paths in the fight against racism, it is essential to recognize that instituting race policies requires a process of policymaking. Turning to the literature on comparative policymaking can therefore help to generate insights into race policy differences between the two countries. In order to account for the trajectory of race policies in these countries, I begin by examining three popular schools of thought on policymaking: the power-interest, problem-solving, and institutional perspectives. Each is fleshed out in detail in the following chapter. In brief, the power-interest school highlights the role of influential actors such as political parties or pressure groups in lobbying for policies that best complement their electoral or other interests. Problem-solving perspectives emphasize the role of groups of actors that cut across bureaucratic, policy expert, and interest group lines to try to resolve policy problems. Institutional theories focus on the role of political structures and path dependent policy legacies in shaping the policy process. Each perspective is compelling on theoretical grounds and has also been substantiated by empirical research in a variety of policy spheres.

While each of these schools of thought sheds light on the policy process, none can successfully account for the range of race policy outcomes in Britain and France. Even taken together these approaches cannot adequately answer two essential questions: What motivated actors to make the decision they made, and why did actors choose such different options in such similar contexts? These are questions that pose problems for the three perspectives not only in the cases presented here, but also in other spheres of policymaking. To explain the content of policies within a country and cross-national differences in policy outcomes, it is necessary to turn to the role of ideas.

[26] For a collection of essays on the topic of ethnic mobilization in Europe, see Rex and Drury (1994). For a seminal text on the role between institutional configurations and ethnic identities and actions, see Nagel (1986).

The key finding of this study is that ideas in the form of *frames* best account for race policies in Britain and France. As I demonstrate through detailed historical case studies, British and French policymakers operated with sets of ideas that significantly influenced the trajectory of their domestic race policies. Moreover, the difference between these sets of ideas explains much of the policy divergence between the two countries. The contents and contours of these race frames will be specified in more detail in the next chapter. They can, however, be summarized as follows: British policymakers have largely accepted the categories of race and ethnicity; they have conceived of racism primarily in "color" terms and have devoted the majority of their energy to fighting access racism; and they have strongly identified their problems of racism with the North American context. By contrast, prevailing French frames have downplayed or denied the categories of race and ethnicity, they have focused more on expressive racism and on anti-Semitism, and they have rejected the North American analogy because of its perceived irrelevance to understanding France's domestic context of racism. French race frames have therefore propelled French policies down a substantially different path from that taken in Britain. In short, it has been the different political and public conceptions of race, racism, and antiracism that have had the most important impact on the precise nature of each country's concrete policies.

In making this argument, this book differentiates itself from studies that focus primarily on the role of political or pressure group interests (Freeman 1995, Money 1999) or national institutional structures (Hansen 2000, Ireland 1994, Soysal 1994) in driving actions in the realm of immigration and integration.[27] Although it prioritizes ideas as the central factor determining outcomes, this study stands in contrast to influential work that underlines the impact on migration or incorporation of international ideas such as liberal rights or norms of universal personhood (Hollifield 1992, Soysal 1994). Race policy decisionmaking processes in Britain and France in the decades after World War II have proven relatively insulated from supranational or transnational forces, perhaps surprisingly for those that have noticed their influence in a variety of domains. Like Favell (1998) and Freeman (1979), I argue that prevailing modes of thought in the two countries are particularly worthy of attention. But whereas

[27] The authors identified with a school of thought are, of course, sensitive to a range of variables in their studies. Boiling down their sophisticated work in this way is therefore a simplification of their arguments. Nevertheless, doing so points out some of the major axes of difference prevalent in explanations of immigration and integration concerns.

Favell's principal goal is to describe each nation's "philosophy of integration" and understand its durability in the face of obvious pathologies, my goal is to analyze the causal relationship between race frames and race policies within each country. And unlike Freeman, who views ideas as falling within a problem-solving rubric and sees them as one among several equally important explanations of cross-national differences,[28] I seek to isolate frames as variables in their own right and to argue that they are the most significant factors accounting for British and French race policy outcomes and divergences.

Demonstrating the impact of frames requires a careful process-tracing of policy developments in each country. Arriving at a comprehensive history of when, how, and why policymaking took the course that it did has entailed examining numerous archives, conducting dozens of interviews, and weighing evidence from books and articles written by hundreds of scholars and race policy participants. Scrutinizing the facts in the light of theoretical perspectives available in the field of comparative public policymaking encourages a skeptical analysis that pays attention to a wide variety of potential influences on each country's policy trajectory. At its base, this study highlights the significance of frames in British and French race policymaking. Yet, it also seeks to reflect on the role of ideas more broadly. To this end, I develop a definition of frames that can be applied to numerous policy spheres; I map out a method for locating frames among actors in a polity; and I examine the questions of where frames originate and when and how they change. This book thus seeks to formulate a model of the interaction between ideas and policymaking that illuminates the influence of frames on the policy process in general.

To accomplish this, the theoretical framework for analyzing the cases is outlined in the following chapter. It sketches the power-interest, problem-solving, and institutional perspectives on policymaking, highlighting their strengths and weaknesses, and explores in depth the ideational perspective, defining frames, and developing tools for understanding their role in the policymaking process. The historical case studies comprise the second part of the study. Chapters 2, 3, and 4 retrace the passage of the British Race Relations Acts of 1965, 1968, and 1976, while Chapters 5 and 6 perform the same task for the French antiracism laws of 1972 and 1990. This segment of the project uncovers the origins and influence of frames on policymaking in each country and examines how frames interact with

[28] See especially Chapter 9 in Freeman (1979), in which he favors the term social learning over problem-solving.

important variables (such as power, interest, and institutions) highlighted by other theoretical perspectives. In order to present the material in a systematic format, each historical chapter utilizes Kingdon's (1995) analytic distinction between two basic segments of the policymaking process: agenda setting and alternative specification.

The third part of the book summarizes the lessons learned from the analysis of the theories and the history. Chapter 7 assesses the role of frames, emphasizing both that they are identifiable and that they are necessary to explain race policy outcomes and cross-national policy differences. Furthermore, it addresses three issues at the heart of debates on the role of ideas in policy analysis. It explores how frames interact with variables associated with the power-interest, problem-solving, and institutional schools of thought in order to integrate ideas into more comprehensive models of comparative public policymaking. It reflects on the conditions under which frames are likely to be most influential in the policy process. Finally, it sketches an outline of the sources of British and French race frames and argues that as a general rule, examining the socialization of key actors is likely to prove the most fruitful first step in understanding the origin of policy frames. This study therefore demonstrates not only that frames matter, but also illuminates how they matter, when they matter most, and where they come from.

Chapter 8 concludes by returning to the overarching questions of race and integration central to the new multiethnic Europe. It touches on the developments in race policy that have taken place in the most recent years in Britain, France, and elsewhere in Europe – developments for which the policy dust has not quite settled. The chapter then reflects upon the costs, benefits, and trade-offs associated with different policies designed to promote harmonious ethnic relations.

I

Perspectives on Comparative Public Policymaking

The Place of Frames

Unlocking a compelling account of race policies in Britain and France requires investigation of policy development over time. To enrich the historical narrative and to uncover the root causes of race policy outcomes, it is essential to analyze the history in light of theories of comparative public policymaking. This chapter therefore begins by outlining three prominent policymaking perspectives. A policymaking perspective refers to a school of thought that accounts for the basic nature and central elements of policymaking, be they specific actors, a theory of motivation, or a conceptualization of constraints on action. The *power-interest* framework, for example, views politics as a function of actors struggling to advance their interests, with outcomes determined largely by relative power resources. *Problem-solving* perspectives interpret politics as a search for policy solutions to concrete problems. *Institutional* approaches typically stress the constraining nature of existing webs of institutions on any new policy under consideration. Each of these perspectives offers useful insights into policymaking and each must be canvassed in order to understand the contours of race policymaking in Britain and France.

Close examination of these perspectives reveals that as informative as each is, none can satisfactorily account for race policy outcomes in these cases. These theoretical frameworks do not successfully illuminate actors' goals or their desired policies. Why did race experts in Britain lobby for positive action and ethnic monitoring, for example, while their French counterparts opposed these policies? To answer this type of question, we need to turn to a fourth policymaking perspective – one based on ideas. The argument presented in this book places special emphasis on *frames* as ideas in the political process. The concept of frames fills the lacuna left by alternative policymaking perspectives, providing a means for understanding actors' preferences and thus for understanding a critical element that shapes policy outcomes.

To lay out the theoretical terrain for understanding race policymaking, section one of this chapter reviews the three mainstream perspectives on policymaking. Outlining the power-interest, problem-solving, and institutional approaches highlights their strengths and weaknesses. Most importantly, these theoretical schools of thought draw our attention to variables that may plausibly account for race policymaking in the cases at hand. As we turn to the historical material, we can investigate the importance of factors such as minority pressure groups versus policy experts, and material interests versus institutional constraints in driving forward the policy process and in shaping policy outcomes. Section two fleshes out the role of frames in politics. It defines frames, discusses where to locate them, and advances an argument about the way ideas and actors relate to one another (a central concern for scholars of ideas). It also recognizes that some readers may be skeptical about the importance of ideas in explaining political outcomes. After all, this argument runs counter to the well-established dictum that politics is about who gets what, when, and how. Therefore, section two establishes explicit criteria for identifying frames and for determining whether or not they impact the policy process. Beyond satisfying skeptics that ideas matter in accounting for race policy outcomes in Britain and France, ultimately it is most important to understand how frames fit together with other theoretical perspectives, and how they can be systematically integrated into theories of policymaking. This chapter thus lays the groundwork for that task.

Power-Interest Perspectives

Power-interest perspectives view policy outcomes as determined by conflict between actors, each trying to advance its agenda. As befits this perspective, power and interests are the elements placed at the center of the analysis, and policy outcomes are seen to depend on the compromises struck between the interests of the most powerful actors. "Social outcomes are the product of social conflict," in political scientist Jack Knight's words, and the resolution of conflicts depends on "how the asymmetries of power in a society influence the evolution of social institutions" (Knight 1992: 16, 14). Analysts arguing from a public choice, group theory, or statist corner can be seen as proponents of the power-interest school of thought. Although they may disagree on whether individuals, interest groups, classes, or state actors are most powerful, they would concur with Macridis' position that "power configuration is basically the configuration of competing and struggling interests . . . and the content of decisions are determined by a parallelogram of . . . forces" (Macridis 1986: 281).[1]

While some theories stipulate that particular actors hold the most sway in society, others simply provide a metric for gauging the power of an actor. Votes, money, number of persons organized or mobilized, institutional resources, military capabilities, or other, less tangible forms of influence may be appropriate for understanding the distribution of power resources. It is also possible to establish a base-line understanding of actors' likely interests. In the versions of power-interest theory that offer the most analytical leverage,[2] these are typically wealth and power. Groups such as business and labor seek to funnel resources toward themselves, thereby ensuring maximum profits or wages. Politicians pursue strategies that draw financial and electoral support for themselves and their parties, thereby enhancing their chances of reelection and of holding political power. Bureaucrats struggle for budget increases and for administrative turf in order to ensure their positions and the influence of their agencies. These interests crop up regularly in the political world and frequently determine policy positions. When actors' goals and relative influence are correctly understood, we can often predict the direction of policy; this makes the power-interest perspective one of the most useful analytic frameworks available.[3]

Because of the importance of power and interests it is necessary to take these variables seriously and to investigate their influence on policymaking in the cases at hand. This school of thought points us to three sets of actors that are most likely to play a role in advancing policy. Groups directly affected by the outcome of the policymaking are likely to be critical to getting an issue on the political agenda and to shaping

[1] For prototypical examples of this perspective, see the literature on the role of group conflict in generating Scandinavian social politics and welfare state policies (Korpi 1983, Stephens 1979, Swenson 1991).

[2] On leverage, see King et al. (1994: 29–30)

[3] It is most insightful in situations where actors' interests entail the pursuit of wealth and influence and when power resources are easy to calculate. For example, when long-term shifts in the international political economy have positive or negative effects on factors such as land, labor and capital (see Rogowski 1989) or on actors that make their living from tradable goods versus nontradable goods (see Frieden 1991), we can expect power resources and policies to shift. When elections approach and swing seats are hotly contested, politicians may respond to influential interest groups in those constituencies in order to retain power (Money 1999).

its final form. In the case of race policies, these actors are minorities and racists. Evidence that minorities' lobbying was influential in creating race policies – or that racists altered the outcome of the policies or kept them off the agenda – would therefore be consonant with the power-interest perspective.[4] Politicians and political parties engaged in electoral politics are the second group of actors commonly highlighted by analysts in the power-interest school. As noted, at the most basic level of motives, these political actors attempt to stay in office and to exercise power. To do this, they search for issues that mobilize voters, show themselves to be capable governors, solidify internal party coherence, or thwart opposing parties. Does the historical record provide evidence that parties: passed antiracism legislation in order to win minorities as new voters; watered-down the content of the laws to mute racist backlash; strove to maintain social order (fearing disruptions caused by racism); or attempted to energize their own party or divide their opponents by "playing the race card?" Finally, following the strand of power-interest perspectives that emphasize the role of bureaucracies in the policymaking process, it is necessary to explore the possibility that race legislation was put on the agenda and shaped by ministries or bureaucracies that, whatever their public posture, were privately intending to expand their turf or maximize their resources.

Theories of the policymaking process must also be able to explain cross-national differences. How can power-interest perspectives account for divergent race policy outcomes between Britain and France? Typically, this school of thought relies on variation in power resources to explain divergent outcomes. According to Korpi and Shalev's (1979) "balance of class power" model, for example, levels and types of societal conflict depend on working class strength and left-party power in government. Translating these insights into the domain of race, we can look to see whether different power resources of minorities, bureaucracies, or parties seeking minority (or antiminority) support in Britain versus France account for divergent race policies across the two nations. If one country had more minorities, a stronger antiracist bureaucracy and a more powerful left party than the other,[5] this may account for more comprehensive race policies.

[4] The U.S. civil rights movement provides a case in which these groups played a vital role. See, for example, McAdam (1988).

[5] This presumes the left party is more sympathetic to minorities, which may not be the case.

As informative as the power-interest school of thought may be, it is also necessary to point out its limitations. Much policymaking takes place outside of the orbit of election campaigns and beyond the gravitational pull of actors' interest in the bottom line. Politicians are not always motivated simply by pursuit of power, bureaucrats by pursuit of turf, or interest groups by pursuit of money. When goals and resources are not so clear-cut, power-interest perspectives lose much of their ability to explain the course of policymaking. We may thus need different maps to help us chart the murky waters of policymaking when we move beyond this perspective's focus on material interests.

Problem-Solving Perspectives

Problem-solving perspectives view political processes not as a power struggle to maximize private interests but rather as the development and implementation of policies that serve as solutions to societal problems. A wide array of policymaking studies make use of problem-solving terminology.[6] Prototypical versions of the problem-solving perspective highlight "coordination" rather than "conflict" as a critical element of politics (Knight 1992: 4–8). A seminal statement of these themes was announced by Hugh Heclo in his work on policy learning in the development of the welfare state in Britain and Sweden. In an oft-cited formulation, he argues that "governments not only 'power' . . . ; they also puzzle. Policymaking is a form of collective puzzlement on society's behalf; it entails both deciding and knowing" (Heclo 1974: 305).[7] Implicit in much of this literature is a vision of actors responding to problems by implementing new and better policy solutions arrived at through processes of learning.

Problem-solving approaches thus view the dynamics of politics through a different lens than their power-interest counterparts. Although analysts working in this vein rarely ignore "powering," they emphasize other aspects of the policymaking process. Specifically, they do two things. First, they point to sets of actors previously overlooked, stressing the role of advocacy coalitions (Sabatier 1987), policy communities (Kingdon 1995), epistemic communities (Haas 1989, Rose 1993), or "middlemen"

[6] Opinions diverge over the extent to which actors consciously seek to solve problems. For a variety of positions on this debate see Lindblom (1959), Shklar (1964), Majone (1989), Cohen, March and Olsen (1972), and Kingdon (1995).

[7] On learning and puzzling, see also Bennett and Howlett (1992).

at the interface of parties, interest groups, and bureaucracies (Heclo 1974: 308–9). In short, problem-solving analysts look beyond parties, interest groups, and bureaucrats to focus attention on coalitions of actors that cross these boundaries to become policy experts in a particular domain. Moreover, these scholars operate with a broader definition of interests than exists in the power-interest perspective. According to the problem-solving school of thought, actors' motives range beyond maximizing their power, budgets, or narrow group interests. This perspective thus opens up new horizons to policymaking researchers, pointing to sets of actors that might otherwise have been overlooked and stretching our understanding of the interests that motivate actors and influence policy decisions.

In the context of race policies in Britain and France, the problem-solving perspective raises the hypothesis that policymaking is generated by groups operating at the interstices of party politicians, interest groups, bureaucrats, and policy experts, rather than by any one or combination of these actors. It also suggests that such policy communities are acting upon their learned expertise in an attempt to solve problems of racism instead of trying to maximize their material interests. Finally, from the problem-solving perspective, cross-national policy variation is most convincingly explained by objective differences in the level or nature of the domestic problems faced. A problem-solving analyst looking at both sides of the Atlantic might argue that if Britain and France have thinner antiracism institutions than those of the United States, it is because European countries have less racism to fight than does the U.S. Accounting for differences on either side of the English Channel, he or she might hypothesize that the type or extent of racism in Britain differs from that in France, and that the policy solutions implemented in each case are therefore a natural function of these problem differences.

Although the problem-solving perspective highlights significant aspects of the race policymaking process in Britain and France, unfortunately it also has its weaknesses. It may highlight the actors that are important and point out that their interests may be multifaceted, yet it does not provide an adequate method for discerning what those interests will be. If the interests are simply to solve the problem of racism, then it is critical to know how racism is defined, what aspects of it are seen as particularly problematic, and which solutions are deemed viable. Because it does not speak to these issues, the problem-solving perspective cannot inform us of the precise content of the policy choices likely to be made.

Institutional Perspectives

Authors working in a third vein share a perspective on policymaking that emphasizes the role of institutions in structuring political life and in influencing political and policy outcomes.[8] For these scholars, understanding the constitutional, legislative, bureaucratic and other rules that structure interactions in society is the key to understanding politics. One important way in which this differentiates institutional analysis from the alternative schools of thought is in terms of identifying politically important actors. Rather than stipulating that certain actors are always likely to be central to decisionmaking, institutionalists examine the prevailing political institutions to understand how power is parceled out (see Immergut 1998: 17, Katzenstein 1978, Weir and Skocpol 1985). As Peter Hall (1986: 264) succinctly states, "some interests will be privileged as a result of the overall organization of interlocking institutional frameworks, while others will receive less attention."[9]

Another key aspect of this school of thought bears more directly on the content of policymaking. One strand of institutionalist analysis offers a compelling hypothesis for explaining policy development. According to this argument, the existing web of institutions – such as pre-existing laws and policy legacies – constrains the shape of any new policy enacted (Weir and Skocpol 1985). Some policies are regarded as more administratively "viable" than others, or "fit" better with prevailing institutions (Hall 1989: 373–4). Policy outcomes are therefore molded by the institutional context. This type of explanation shares a close affinity with those that highlight the effects of path dependence on policy outcomes (Krasner 1984, Mahoney 2000, North 1990, Pierson 2000). Such arguments sometimes emphasize the constraints and lock-in effects of past policies that tend to create a bias toward policy continuity.[10] Institutionalist approaches thus bring out important aspects of politics

[8] As numerous review articles emphasize, (new) institutionalists can be divided into several subcategories, such as "rational choice," "historical," and "sociological" (see Hall and Taylor 1996, Immergut 1998, Kato 1996, Koelble 1995). Many sociological institutionalists define certain types of ideas (such as norms) as institutions. Because these institutionalized ideas are so different from other forms of institutions, I do not treat them in this section.

[9] To the extent that institutionalists focus on power and interests, they share an affinity with power-interest theorists. The overlap is especially visible in the case of rational choice institutionalists who emphasize institutions principally to demonstrate how they constrain interest-motivated actions.

[10] Mahoney's (2000) work also demonstrates how path-dependent reactive sequences can engender policy change rather than policy continuity.

underemphasized by the previous perspectives. Recognizing the role of the "rules of the game" in determining power resources and in constraining the range of policy choices open to policymakers is vital to a complete understanding of the policy process.

What do institutionalist approaches draw our attention to in the cases of race policymaking at hand? To explain the extent of race policies, it is necessary to examine how institutions allocate power to interested parties in each country. For example, do Britain's two-party parliamentary system and moderately strong race bureaucracy and France's multiparty (Fifth Republic) semipresidential system and absence of a race bureaucracy privilege some voices over others? Are racial minorities particularly strong in one system and shut out in another because of the rules of the game? If so, this may account for differences in the scope and nature of each country's race policies.

Looking beyond institutional allocation of power, what influence do policy legacies and preexisting institutions have on policy outcomes? It is possible that the difference between the British common law tradition and the French Romano-Germanic legal model (David and Brierley 1985) affected decisions about whether to enact civil or criminal penalties for racist infractions. Perhaps the relatively stronger race bureaucracy in Britain is the product of a set of political institutions that make it easy to establish new public organizations in Britain, whereas French administrative rules render it virtually impossible to erect such structures. If this kind of an institutional argument is correct, new policies in Britain will not be administratively viable in France and vice versa. Moreover, any attempts to break down the policy legacy or to radically overhaul the institutions will likely encounter high hurdles because of the constraints established by previous policy choices.

Institutionalism thus suggests some avenues for explaining the trajectory of race policymaking in Britain and France. Yet, as with the other theoretical approaches, institutionalism has its weak points. For example, although it may indicate which policies are wholly out of bounds, the policy legacy approach cannot help us understand why, given a range of options, one particular policy path is chosen over another. Institutional approaches do not purport to account for actors' underlying policy goals. In terms of tracking the evolution of policy, institutional lock-in and path dependence may help us understand stability over time. However, it is sometimes assumed that where there is stability, institutional forces are the root causes, whereas many variables may underpin policy continuity. As with its predecessors, the institutional perspective tells us important things about the policy process, but it is insufficient for understanding policymaking and policy outcomes.

An Ideational Perspective – The Role of Frames

Although the three approaches examined thus far say a great deal about policymaking, subsequent chapters demonstrate that they are inadequate in the cases at hand principally because they do not account for the goals of policy participants. Ideational perspectives can help overcome this weakness of other schools of thought. Political scientists' interest in ideational explanations has blossomed in recent years (for reviews, see Berman 2001, Blyth 1997, Checkel 1998, Finnemore 1996b, Finnemore and Sikkink 2001, Jacobsen 1995). Much of the existing literature on ideas and politics offers useful building blocks for constructing a better understanding of comparative public policymaking. In particular, the concept of frames has drawn increasing attention for its ability to illuminate developments in a variety of spheres.[11] Although no single definition of the term has come to be accepted across all fields (Entman 1993), Rein and Schön (1993: 146) capture the essence of a frame as "a perspective from which an amorphous, ill-defined, problematic situation can be made sense of and acted on."[12]

Even when the term "frame" does not figure explicitly in the analysis, scholars have developed similar variables to help account for policy outcomes. Hall (1993: 279), for example, defines a *policy paradigm* as "a framework of ideas and standards that specifies not only the goals of policy and the kind of instruments that can be used to attain them, but also the very nature of the problems they are meant to be addressing."[13]

[11] For references to the antecedents of policymaking's use of frames, see Rein and Schön (1993). For other works that make use of the concept in a wide variety of fashions, see Goffmann (1974), Tversky and Kahneman (1986), Iyengar (1991), Gamson (1992), Schön and Rein (1994), Cappella and Jamieson (1997), Tarrow (1998), Cruz (2000), Payne (2001), and Saguy (in press).

[12] Goffmann (1974: 21) illustrates his use of frames by stating that "When the individual... recognizes a particular event, he tends... to imply in this response (and in effect employ) one or more frameworks or schemata of interpretation of a kind that can be called primary... a primary framework is one that is seen as rendering what would otherwise be a meaningless aspect of the scene into something that is meaningful." For additional references which touch on framing or related concepts, see Baumgartner and Jones (1993), Jones (1994), and Stone (1989).

[13] The source of the paradigm terminology, Thomas Kuhn, uses the concept in a number of ways. Paradigms approach today's prevailing meaning of frames when Kuhn states that one may suspect that "something like a paradigm is prerequisite

Sabatier (1987: 660) advances the concept of a *belief system* as "a set of basic values, causal assumptions, and problem perceptions." For Muller (1997), a *référentiel* can be summarized as a "mechanism of fabrication of images, ideas, and values that constitute a vision of the world."[14] Each sees these ideational variables as central to the policymaking process.[15]

As useful as these analyses have been, none has sought to construct a comprehensive model of the relationship between ideas and policymaking, leading one friendly critic to conclude that "so far studies of ideational variables add up to less than the sum of their parts" (Berman 2001). This book therefore attempts to develop a general framework for analyzing whether and how ideas affect policymaking by pointing to the kinds of ideas likely to impact the policy process and by illuminating the causal pathways through which ideas have their influence on policy outcomes.[16] In order to understand the role of frames in policymaking, it addresses a series of questions. What precisely are frames? How do we locate these ideas with specific actors that carry them? What is the relationship between actors and frames – do frames constitute actors, or do actors simply use frames strategically to advance their material interests? How do we identify the frames that actors are carrying? How do we judge whether frames are actually important in the policymaking process or whether they are merely window dressing compared to the influence of other, more important forces? I tackle each of these in turn.

Defining Frames

Building on the groundwork laid by Rein and Schön, Hall, Sabatier, Muller, and others, I define a frame as a set of cognitive and moral maps that orient an actor within a policy sphere.[17] Frames help actors identify problems and specify and prioritize their interests and goals; they point actors toward causal and normative judgments about effective and

to perception itself. What a man sees depends both upon what he looks at and also upon what his previous visual-conceptual experience has taught him to see. In the absence of such training there can only be, in William James' phrase, 'a bloomin' buzzin' confusion' " (Kuhn 1996 [1962]: 113).

[14] In Jobert and Muller's (1987: 51–78) work, the *référentiel* is defined as "the representation of the policy sphere, as well as its place and role in society" (1987: 63), or as "the ensemble of norms or referents of a policy" (1987: 52).

[15] For a review of these three authors, see Surel (2000).

[16] For one attempt to do this, see Goldstein and Keohane (1993).

[17] Because the concept of frames is used by scholars in a number of contexts, it may be useful to call this a policy frame, in order to distinguish it from collective action frames, injustice frames, media frames, and other types of frames.

appropriate policies in ways that tend to propel policy down a particular path and to reinforce it once on that path; and they can endow actors deemed to have moral authority or expert status with added power in a policy field. In this way, frames give direction to policymaking and help account for policy outcomes.

As cognitive maps, frames encompass definitions, analogies, metaphors, and symbols that aid actors in conceptualizing a political or social situation, identifying problems and goals, and charting courses of action. They provide an answer to Goffman's (1974: 25) question "What is it that's going on here?" For example, terms such as race, racism, and discrimination can be defined in different manners. Race may refer to biological or to cultural traits.[18] "Biological" races may be identified by skin color, head shape, presumed descent or some other factor or combination of factors. The meaning of racism is also open to interpretation. Countries or individuals concerned about racism may conceive of the issue in significantly different ways. The word racism may trigger visions of skinheads beating foreigners, of politicians railing against Jews, or of employers turning away job applicants of a certain hue – each to the point where they crowd out alternative definitions of the term.

Analogies, metaphors, and symbols are components of frames when they are employed to conceptualize a political or social situation, when they identify problems and goals, and when they chart courses of action. An analogy, as Khong demonstrates in his study of the American war in Vietnam, can "help define the nature of the situation confronting the policymaker" (1992: 10). Analogical reasoning can also constitute a cognitive screen for interpreting events. As Kingdon (1995: 94) notes, raw information does not speak for itself. Whether ten acts of racist violence per year is perceived as high or low depends on the context within which one assesses such a figure. Does one compare this data with that of the previous year, the previous decade or with that of a neighboring country? Analogies help an actor determine the relevant comparative context. Metaphors, too, serve to generate an understanding of the surrounding world and possible responses to it. In the realm of immigration policy, for example, aquatic metaphors of waves, streams, or floods of migrants have often been employed to justify turning off the taps of immigration to avoid swamping.

Frames are also critical for helping to interpret problem indicators, crises, and feedback (see Kingdon 1995: 90–103). Frames assist actors

[18] On cultural racism, see especially Barker (1981).

in sorting through the facts of life, drawing their attention to particular bits of information that are endowed with special salience (Entman 1993: 52–3). Frames can thus influence not only what type of information is gathered by policymakers, but also how heavily different information is weighed. If the context for understanding racism is exclusively domestic, for example, one is less likely to look to and to learn from international experiences. Different understandings of the problem at hand and differential attention to the range of possible solutions can affect the eventual policy enacted.

As moral maps, frames assign a valence to terms and to courses of action and can allot authority to speak for a cause. Concepts like race and discrimination may have positive, neutral, or negative connotations, generating (or not) what Gamson (1992: 7) refers to as the hot cognition of moral indignation at injustices. Identifying race as a socially meaningful category may seem natural and necessary to those concerned with fighting racism, or race may be rejected as a meaningless and pernicious term. There are individuals for whom discrimination is an acceptable fact of life; for others it must be eradicated root and branch. In addition, frames may vest certain individuals or groups with authority in representing a cause, either because they are members of a harmed party or because they have established their credentials as honorable advocates.

Frames stand on a middle rung of the ideational ladder of abstraction. They are not as broad as political culture, which refers to factors such as societal levels of trust, willingness to participate in the public sphere, adherence to democratic values, feelings about government, and/or views about hierarchy (Almond and Verba 1989 [1963], Inglehart 1977, Putnam 1993, Wildavsky 1987).[19] They are not as comprehensive as ideologies, which represent total visions of the world (Berman 1998: 20), or as worldviews, which embody conceptions of possibility that include "views about cosmology and onotology as well as about ethics" (Goldstein and Keohane 1993: 8). Yet frames are more than a single causal belief, policy position, or normative proscription. They involve a body of such micro-ideas situated within the context of broader political culture, ideology and worldviews. Frames can be distinguished from other middle-range ideas – such as Berman's (1998) concept of "programmatic beliefs" – by their focus on a particular policy sphere.

[19] The definition of political culture often differs significantly by analyst. For a variety of perspectives on the topic see the overviews by Berezin (1997), Wilson (2000) and Formisano (2001).

In sum, frames are the set of interpretations, cognitive schemas, linguistic tools, causal beliefs and normative sensitivities that an actor applies when conceptualizing a policy domain.[20] They are multidimensional ideas relevant to a particular policy sphere that serve to organize information, empower certain actors, define goals, and constrain actions. As cognitive maps, they include definitions, concepts, metaphors, symbols, and analogies that crystallize the salient dimensions of an issue. As moral maps, they provide value assessments of events, indicating right and wrong policies. Frames help actors specify and prioritize goals, define problems, and interpret events. They point actors toward causal and normative judgments about effective and acceptable policies. In this way, frames help to define the terrain of action and then influence action within that terrain.

Frames and Actors

It has become a mantra in the field of political science to assert that "ideas do not float freely."[21] In order to factor them in to political models, ideas are typically grounded through their attachment to specific carriers.[22] In order to estimate the importance of frames, therefore, it is necessary to outline their relationship to individual actors and to broader social groups.

Each person has his or her own particular configuration of cognitive and moral maps surrounding an issue such as race. These individual frames can be assessed through a variety of methods, including survey research and in-depth interviews. As with Bourdieu's (1990) perspective on the *habitus*, because no two persons share precisely the same experiences, no two individuals' frames will be exactly the same if they are viewed at their most microscopic level. However, frames may also be analyzed at a group level. Although individuals' frames will not be alike in each of their dimensions, it is possible to speak of a frame held by a group of individuals or even by a society as a whole if enough elements of the frame are shared. As we draw back from the individual level, we begin to see similarities and differences in frames at increasing levels of aggregation, just as if we moved from comparing two leaves of an oak tree to

[20] These microelements can and must be distinguished from one another, and may themselves interact with one another. Taken together they amount to frames when they are relatively stable and durable.

[21] See Risse-Kappen (1994), but note that some analysts would take exception to this position. For the counter-argument, see Wendt (1999: 172–6).

[22] Berman (1998: 22) also emphasizes this point.

comparing the leaves of neighboring oak and maple trees, to comparing deciduous and coniferous forests.

Conceptualizing frames in this way means that there is no a priori assumption that all members of a nation, a culture, or a civilization share precisely the same frames.[23] It raises the possibility that groups within each society – elites and masses, policy experts and the uninitiated, liberals and conservatives, blacks and whites – may hold different frames.[24] In short, we must look to see how frames are distributed within a society and across societies. In some cases it will be possible to talk about frames at the national level, and in some cases it will not. Policy frames may be more or less coherent in different policy spheres, at different times, and in different countries. This is an empirical question.

Beyond understanding that frames can be distributed unevenly within and across societies, it is also crucial to grasp precisely how they affect those individuals or groups that hold a particular frame. For scholars that accept the notion that ideas are important in political life, there are two fundamental perspectives on their role. First, ideas are seen to matter because they can be useful to actors. Viewed through this lens, ideas are used as weapons to try to win political battles,[25] they serve as focal points in coordination games, allowing actors to agree on outcomes that ultimately serve their interests (Garrett and Weingast 1993, Schelling 1980: 54–8), or they are useful as road maps, guiding actors down the most stable or productive path of action (Goldstein and Keohane 1993; McNamara 1998). This perspective begins with the actor and presumes an interest, only then bringing ideas into the picture as a tool for achieving those interests. This is in sharp contrast to the second point of view, which states that ideas constitute actors, forming their identities, determining their roles, and helping them define their interests.[26] Ideas factor into politics

[23] In the field of political culture this assumption seems to be held by Huntington (1993), but is not held by Inglehart (1997).

[24] Entman (1993: 52–3) makes a similar point with respect to frames in the communication process, stating that frames have at least four locations: communicators, texts, receivers, and the culture.

[25] One example of this is Thatcher's use of monetarism as a weapon to attack both the leadership of her own party in the mid-1970s and then the opposition Labour party in the 1979 election (Hall 1993: 286).

[26] The literature that reflects this perspective ranges widely from the new institutionalism in sociology (see Finnemore 1996b; March and Olsen 1989; Powell and DiMaggio 1991) to constructivism in international relations (see Checkel 1998; Katzenstein 1996; Wendt 1999).

at the earliest stage, in a sense before actors even enter the scene. This perspective places ideas at the center of analysis, showing not how actors use ideas, but how ideas "use" actors.[27]

Which of these conceptualizations of ideas is correct? From the definition of frames announced above, it should be clear that frames matter precisely by constituting actors' identities and helping them define societal problems and their personal goals. The empirical evidence presented in the next five chapters demonstrates that ideas such as frames do orient actors and propel policy in a particular direction. However, the empirical evidence demonstrates that actors also use ideas to try to advance their interests. In fact, the ideas that they use may be elements of the very frames that help generate actors' identities and interests. There is no necessary contradiction between the two perspectives. Both in theory and in fact, they are simultaneously true.[28]

The relationship between frames and actors is interactive. Frames constitute actors in the sense that they can provide identities and direct interests, but actors are not social dupes that dance to the tune called by free-floating ideas. Individuals can recognize the importance of the ideas that structure their thinking and their social world, and turn around and use those ideas strategically to advance their interests.[29] Frames therefore can have a causal effect on actions, but at the same time actors are free to maneuver within the structure of ideas and to attempt to manipulate them for their own purposes. Frames thus influence political outcomes in two ways: first, because they help formulate actors' interests, and second, because actors can tap into existing frames to try to obtain their goals.[30]

[27] The tension over the analytical relationship between actors and ideas has interesting analogs in the fields of sociology and anthropology. Sociologists have long debated the primacy of agents or structure in theories of action. Anthropologists have deeply rooted disagreements over whether identity is instrumental (responding to the instrumental interests of actors) or primordial (a vision which states that actors' identities are essentially determined by their social world).

[28] Here I draw on the insights of structuration theory (see Giddens 1979, Wendt 1987). The interactive nature of actors and ideas (as a part of structure) is further developed by Sewell (1992).

[29] Finnemore and Sikkink's (2001) overview of constructivism in the field of political science demonstrates that a number of authors also use as their starting point these assumptions about the dual role of ideas.

[30] One example of this kind of interactive dynamic can be seen when actors motivated by norms (such as international human rights) socialize others into believing in those norms or at least into obeying their prescriptions. See, for example, Finnemore (1996a).

Identifying Frames and Their Impact on Policies

In addition to understanding the theoretical bases underpinning the concept of frames, several practical questions must be answered in order to make frame analysis useful in the study of policymaking. How do we pinpoint an actor's policy frame? How do we know if there is a prevailing frame in a country, and if so, is it possible to identify that frame? How do we judge if frames are important in explaining domestic policy outcomes or cross-national policy differences? In short, it is important to know not just where to look for frames, but how to determine precisely what they are; and we need to understand what the patterns of policymaking will look like if frames are important in the process.

Identifying frames can be done in a number of ways. The principal method is to examine the statements of actors in order to gauge their cognitive and moral maps with respect to a particular policy area. Concretely, in the field of race policies, we must discern how they employ and judge terms such as race, racism, and discrimination. Is race seen as a meaningful social category? How is a race or ethnicity constituted? What acts are the prototypical racist acts? Is discrimination an important form of racism, or is it a socially acceptable practice for determining whom we like and dislike? To establish an individual's and a society's frames, it is possible to conduct interviews, examine the public record (through the media and through political transcripts), and comb private documents and archives. Naturally, rhetoric expressed publicly may not always reflect privately held frames and that there may be an uneven distribution of frames within societies. To avoid drawing hasty conclusions, therefore, it is useful to cast a wide net in gathering evidence before judging the contours of an individual's or a society's frames.

If frames are important in determining race policies, the empirical record will show several things. First, actors in each country will hold coherent race frames rather than merely congeries of unrelated or constantly shifting ideas. Frames may evolve over the medium or long-terms (and these evolutions can prompt policy changes), but if they change rapidly and incessantly, their impact on policymaking is likely to be minimal. Second, race frames will precede policymaking episodes and will be evident during policymaking decisions. It may be the case that not every actor involved holds a race frame firmly at the time policy is made. Policy decisions themselves can help cement certain frames with peripheral or uncommitted actors. Yet for frames to be important in the policymaking process, a core group of significant actors must be operating with identifiable frames prior to and during policy negotiations.

Third, new policy initiatives will be in keeping with the implications of the policy frame. If the frame implies that one form of racism is the prototypical form and demands the most energetic policy responses, that form of racism will draw primary policy attention. If the race frame entails a metaphor that implies that policy must change over time or an analogy that links policy developments to other spheres where policy is changing, policy will change. Finally, cross-national variation in policy outcomes will be a function of different prevailing frames. Policy outcomes within each country will depend on frames, and differences between countries will be explained by variation in these frames. Actors in the two countries will talk about race, racism and discrimination in different terms, develop different metaphors and analogies when thinking about race, conceptualize societal problems of racism differently, formulate different policy goals, and enact different race policies.

Conclusion

Examining power-interest, problem-solving, and institutional schools of thought draws attention to factors that shape policy outcomes in a variety of settings. Because the variables they identify have proven important in a wide array of policy spheres, they must be examined carefully in the cases studied here. Each perspective illuminates important aspects of race policymaking in Britain and France, although not every insight from these schools of thought is equally valuable. Even together, however, these theoretical perspectives cannot account for important dimensions of race policy outcomes in these two countries. Given similar constellations of interests, political power, problems of racism, and institutions, key actors in each country pushed for substantially different race policies. As the history of the cross-Channel neighbors demonstrates, this is due in large measure to differences in British and French race frames.

Laying the groundwork for this argument, this chapter has identified the kinds of ideas that matter in the policy process and has fleshed out just how they matter. To that end, it defined a frame as a set of cognitive and moral maps that orient an actor within a policy sphere; it conceptualized the relationship between ideas and actors as interactive, with frames constituting actors but with actors also able to draw on existing frames for their purposes; it argued that frames are ideas held not only by an individual but also distributed across groups; and it provided concrete means for identifying actors' frames and for judging whether they impact the policymaking process. Frames influence policy outcomes by shaping actors' goals, by molding their perceptions of societal problems, and by reinforcing a particular path along which policy is likely to develop. Frames are not alone in determining policy outcomes, but they are more than a mere addendum to other theoretical perspectives – they are necessary variables in complete accounts of policymaking. The trajectory of race policy development in Britain and France demonstrates this point.

2

The Birth of British Race Institutions

1945 to the 1965 Race Relations Act

The 1965 British Race Relations Act was a whimper of a law that arrived with a bang. By contemporary standards it was a narrow and weakly enforced attempt to ban racism. Passage of this act, however, was neither a banal event nor a foregone conclusion. Regulating behavior based on personal preferences or aversions was long and strongly opposed by many of the political elite. Britain's first Race Relations Act was therefore a significant philosophical departure from reigning British public policy. Moreover, action perceived to favor minorities – who at the time were caught in a maelstrom of anti-immigrant electoral sentiment – was not politically popular. Establishing antiracist provisions was thus a risky step for a Labour government with a thin two-seat majority.

The 1965 act had long-term implications for the future of British race institutions, laying the foundations for many present-day British race policies. As the following chapters suggest, the decision taken in 1965 to establish an administrative model (backed by the civil law) to punish access racism was critical to British institutional development and marked a significant departure from the criminal law model later selected in France. Britain's administrative and civil law approach has resulted in significantly higher numbers of complaints, settlements, and verdicts in cases of discrimination than France's criminal law structures. Yet, the content of British institutions was by no means predetermined. Several different formulas for punishing racism were floated and sunk throughout the intense year-long time span between Labour's election in 1964 and the final stage of the Parliamentary process in 1965.

In order to understand the origins and trajectory of British race policies, we need to answer several questions: What factors led British lawmakers to put race on the Parliamentary agenda; who favored the legislation and how did they succeed in enacting this law; what finally determined which types of acts were to be outlawed and what form the antiracism structures would take? This chapter reconstructs the history of the passage of the 1965 British Race Relations Act to answer these questions. It demonstrates that the Labour government passed the law in large part as a reaction to the restrictive immigration context of 1960s Britain. Anti-immigrant public sentiment during this era had two principal effects. First, for electoral reasons, it compelled Labour to accept policies that limited ethnic minority arrivals from overseas. Second, it highlighted the potentially devastating current of racism rippling through British society. The Labour Party therefore constructed the 1965 act as part of a "package deal."[1] Its central purpose was twofold: to appease Labour supporters who bridled at immigration restrictions, and to head off troublesome problems of racism.

The history of the first round of race policymaking in Britain demonstrates that problem indicators and electoral political issues were central to placing race on the agenda. The 1958 riots in Nottingham and Notting Hill, the 1962 Conservative crackdown on immigration, and the 1964 election in the district of Smethwick each helped to persuade the 1964 Labour government to enact the first round of race relations legislation. Each event ratcheted race up the political agenda by raising the public profile of interactions between the white majority and nonwhite minorities. Although frames were important at the agenda-setting stage for helping to interpret events in terms of race, it is also apparent that there was a wide diversity of race frames in Britain in the 1940s through the 1960s. Politicians, policymakers, and experts tended to disagree over the extent and types of racism that gripped British society, and held divergent opinions about the relevant context for analyzing policy options.

One strand of British race frames, however, played a pivotal role in the negotiations over the antiracism institutions eventually implemented. A group of Labour Party activists and politicians came to see British problems of racism as quite similar to problems of racism found in North America and even South Africa. The roots of this frame can be traced back to the mid-1950s, and the influence of this perspective on the 1965 Race Relations Act was decisive. By teaming up with Labour backbenchers, ethnic minority activists, the media, and the opposition Conservative Party, a

[1] On the package deal in particular and the 1965 Race Relations Act in general, see also Hansen (2000: ch. 6).

core group of Labour Party experts convinced the government to abandon its proposed criminalization of access racism in favor of the "North American" solution of administrative and civil law procedures. In this case, actors were driven to seek particular policy outcomes by their frames. These actors also used these frames to rally a coalition of sympathetic allies (such as Labour backbenchers) and electorally interested parties presumed to be hostile (such as the Conservatives) around their preferred policy solution. Here, the combination of specific ideas and the "powering" of an eclectic set of interested actors overturned the government's legislative proposals and established a core element of British anti-racist institutions.

This chapter begins by outlining the demographic and immigrant context of the years 1945 to 1965 in Britain. If London held open the doors to members of its far-flung empire in the immediate postwar era, over time its welcome became less and less warm. Immigration was increasingly seen as a problem closely associated with issues of race and racism. Section two discusses efforts in Britain in the 1950s and 1960s to pass antidiscrimination legislation, suggesting that these had not garnered much enthusiasm or support among the political elite early on. Turning to the underlying causes for the increasing attention to race, the third part of this chapter focuses on the 1958 anti-immigrant, antiminority riots as an early turning point in Labour Party policy. It argues that this incident, coupled with the party's backtracking on its moral and political promises made during passage of the 1962 Commonwealth Immigrants Act and a stark example of racist rhetoric seen in the 1964 election in the constituency of Smethwick, convinced Labour that passing antidiscrimination provisions was necessary in spite of the potential political risks. Section four details the process of passing the law, explaining the dramatic reversal in the government's position on its own bill. It highlights the role of a specific race frame as a gathering point for actors interested in shaping the final version of the legislation. Section five briefly summarizes the institutions established by the 1965 Race Relations Act. It reviews the relevance of policymaking theories to the case at hand and suggests that although the 1965 act had generated much noise, this law was not enough to silence the problems of racism on British shores.

The Immigration Context: 1948 to 1965

Like most European countries, Britain experienced a labor shortage in the years following World War II. Hundreds of thousands of immigrants arrived on the sceptered isle to take up jobs between the late 1940s and the early 1960s. Initially, many came from Ireland, the "Old Commonwealth" (Canada, Australia, and New Zealand), and other non-Commonwealth countries (Freeman 1979: 47). Later increasing numbers came from "New Commonwealth" countries, comprised primarily of nonwhite populations (Freeman 1979: 23, Layton-Henry 1992). It was these later immigrants who prompted much of the political debate over immigration policy and who ultimately induced Britain to develop domestic race policies.

As they recruited workers from beyond their shores, British leaders periodically raised questions about the "best" immigrants for Britain. These discussions percolated into the public domain when the first boatload of Jamaicans sailed into Britain on the Empire Windrush in 1948 containing, in *The Times*' words, "singers, students, pianists, boxers, and a complete dance band. Thirty or forty of [the immigrants] have already volunteered to work as miners" (*The Times*, June 23, 1948). Although the Minister of Labour was short on workers, he declared that he hoped "no encouragement is given to others to follow their example" (quoted in Foot 1965). Race thus played a role in debates and calculations about appropriate immigrants, although it was rarely the sole factor considered (Great Britain: Royal Commission on Population 1949: 124–5, 130; Miles 1993: 150–69).[2] Concerns about absorbing racially or culturally different newcomers exposed an underlying tension throughout the postwar era between those who favored white immigrants of "good stock" to the exclusion of "coloured" immigrants, and those who felt a strong commitment to the multiracial Commonwealth (Katznelson 1976: 127). As Randall Hansen's work demonstrates, immigrants from the Commonwealth and colonies had a privileged status on British shores.[3] They were legally and psychologically (in theory at least) more part of the national community than "aliens,"[4] irrespective of race. As British subjects, they obtained full civil, political, and social rights upon establishing residency in Britain. They had the right to work, the right to vote, and

[2] The Royal Commission on Population, for example, doubted that immigration was a viable solution to problems of low domestic population given that "the sources of supply of suitable immigrants for Great Britain are limited, as is also the capacity of a fully established society like ours to absorb immigrants of alien race and religion" (Great Britain: Royal Commission on Population 1949: 130).

[3] It is of course illogical to refer to a country's citizens or subjects as immigrants merely because they move from one place to another within the country or Empire. Nevertheless, it is standard practice to refer to non-British Isles British citizens and subjects as immigrants if they relocate from a colony or Commonwealth country to Britain. I therefore retain this convention.

[4] Migrants to the UK from countries outside the Commonwealth or colonies.

the right to access Britain's new national health care system as well as all the social services the UK had to offer. In the early postwar years of the late 1940s and 1950s – in spite of egregious examples of racialist reasoning[5] – it is safe to say that pro-Commonwealth advocates had the moral and political upper hand and that Britain admitted subjects of the Crown regardless of their race or religion (Hansen 2000).

This does not mean that race was not in the public eye. Subjugation of the "darker races" and notions of the "white man's burden" were well known to elites who had traveled to the colonies and to school children reading about Britain's far-flung empire (Tomlinson 1990: 71–86). In addition to popular (and often negative) assessments of minorities in this era, a small group of British anthropologists and other interested parties began to construct and to investigate notions of race defined around the color line, often drawing on American and African inspiration. This era gave rise to books such as *Negroes in Britain* (Little 1948) and *The Coloured Quarter* (Banton 1955) and to the founding of the Institute of Race Relations in the 1950s (Rich 1986: 193–200). For these experts, race carried no nefarious overtones; rather, it was simply a sociological phenomenon to be studied and understood. Although an interest in race and color was burgeoning in these circles in the 1950s and lurked in the back of the public consciousness,[6] thinking in such terms had not yet come to dominate British postwar culture.

Closely related to concerns about the racial composition of Britain, immigration increasingly became a subject of public and political debate. Over time, and as the numbers of ethnic minority immigrants rose, the balance shifted between those who favored an inclusive policy toward members of the Commonwealth and colonies, and those who argued for restrictions.[7] The electorate put more pressure on mainstream politicians to halt the influx of immigrants (Money 1999).[8] Fears of a clampdown generated a surge of ethnic minority immigrants in the early 1960s, as individuals from the Commonwealth and colonies rushed to Britain to

[5] For examples of race prejudice among political and policy leaders, see Carter et al. (1987), Miles (1990), Miles (1993: 157–64), and Carter et al. (1996).

[6] It could also be witnessed in Whitehall, although again, within limited circles (Carter, Harris, and Joshi 1987, Paul 1997).

[7] On the seeds of changing opinion, see especially Dean (1992).

[8] The rising political temperature has to be seen in the historical context of the economic downturn of the late 1950s, the long-standing competition for housing, and the anti-immigrant sentiment expressed during the 1958 disturbances in London and Nottingham (Layton-Henry 1992: 36–41, Rex and Moore 1967, Sked and Cook 1990: 152–4, 178–9).

"beat the ban" announced by the Conservative government in 1961. Immigration from the New Commonwealth climbed from 57,700 in 1960 to 136,400 in 1961 to 94,900 for the first six months of 1962 before controls were introduced (Layton-Henry 1992: 13). Immigration of ethnic minorities into the United Kingdom dropped dramatically thereafter. In 1966, for example, Ministry of Labour voucher holders admitted from the West Indies, India, and Pakistan (the three largest sources of immigrants) totaled 3,782 (Freeman 1979: 24–5). Restrictionists seemed to have won the day on the issue of immigration. Once the initial immigrants had settled in Britain, however, they began to bring over their families, thereby engendering a stream of immigration not stringently controlled by state policies.[9] By 1966, there were approximately one million ethnic minority individuals resident in the United Kingdom, a figure that firmly entrenched Britain's status as a newly multiracial and multicultural nation (Rose 1969: appendix Table III).

The Politics of Antidiscrimination before 1965

Although antidiscrimination laws were rarely visible on the political agenda prior to 1964, there was virtually constant low-level attention to the topic preceding the 1965 Race Relations Act. Two efforts to enact British legislation prohibiting discrimination predate the end of World War II,[10] each of which, however, illustrated the reluctance of British policymakers to encode race into British laws. The Public Order Act of 1936 – designed to punish insulting words likely to lead to a breach of the peace – was written in the context of anti-Semitic statements and violence by Oswald Mosely's British Union of Fascists (Cross 1961: 161, Lester and Bindman 1972: 350). Although passed because of ethnic tensions, Parliament ultimately decided not to include explicit provisions against incitement to *racial or religious prejudice* in the bill, punishing instead generic acts of incitement to *disorder* (Hansard 318: 638–54).[11]

[9] Dependents from the West Indies, India, and Pakistan admitted in 1966 totaled 32,554 (Freeman 1979: 24–5).

[10] In addition, see Lester and Bindman (1972: 383–418) on antidiscrimination legislation for India which was passed in the nineteenth century, but was never fully implemented. There were also common law provisions which in theory (but not necessarily in practice) prohibited discrimination in certain domains (Jowell 1965: 171–5).

[11] The act banned the wearing of political uniforms under most circumstances, forbade the use of stewards at open air meetings, strengthened the existing law against using words likely to lead to a breach of the peace and gave the police power to ban

Similarly, a law proposed in 1943 to ban racial discrimination on British soil was ultimately rejected on the grounds that it was seen as contrary to public policy to give preferential treatment and protection to just one segment of the national population (Lester and Bindman 1972: 21).

Concerns over racism thus evoked a tension within the British elite. On the one hand, there had been enough interest in policies that sought to combat racism to place them on the political agenda in the 1930s and early 1940s; on the other hand, the idea that the state had a duty to be race-neutral had carried the day in each instance. In its dealings with the colonies and in popular perception, race was a category that Britons recognized and utilized, yet there was an overriding desire to avoid overtly race-based domestic policies. As with the rising interest in the topic in academic studies, however, the 1950s and early 1960s saw a gradual evolution with respect to political leaders' opinions on the place of race in state structures.

After the war, segments of the Labour Party began to turn their attention to questions of racism. In the early 1950s, the party commissioned two reports on race issues, each of which advocated legislation against racial discrimination. The Labour leadership shelved both reports, however, and took no action (Hepple 1968 129–30, Hindell 1965: 390–1, Lester and Bindman 1972: 108). By the mid-1950s, party literature contained periodic statements against racial discrimination, although it shied away from proposing legislation (Foot 1965: 167–8, Katznelson 1976: 128–9).[12] Furthermore, a small number of individual Labour Members of Parliament repeatedly proposed antidiscrimination laws. In the early 1950s, Reginald Sorensen and Fenner Brockway each introduced "colour bar bills" designed to prevent discrimination against blacks on British soil. Between 1953 and 1964, Brockway introduced nine similar bills, two other Labour MPs[13] put forward slightly different versions in the House of Commons, and Lord Walston introduced a 1962 bill in the House of

marches if they were deemed likely to lead to a breach of the peace (Cross 1961: 161). The MP who moved the amendment to include wording about racial and religious hatred did so arguing that this was the true problem and the true purpose of the bill, and that other forms of opinion or speech should not be outlawed. The Attorney General responded that the importance of the initiative was in banning acts that would lead to breaches of the peace, no matter what type of speech was used (Hansard 318: 638–54).

[12] In addition, Labour Party insiders in the late 1950s were considering the benefits of a ban on racial incitement in the hopes that it would "prevent racial discrimination getting a foothold in the social organisation of this country" (Dean 1993: 65).

[13] J. Baird in 1958 and Leslie Plummer in 1960.

Lords (Hepple 1968: 129, PRO HO 342/82). But bills such as these, especially coming from Labour benches under the Conservative governments of 1951–64, had very little chance of becoming law. Of all of these bills, only one (Brockway's 1957 bill) made it to the second stage of the Parliamentary process, where it was disqualified because fewer than forty of the six hundred and thirty MPs were present for the debate (Lester and Bindman 1972: 109).

The pockets of the British public and of the Labour Party committed to legislative action were therefore very limited and relatively inconsequential. In the years after the war and leading up to the passage of the 1965 act, there were many reasons to doubt enactment of race relations provisions. In the anti-immigrant context of the mid-1960s, there was little electoral support for a law commonly understood as proimmigrant (Hindell 1965: 398, Lester 1996, Lester and Bindman 1972: 15). Pressure group support prior to the Labour government's announcement of forthcoming legislation in 1964 was confined to low-level lobbying from Jewish organizations which archives demonstrate had little impact on the government's thought or actions.[14]

Perhaps most importantly, there remained strong institutional biases against incorporating race provisions into British law, which was seen as "the quintessence of colour blindness" (Rose 1969: 200). During the 1964 election campaign, for example, Conservative Prime Minister Sir Alec Douglas-Home stated that "those who ask for special legislation [dealing with racial discrimination] ignore the fact that at present all British citizens, irrespective of race, creed or colour, are equal under the law" (cited in Deakin 1965: 10).[15] Moreover, British law was seen to play a linchpin role in upholding freedom of contract and property (Jowell 1965: 179, Lester 1996, PRO HO 342/82). This principle was invoked in the late 1950s, when a British court ruled that a Wolverhampton ballroom

[14] During the late 1950s and early 1960s Jewish groups sought laws against anti-Semitic public speeches made during this era (Lester and Bindman 1972: 109, NCCL: National Council for Civil Liberties 1960), but there is little evidence that this pressure achieved substantial results. Lester and Bindman (1972: 109) do note that the anti-Semitic speeches prompted Brockway to include an anti-incitement provision in his 1961 bill, which was supported by the Board of Deputies of British Jews. But while the disorder prompted by far right rallies in 1962 led to the 1963 strengthening of the 1936 Public Order Act, it did not lead to provisions against incitement to racial or religious hatred (Lester and Bindman 1972: 353, PRO HO 342/83).

[15] See also the similar objections of the Conservative Home Secretary, Henry Brooke, voiced in 1963 (referred to by Jowell 1965: 180).

could legally maintain a "colour bar" in its business interests (Lester and Bindman 1972: 53). Internal memos during the Conservative Party's terms in office show that there was also reluctance to pass such laws on the grounds that they were unenforceable and as such would only bring the law as a whole into contempt (PRO HO 342/82). Given the relative indifference to discrimination as a public phenomenon and the overwhelmingly anti-immigrant context of the early 1960s, passage of the 1965 act was in no way preordained. What factors, then, turned the tide and placed race on the legislative agenda?

The Parliamentary Labour Party bears primary responsibility for taking the race initiative. They first formulated proposals for banning discrimination while in opposition in 1958 and carried them into policy upon attaining office in 1964. Yet identifying the actors does not explain the action. The party's motives for overturning precedent cannot be accounted for in terms of an appeal for votes. Instead, they were related to four central factors. First, the party leadership was concerned with preserving social peace by minimizing interracial tensions. Second, Labour MPs felt substantial guilt over their acquiescence to the Conservative Party's 1962 immigration restrictions. These two factors led politicians to insist on integrating immigrants into British society, a constant theme in 1960s British political discourse.

Third – and linked to the previous motives – party leadership changed its views on British tolerance. Whereas prior to the late 1950s Britons were viewed as almost universally tolerant of immigrants, the increasing social tensions in this era made politicians aware of British intolerance and the need to curb the intolerant. Finally, the Labour Party wanted to remove race from the political and electoral sphere. The 1965 Race Relations Act was seen to respond to all of these goals. Three central events and their aftermaths forged this line of reasoning within the Labour party: the 1958 riots, the 1962 Commonwealth Immigrants Act, and the 1964 election in the borough of Smethwick.

The 1958 Riots

Labour's first public support for antidiscrimination legislation came in the wake of the "race riots" of the summer of 1958 (Foot 1965: 167–9, Hepple 1968: 130, Hindell 1965: 392).[16] In late August and early September of

[16] See also LPA, File Box: "Race Relations and Immigration / Racial Discrimination Debate 1958 / Notes and Memoranda 1958 / Press Cuttings 1960–1 / Memoranda etc. 1962–3, 1965."

that year, a series of conflicts erupted in Nottingham and the Notting Hill section of London. The disturbances encompassed actions such as altercations between small groups, and the mobilization of hundreds of whites, hurling missiles and physically attacking West Indian immigrants. As Robert Miles states in his study of the riots, "one can conclude that the West Indians were primarily the victims of attack by British-born residents" (Miles 1984: 255). Miles (1984: 262–4) illustrates how the reaction of the political class and the media came to be framed by MPs who argued that the events demonstrated a "race problem" in Britain, the solution to which was immigration control.[17] Cyril Osborne, a Conservative MP, went so far as to proclaim that Britain was "sowing the seeds of another 'Little Rock' and it is tragic. To bring the problem into this country with our eyes open is doing the gravest disservice to our grandchildren, who will curse us for our lack of courage. I regard the Nottingham incident as a red light" (*The Times*, August 28, 1958). The overriding short term aim of the government in the days surrounding the events remained, however, the restoration of public order (Miles 1984: 257).

Although Labour's initial response to the riots was confused, by the end of September (one month after the onset of the disorders) it had issued a policy statement committing itself to legislate against racial discrimination (Lester and Bindman 1972: 109, Miles 1984: 265).[18] Having formulated a prolegislation policy, Labour followed through by urging the Conservative government several times during the next few years to pass antidiscrimination legislation. In spite of this apparent commitment to the cause,

[17] The "solution" to an anti-immigrant riot was therefore seen – some would say ironically – to be anti-immigration policies.

[18] The Labour Party pledged to legislate against discrimination in "all places to which the public have access" – a seemingly incongruous solution to the problems of physical racism exhibited during the riots of 1958. The party proposed to ban access racism and not physical racism in part because it had already established an internal subcommittee to monitor acts of racism in Britain. As of 1958, the committee had fielded several complaints of access racism, but had not been asked (or forced) to handle issues of physical racism. Although no detailed records exist in the Labour Party archives, it is possible that when the party turned to the committee for an immediate policy proposal, the committee responded with its ideas to outlaw access racism. This incident therefore illustrates an interesting institutional influence on solution choice since the party turned for proposals to its institutionally established experts. It is also possible that since the purpose of legislation was most likely to make a strong statement against generalized racism, the form of the law would be less important than the fact of its existence. For more information, see LPA, File Box: "Race Relations and Immigration / Racial Discrimination Debate 1958 / Notes and Memoranda 1958 / Press Cuttings 1960–1 / Memoranda etc. 1962–3, 1965."

their lack of support for the Labour backbencher Brockway's bills suggests that this issue was not at the top of their agenda (Lester and Bindman 1972: 109, Rose 1969: 222). Nevertheless, the social disorder exhibited during the 1958 riots engendered a sense within the Labour Party that the state needed to take action to preserve the peace.[19] In the words of Home Secretary Soskice during passage of the 1965 Race Relations Bill, the Party learned that: "Overt acts of discrimination in public places, intensely wounding to the feelings of those against whom these acts are practised, perhaps in the presence of many onlookers, breed the ill will which, as the accumulative result of several such actions over a period, may disturb the peace" (Hansard 711: 927). For Soskice, race relations legislation was in large part related to concerns of public order, a lesson first learned by the party in 1958.

The 1962 Commonwealth Immigrants Act (CIA)

Under increasing pressure from its backbenches, party faithful, and cabinet members, the Conservative government announced during the Queen's Speech on October 31, 1961 that it would introduce legislation "to control the immigration to the United Kingdom of British subjects from other parts of the Commonwealth" (Hansard 648: 6).[20] Although the Conservative Party had been persuaded of the need for what was to become the 1962 Commonwealth Immigrants Act, the same was not true for Labour, which loosened all of its rhetorical and procedural cannons in an effort to sink the project. It proposed wrecking amendments, opposed the imposition of the guillotine, and wrangled for concessions during the committee stage (Foot 1965: 171–3). Labour leaders excoriated the Conservatives. Hugh Gaitskell rose during the Second Reading Debate in Parliament to denounce "this miserable, shameful, shabby bill" which was "a plain anti-colour Measure" (Hansard 649: 803, 799). The bill was seen as embodying pure race restrictions not only because it came in response to public statements about preserving British "whiteness," but also because it exempted the Irish from immigration control (even though hundreds of thousands of Irish immigrants were entering Britain

[19] The 1958 riots were not the first instances of racial tensions in the postwar era. Disturbances had occurred in the late 1940s in Liverpool, Deptford, and Birmingham, typically involving fights between blacks and whites (Hansen 2000: 58).

[20] For detailed studies of the Conservative Party's positions on immigration in the 1950s and early 1960s, see Dean (1992) and Dean (1993).

in the same era).[21] When Conservative Home Secretary R. A. Butler tried to temper the exception by offering that the government reserved the right to control Irish immigration, Patrick Gordon Walker retorted for Labour: "Why did the right hon. Gentleman put this in the Bill in the first place?...I think I know. He put it in as a sort of fig leaf to preserve his reputation for liberalism. Now he stands revealed before us in his nakedness. He is an advocate now of a Bill which contains barefaced, open race discrimination" (Hansard 649: 706). Labour had energized its activists and taken a strong moral line. In early 1962, speaking before a mass meeting of Commonwealth organizations in Britain, front-bench spokesperson Dennis Healey "gave a solemn pledge that a Labour government would repeal the Immigration act" (Foot 1965: 173).

But this moral and political commitment was soon to lose its force. By late February 1962, Healey was hedging on his promise. Labour refused to commit itself in Parliament to repealing the act, and implied that it would accept restrictions, "if the information collected by a serious survey of the whole problem revealed that immigration control was necessary..." (Hansard 654: 1271). By late 1963 the party (under the leadership of Harold Wilson following Gaitskell's death in January) no longer officially contested the need for control of immigration (Foot 1965: 175–6, Katznelson 1976: 146). By 1964 Home Secretary Soskice had taken this a step further by declaring that "the Government are firmly convinced that an effective control is indispensable. That we accept, and have always accepted" (Hansard 702: 290). And by late 1965 the party had co-opted the rhetoric used by the Conservatives in 1961, speaking of "the need to control entry of immigrants to our small and overcrowded country" (Great Britain: Home Office 1965: 5), marking a substantial reversal from its earlier position.

For many in the party, this hard line was distasteful. The preferred method of assuaging Labour's guilty conscience was to emphasize the "positive" aspects of its immigration policy, defined as "integration." The goal of integrating immigrants was supported by both parties, as British leaders sought a respite for the nation to come to terms with the island's new inhabitants (Katznelson 1976: 140–1). Although several observers have commented on the contradictions of this dual strategy (see Foot 1965: 185, Katznelson 1976: 150), it gained credibility among the

[21] See Carter, Green, and Halpern (1996: 151), Foot (1965: 139–40), and Miles (1993: 130–1, 154–5).

party faithful. Roy Hattersley captured the mood best with the aphorism: "Without integration, limitation is inexcusable; without limitation, integration is impossible" (quoted in Rose 1969: 229). Immigration controls and positive integration measures (such as antidiscrimination legislation and aid to areas affected by immigration) were pitched – and well-received – as two sides of the same coin.[22]

In spite of the development of the dual strategy (which Home Secretary Soskice would term the package deal),[23] by the time Labour came to power in late 1964, it was under little pressure and had little incentive to follow through on its pledge to legislate against discrimination. There was much opposition or ambivalence in the electorate to perceived prominority laws. Yet Labour's rejection of the 1962 CIA and then its acceptance of immigration controls left a residue of guilt in the party and resulted in modest pressure for proimmigrant policies. The party's left wing cast 1.5 million votes against the government's restrictionist immigration line at the 1965 Labour conference (Ziegler 1993: 200). As Wilson's official biographer notes, "Wilson had considerable sympathy with his left wing on this issue. He disliked the legislation and would have liked at least to accompany it by measures that would ensure that those immigrants who were allowed in were treated properly. He argued for a law that would prohibit any sort of racial discrimination" (Ziegler 1993: 200).[24] Being tough on Commonwealth immigrants at the borders was a new tactic for the party. It militated against Labour's commitment to the Commonwealth, its commitment to open immigration and its ideal of nondiscriminatory policies. As the first chairman of the Race Relations Board wrote, "It was in response to this combination of pressures, some political, others his-

[22] Years later during the 1976 Race Relations Bill debates, then Home Secretary Roy Jenkins framed the trade-off in just these terms: "Together with that strong control over immigration, we must have a most determined and liberal policy of complete equality for those settled in this country. I regard these matters as two sides of the same coin." (Hansard 905: 596).

[23] PRO HO 376/68, Hansen (2000: 137).

[24] Kushnick (1971: 240) suggests that acceptance of the 1962 restrictions was "bound to create a storm of opposition within the Labour Party," and that given a thin House of Commons majority an antidiscrimination bill was important to preserving party unity. Moreover, Howard (1963: 726) notes that passions were still running high against the 1962 act in Labour quarters. While concerns of party unity undoubtedly played a role in Soskice's desire to introduce a "package deal" on immigration issues, antidiscrimination laws were a tough electoral bullet for Labour to bite given widespread popular anti-immigrant sentiment in this era. Absent guilty consciences and other additional factors, it is doubtful that the Race Relations Act would have seen the light of day.

torical, and others prompted by guilt, that the [1965 Race Relations Act] emerged" (Bonham Carter 1987: 3).

The 1964 Election in Smethwick

The general election of 1964 returned Labour to power for the first time since its loss in 1951. On the strength of a national swing to Labour of 3.5 percent, the party garnered 317 of 630 seats in the House of Commons (Sked and Cook 1990: 194). Immigration and race, however, were not particularly salient national electoral issues, making an impact in only twenty-four Parliamentary races that year (Deakin 1965: 157). Yet the racialized tenor of the campaign in just one constituency – Smethwick – sent tremors through the nation's political elite. For the first time and in the starkest terms, the battle for a Parliamentary seat went beyond discussion of immigrant flows to purely racial issues. In an interview given to *The Times* in March 1964, the Conservative candidate Peter Griffiths spoke about the slogan "If you want a nigger neighbour, vote Liberal or Labour." He declared "I should think that is a manifestation of the popular feeling. I would not condemn anyone who said that" (quoted in Deakin 1965: 8–9, Hansen 2000: 132).

Griffiths not only won the seat with a large (7.2%) electoral swing to the Conservatives (Deakin 1965: 159), he also defeated Patrick Gordon Walker, a defender of liberal policies during the 1962 immigration debates, and Labour's shadow foreign secretary.[25] As one of the foremost observers of race politics in Britain notes, Smethwick sent shock waves through the party and the political elite, making "colour and race major factors in British politics for the first time" (Deakin 1965: foreword). Griffiths was branded a "Parliamentary leper" by Wilson (Hansard 701: 71). To add insult to injury, Gordon Walker failed in his subsequent bid for a "safe" Labour seat, a fact at the time widely attributed to the race issue (Deakin 1965: 157–8, Rose 1969: 225).[26] Labour's majority subsequently shrank to two seats.

The Labour Party drew two lessons from this experience. First, Britain was not as welcoming to racial minorities as previously thought. It was clear that British tolerance, upon which arguments against race legislation

[25] During the 1962 debates an astute Gordon Walker recorded in his diary that he feared losing his seat due to the difficulties in his constituency "owing to colour" (quoted in Dean 1993: 72).

[26] The loss was not necessarily due to race factors, though. Hansen (2000: 133) argues that carpetbagging and poor campaigning skills were likely more prominent concerns of the constituency.

rested, did not hold uniformly for every Briton. Speaking for the government during the Second Reading Debate on the 1965 bill, David Ennals declared that "no one who has studied the facts can deny that there is discrimination in some parts of Britain today" (Hansard 711: 167). Certainly the party had learned the limits of British tolerance during the 1958 riots, but the Smethwick election served as a ringing reminder. Moreover, Griffiths' success was viewed as a stain on British politics. In a letter to the archbishop of Canterbury, Wilson wrote about anti-immigrant feelings, stating that "unless this problem is dealt with head on, I am afraid that it will foul our politics not only in the next Election but over a very considerable period of time" (quoted in Ziegler 1993: 174). Smethwick thus alerted Labour leaders to the lurking "monster" of race prejudice (Hindell 1965: 395), helping to convince them of the necessity of legislation.

Second, the party realized that it would benefit from eliminating race as a partisan issue. The mood of the electorate was particularly hostile to immigrants, and in closely fought races under conditions of thin Parliamentary majorities, Labour would lose votes for being seen as prominority.[27] Yet if Labour's strategy was to neutralize race as an electoral issue, its tactic of passing antidiscrimination legislation was not self-evident. Although some observers have argued that the eventual structures served as "buffer institutions" depoliticizing race tensions (Katznelson 1976: 150–1), the choice to elevate the topic to national prominence through a Parliamentary debate was highly risky. It was clearly in the Conservative Party's interest to oppose the Race Relations Act as a proimmigrant policy. This tactic evoked great public sympathy when pursued in the late 1960s by Enoch Powell (see Layton-Henry 1992: 79–83).[28] Labour therefore judged that the only way it could settle the race issue and defuse the ticking bomb was by pursuing bipartisan Parliamentary consensus over an antidiscrimination law.

From the Agenda to the Law

The Labour Party officially committed itself to legislate against racial discrimination during the Queen's Speech of November 1964 (Hansard 701: 37–41).[29] The course of events that had placed race on the government's

[27] See Money (1999) for an elaboration on the dynamics of immigration politics under conditions of close elections.

[28] For works on Powell and Powellism, see Cosgrave (1990) and Shepherd (1996).

[29] Harold Wilson began speaking publicly of Parliamentary action as of 1963 (Hindell 1965: 390, Kushnick 1971: 239), and the party had included a short sentence in

agenda, however, did not necessarily dictate the precise form of the institutions that were to result from the law. In many ways, these decisions were even more important to the future of British race policies than the factors that motivated the agenda-setting process. The results of the 1965 struggles over race law had lasting implications for British institutions, driving them in a different direction from those later adopted in France.

Expressive Racism: Incitement to Racial Hatred

Although rarely the foremost concern of British race policies, banning expressive racism (formulated as incitement to racial hatred) was an early goal of the Labour Party. As Shadow Prime Minister, Wilson had claimed in April 1964 that his government would legislate against incitement; yet the November Queen's Speech conspicuously avoided mention of the topic, limiting its pledge to a ban against racial discrimination (PRO HO 376/3, Hansard 701: 37–41). As it turns out, the government was sympathetic to enacting expressive racism prohibitions but it was uncertain that satisfactory legal provisions could be crafted.[30]

Its hesitation was due in large part to the reluctance of the Home Office bureaucracy to institute anti-incitement provisions. Civil servants had claimed that a law to punish incitement on racial grounds was unworkable; they forwarded their reservations about legislation to the Labour government in the form of strongly worded internal memos (PRO HO 342/82, PRO HO 342/83). When pressed by the new Home Secretary to consider options against incitement, the Home Office bureaucrats responded reluctantly by stating that "the working party's view is that the case for legislation is not at present made out" (PRO HO 376/68). In the face of continued pressure, however, they conceded that "the least

the 1964 election manifesto pledging to legislate against racial discrimination and incitement (Craig 1975: 268). Moreover, in early 1964 the party had asked both the shadow Labour cabinet and the Society of Labour Lawyers to draft proposals to fulfill Labour's pledge (Lester and Bindman 1972: 110). But given electoral hostility to immigrant issues, the party's lack of prioritizing such legislation since its first commitment of support in 1958, and its shelving of similar reports generated in the early 1950s (Hindell 1965: 390–91), it was the Queen's Speech that finally cemented the party's pledge to legislate.

[30] The minutes of the cabinet meeting of October 29, 1964 state: "The action against racial discrimination which was foreshadowed in the speech should, if possible, deal also with incitement to racial hatred. But, in view of the difficulties of devising satisfactory legislation for this purpose, no commitment on this point should be accepted at this stage" (PRO CAB 128/39 Part I: C.C. 4[64]).

objectionable course" was creation of a new offence of written incitement of hatred between groups of different race or color (PRO HO 376/68).

During the subsequent back-and-forth between the bureaucrats and Home Secretary Soskice over the incitement portion of the bill, there was a particularly interesting, if relatively fleeting, tension over the nature of the social problems the provisions were designed to counter, and over whether countering specific social problems was the major purpose of the bill. Most of the relatively low-level societal pressure for anti-incitement provisions emanated from the Jewish community.[31] By 1964, however, Home Office bureaucrats argued that Jews were more concerned with swastika-daubing than with major anti-Semitic public statements of the kind made in earlier years (PRO HO 376/68). The bureaucrats were primarily interested in whether these types of acts could be adequately penalized by a law. Soskice too had his concerns about whether and how such acts could be effectively punished, but wrote that "the only justification and need for the legislation is as part of a big package deal, together with [other measures] to integrate the coloured immigrants" (PRO HO 376/68). Soskice was arguing, in effect, that the problems were not narrowly confined to those identified by the Jewish community. Rather, they were more broadly related to immigrant integration. In emphasizing the term package deal and deemphasizing the practical working of the law, however, Soskice was also clearly responding to the political imperative of making palatable the immigration restrictions so distasteful to many in the Labour Party (Hansen 2000: 137–8).

In the end, the Home Secretary's and the party's insistence won out over the Home Office's reluctance. Anti-incitement provisions were to be formulated and included in the law, as problematic as they may have been.[32] Yet although much bureaucratic energy was expended discussing how such provisions could be made legally and practically enforceable, and although substantial time was allotted in the 1965 Parliamentary debates to incitement and free-speech concerns (Hansard 711: 926–1060), the majority of the attention devoted to race relations

[31] Public pressure for action peaked following Colin Jordan's anti-Semitic public speeches during the summer of 1962, when 430,000 signatures were collected calling for legislation against racial incitement (Kushnick 1971: 242). Although this did not sway the Conservative government, Kushnick (1971: 242) asserts that these efforts strengthened Labour's resolve to pass anti-incitement legislation.

[32] The decision was taken at the cabinet meeting of February 22, 1965 (PRO CAB 128/39 Part I).

legislation in Britain has not centered on expressive racism. After being passed in 1965, anti-incitement provisions have taken a consistently low profile compared to issues of access racism and concerns about color.[33]

Access Racism: Choosing Institutions

When Reginald Sorensen submitted his "colour bar bill" to Parliament in 1950, it sounded what was to become a recurring note. Criminalizing access racism was to be the default proposal of virtually all subsequent Parliamentary bills (Lester and Bindman 1972: 107–13).[34] When the Labour government published its Race Relations Bill on April 7, 1965 it too was predicated on the use of criminal law to punish access racism. This not only followed the precedent of earlier drafts from a variety of sources, it was also "more in line with [British] legal tradition," in the eyes of Home Secretary Soskice (Hepple 1968: 133, Hindell 1965: 398).

Yet the final version of the 1965 Race Relations Act differed dramatically from the initial bill. By the time the law was given the Royal Assent in November 1965, the criminal provisions against access racism had been excised and replaced with a process which relied on administrative procedures and conciliation in the first instance, backed ultimately by civil court enforcement. Such a substantial policy tack mid-stream in the legislative process is virtually unknown in Britain, and it prompted some opposition members of Parliament to call for the government to withdraw its project and to resubmit a new bill.[35] Moreover, the practical implications of the different systems are substantial. Obtaining convictions using criminal procedures proves extremely difficult, whereas using an administrative approach and the civil law facilitates the airing of grievances (Banton 1994). The 1965 selection of an administrative approach to

[33] When it came time to legislate the 1976 Race Relations Act, the Home Office (in its 1975 White Paper) devoted only a brief section to issues of "Racial Incitement and Public Order," stressing their fundamental differences from the main focus of the upcoming act: "These offences are entirely separate from the antidiscrimination provisions of the race relations legislation. They deal with the stirring up of racial hatred rather than with acts of racial discrimination; they are criminal rather than civil; and they are enforced in the criminal courts rather than by the Race Relations Board in the civil courts" (Great Britain: Home Office 1975: 30).

[34] Brockway's bills took slightly different shapes over the years, and in some cases included the provision that the victim could recover damages in a civil action (Lester and Bindman 1972: 108–09).

[35] Standing Committee B, Race Relations Bill; 1st Sitting, May 25, 1965, cc. 6–8.

handling access racism went on to become the foundation upon which future British race institutions were built, and marks one of the most important differences between British and French race institutions.[36]

How, then, did this transformation occur? Three groups of actors combined to produce this unusual turn of events. First, a small group of Labour lawyers introduced a new policy idea into the British debate. Having framed British problems of racism as similar to those in North America and having studied American and Canadian policies, this group lobbied for administrative machinery and conciliation as the most effective means of resolving problems of access racism. Second, Labour backbenchers and the Conservative opposition each (for different reasons, discussed below) took up the banner of the alternative policy proposal. Finally, faced with pressure from left and right, the government – with a razor thin majority and wanting to avoid confrontation over an electorally unpopular issue – agreed to revise its proposed bill between the Parliamentary Second Reading and the committee stage, rejecting its plans for criminal provisions and embracing the administrative approach.

The original idea for a statutory agency to deal with discrimination complaints can be traced to a group of Labour lawyers and to their exposure to American race relations policies. Prior to the mid-1960s there was little knowledge in Britain of the U.S. institutional mechanisms for dealing with racism. As Britain's Institute of Race Relations Director Philip Mason noted, whereas in the United States at this time "there was too much information" on race issues, in Britain there was "nothing like enough" (Rose 1969: xx).[37] When the Labour Party's National Executive Committee solicited two proposals for legislation in 1964, one group – the

[36] The 1976 modifications to the pure administrative model are addressed in Chapter 4.

[37] There was, however, some information available, notably through scholars such as Kenneth Little, who made policy recommendations to the Labour Party in the early 1950s (see Hindell 1965: 390–1). Also, there were sporadic contacts between the Labour Party and Home Office bureaucrats and various U.S. race relations agencies in the 1950s and early 1960s. In addition, the Institute of Race Relations (IRR) began releasing press summaries in March 1958 on "Coloured People in Great Britain." The IRR seems to have taken over from the Royal Institute on International Affairs, whose "Board of Studies on Race Relations" started putting out a monthly report on "Coloured People in Great Britain" in March 1955. See LPA, File Box: "Race Relations and Immigration / Racial Discrimination Debate 1958 / Notes and Memoranda 1958 / Press Cuttings 1960–1 / Memoranda etc. 1962–63, 1965," File Box: "RIIA – Race Relations / Institute of Race Relations / 1955–59," and PRO HO 342/82.

shadow cabinet working committee, which included the future Home Secretary Frank Soskice – focused mostly on issues of incitement (Hindell 1965: 392–3, Lester and Bindman 1972: 110) and suggested access racism provisions that employed the traditional tools of criminal punishment. As Hindell (1965: 393) explains, they did not "indicate any awareness of foreign experience or legislation." This group's proposals constituted the foundation for the government's April 1965 Race Relations Bill.

Members of the second committee,[38] however, had taken notice of events and institutions in North America, having identified British problems of racism with those in America and even South Africa (see Hindell 1965: 393–4, Lester and Bindman 1972: 110–11; interviews with Jowell, Lester, July 8, and July 23, 1997).[39] A key participant in this group was Anthony (now Lord) Lester, who went on to play a pivotal role in lobbying efforts for administrative machinery in the 1965 act. Lester had been exposed to American influences (as had several of his committee colleagues) while studying law at Harvard University. In his own words, he spent "two profoundly influential years" in the United States in the early 1960s, witnessing both the civil rights movement and entrenched patterns of racial discrimination and disadvantage (Lester 1996: 1). After returning from an Amnesty International mission to the American South in 1964, he "was more than ever convinced that the affliction of racism in the United States was taking root" in Britain (Lester 1996: 1).

Lester and others had studied and been greatly influenced by the American and Canadian models of race relations (see especially Jowell 1965, also Hindell 1965: 395, Lester and Bindman 1972: 110–11). In 1964, Jeffrey Jowell spent an extended period of time in North America studying in tremendous detail the workings of state and provincial race laws. Although the influential 1964 U.S. federal Civil Rights Act had just been passed when Jowell traveled overseas, by 1960 seventeen states and several Canadian provinces had agencies such as Fair Employment Practice Commissions that administered comprehensive antidiscrimination legislation (Skrentny 1996: 29). The usual procedure under these structures involved an individual complaint, followed by an investigation by the commission. If probable cause were determined, conciliation would result. If this failed to secure a satisfactory outcome, the next step was a public hearing

[38] Known as the Martin committee of the Society of Labour Lawyers.

[39] Signs posted in shop windows advertising rooms for "whites only" or stating "no coloureds" triggered recognition of racism and comparisons in at least one observer with the situation in South Africa (interview with Jowell, July 8, 1997; see also Jowell 1965: 175).

ultimately backed by the threat of a cease and desist order, and a finding of contempt of court for noncompliance (Skrentny 1996: 29).

Jowell concluded from his research that use of administrative machinery was the most effective method of countering discrimination (Jowell 1965). He criticized the government's April 1965 bill by saying that it was "the sort of measure which has long been abandoned as ineffective by progressive governments in the United States and Canada" (Jowell 1965: 179). The Lester group (an outgrowth of the Labour Party sponsored committee) therefore advocated establishing an administrative body known as a "Citizen's Council" and using conciliation rather than criminal proceedings to punish access racism (Lester and Bindman 1972: 111).[40] Since the April 1965 Race Relations Bill contained none of these elements, Lester and his colleagues continued their intense lobbying campaign (begun in late 1964) in an attempt to bring the provisions of the bill into line with the lessons learned from North American experiences.

Several members of this group became members of the legal committee of the Campaign Against Racial Discrimination (CARD) (Heineman 1972: 115, Lester and Bindman 1972: 112).[41] CARD, formed in December 1964 as a pressure group for immigrant interests, adopted and advocated the Lester-group proposals.[42] They lobbied the media, other specialist organizations, and Members of Parliament (see Heineman 1972, Hindell 1965, Lester and Bindman 1972, Rose 1969). Those advocating the American ideas had thus established an institutional home in the CARD which was then used as a beachhead for pressing into the Parliamentary interior.

The proposals for conciliation rather than criminalization drew support from the media, which criticized the government's bill as a "botched job" (Heineman 1972: 118). But more importantly, noncabinet Labour

[40] They advocated that it be modeled on the Press Council, and that it be empowered to investigate discrimination in a broad range of areas (see Lester and Bindman 1972: 111).

[41] CARD was emblematic of the British political situation with respect to race issues in the mid-1960s in that it took much of its inspiration and ideas from the American context (Martin Luther King Jr.'s visit served as a catalyst for its foundation [Heineman 1972: 16]), while at the same time recognizing substantial differences between the two countries (see Heineman 1972).

[42] CARD, like the Lester group, also advocated extending the legislation to ban discriminatory acts in employment, housing, insurance, and credit facilities (Heineman 1972: 31). In this, Lester and CARD were unsuccessful in 1965, although the 1965 act included a limited provision against discriminatory covenants in housing (see Lester and Bindman 1972).

frontbenchers and backbenchers began to express sympathy for administrative machinery and conciliation procedures. Lobbying by Lester and colleagues convinced core Labour supporters – including most notably Maurice Foley, Parliamentary Under-Secretary at the Department of Economic Affairs, recently made responsible for coordinating the government's immigrant integration programs – that conciliation was more effective in dealing with access racism than criminalization. As Lester and Bindman (1972: 115) note, "all the Labour Members who spoke during the debate also favoured the principle of enforcement by conciliation and civil proceedings, and several of them referred to CARD proposals and to North American experience" (see also Hansard 711: 926–1060). The government was thus faced with pressure from the media and from within its own party to adopt administrative procedures.

Why Labour MPs were so receptive to this proposal possibly turns on two issues: the credibility of the information source, and sympathy to American ideas. The Society of Labour Lawyers was undoubtedly perceived by MPs as a reliable source of information, and the personal status of its members was high. Moreover, identification with the United States was reportedly strong among a segment of the Labour Party that comprised significant numbers of American-style liberals, some of whom (such as Shirley Williams) had exposure to the United States (interview with Jowell, July 8, 1997; personal communication with Williams, July 28, 1996).[43] These MPs were likely to be intellectually sympathetic to progressive American policies in the civil rights era. Moreover, the parallels to America seemed natural to many in Britain, who had come to conceive of their race problems in color terms. The riots of 1958, the Commonwealth Immigrants Act of 1962, and the 1964 election results in Smethwick had convinced many in the party that color racism was a significant issue in Britain. Segments of the British elite (including certain Labour MPs) had framed British problems in American terms, and were therefore likely to be receptive to progressive American solutions.

Although media and Labour opinion was shifting in favor of administrative and civil law procedures, the critical breakthrough came when

[43] Shirley Williams, Junior Minister in the Home Office during the late 1960s and future Secretary of State for Education in the 1970s, stated: "I have always personally been very interested in the question of race relations, partly because of my background as a schoolchild and then as a graduate student in the United States. It has always been a topic of great importance to me since I returned to Britain and found the rapidly rising number of ethnic minorities in this country in the fifties, and in particular the sixties" (personal communication, July 28, 1996).

Lester and his allies convinced the opposition to take on board the spirit of the proposals. The CARD Legal Subcommittee met with the Conservatives in late April, at which time the Shadow Home Secretary (Peter Thorneycroft) expressed interest in conciliation as opposed to criminalization (Heineman 1972: 119). Conciliation appealed to the opposition because they could publicize the failings of the existing bill and use the alternative proposals as a rationale for opposing the government's proposal altogether.[44] As Lester and Bindman (1972: 113) note, "it was a subtle strategy, for it enabled the opposition to avoid appearing to be wholly negative in rejecting any kind of legislation." Thus in the Second Reading Debate, Thorneycroft moved an amendment to sink the original Soskice bill "which introduces criminal sanctions into a field more appropriate to conciliation" (Hansard 711: 943). Such a statement also highlights a second point: Although the Conservatives showed little enthusiasm for any form of race relations legislation, if it were to be passed, they judged that conciliation by an administrative agency would be weaker, less confrontational, and therefore more palatable than criminal sanctions (interview with Jowell, July 8, 1997).[45] The liberals in the CARD group and in the Labour Party felt, by contrast, that administrative procedures would be *more* effective. Out of these differing interpretations of the impact of administrative conciliation, a coalition of Baptists and bootleggers was born, and the pressure was directed at the government from all sides.

The government came under heavy fire during the Second Reading Debate in the House of Commons for its proposal to criminalize access racism. When put to a vote, the bill survived by only a nine-vote margin (Hepple 1968: 133).[46] Wanting to avoid protracted and high-pitched public controversy over the sensitive and electorally unpopular topic of race, the government bowed to its critics and redrafted the bill between the Second Reading and committee stages of the Parliamentary process (see Hindell 1965: 398, PRO CAB 129/121). During the first committee meeting, the Conservative Shadow Home Secretary appeared stunned by this turn of events. He exclaimed: "We have the Government suddenly saying, 'We have changed the principle of the Bill'. I find that astonishing,

[44] Heineman (1972: 119) states that they wanted to "use the concept of conciliation as a switch with which to annoy Soskice."

[45] This was undoubtedly true not only of the Conservatives, but also in the public at large and possibly in sections of the Labour Party. As Kushnick (1971: 241) states, "in the debate both within Parliament and outside ... conciliation came to be seen as an end in itself ... almost, indeed, as the alternative to sanctions themselves."

[46] The vote was 258 to 249, with the Liberals voting with the government.

because the Home Secretary and I both know the way in which Bills are prepared. . . . It is astonishing to produce a Bill and then half-way through to change the basic principle on which it has been produced."[47] Given that the project was rewritten according to their specifications, however, there were limits to the permissible scope of opposition and Labour backbenchers' complaints.

In the following negotiations, Labour critics pushed for a stronger enforcement agency and for extension of the antidiscrimination provisions to cover housing and employment. Conservatives sided with the government to oppose these changes, resulting in only minor alterations to the substance of the bill.[48] The 1965 race relations institutions were set: In dealing with access racism, the law was to be based on conciliation via administrative machinery and ultimately enforced in the civil courts.

The 1965 Race Relations Act

The final version of the 1965 Race Relations Act dealt explicitly with expressive and access racism. People who used threatening, abusive or insulting written or spoken expressions with intent to stir up hate against others on the grounds of color, race, or ethnic or national origins were subject to a maximum prison sentence of two years and a maximum fine of £1,000. In contrast to French policies established in the 1970s, the decision to prosecute could be made only by the state's representative, such as the Attorney General in England or Wales, or the Lord Advocate in Scotland (Lester and Bindman 1972: Appendix 2). Access racism provisions were limited primarily to discrimination in public places (such as pubs or hotels) and did not include employment discrimination, or racism in the banking or insurance areas, and only touched cursorily on housing concerns.[49] As with incitement provisions, discrimination was made unlawful on color, race, ethnic or national grounds (but not, notably, on religious grounds).[50] Finally, the act established a three-person national Race Relations Board (RRB), designed to create Local Conciliation

47 Standing Committee B, Race Relations Bill; 1st Sitting, May 25, 1965, c. 6.

48 Standing Committee B, Race Relations Bill; see also Hindell (1965: 401–5) and Lester and Bindman (1972: 116–18).

49 It banned enforcement on racial grounds of restrictions on the transfer of tenancies.

50 During the Parliamentary debates, the government argued in response to several MPs' questions that Jews, though difficult to classify, would be protected under the law as being caught either by the term ethnic or racial (Hansard 711: 932–33, 1044). See also Lester and Bindman (1972: 156–8).

Committees (LCC) which would receive and manage specific complaints of discrimination. If conciliation failed, only the Attorney General in England and Wales or the Lord Advocate in Scotland had the power to undertake proceedings to restrain individuals from discriminating.

The act was therefore weak in many respects. It provided for an infant administrative agency, with correspondingly few teeth. It was not a Statutory Commission with powers of subpoena and investigation (see Hindell 1965: 400). Courts could be used to punish racists only after a lengthy process which included approval from the state gatekeeper. Only certain acts of access racism were penalized, and employment and most housing discrimination were intentionally excluded from the 1965 act. Religious discrimination was not covered, nor did the law extend to Northern Ireland. These limitations, however, were by design and not by accident.[51] Most politicians hoped that the simple declaratory function of the 1965 Race Relations Act would suffice to curb the existing discrimination in Britain (Kushnick 1971). As Home Secretary Soskice declared in winding up the debates over the 1965 act, "We have taken what in a sense is a first step. I hope that events will show that it is not necessary to take any further step and that this may be the last step.... It would be an ugly day in this country if we had to come back to Parliament to extend the scope of this legislation" (Hansard 715: 1055–6).

Conclusion

The 1965 Race Relations Act grew out of the immigration context of the postwar era. Ethnic minorities reversed the centuries-old patterns of colonial migration and began arriving on British shores by the hundreds of thousands. Although this may appear to be a sufficient explanation for what was to follow, the fact of immigration itself was not enough to prompt antiracism legislation. As we will see in Chapter 5, the influx of nonwhite settlers was not the primary impetus behind the foundational French antiracism law of 1972. Moreover, for over a decade in Britain, calls by lonely backbench politicians for protections against racism went unheard and unheeded, as government spokespersons argued that British law was being virtuous by being race-blind.

This chapter illustrates the fact that that the electorate, minorities, and bureaucrats played surprisingly minor roles in instigating the process

[51] See PRO HO 376/68; PRO PREM 13/383; PRO CAB 128/39 Part I; PRO HO 376/69; PRO CAB 134/2183.

and in supporting the legislation. There is no evidence of popular support for race relations measures in this strongly anti-immigrant era, nor was there substantial pressure from ethnic minorities suffering the effects of racism, as there was at this time in the United States. Moreover, race laws did not arise because they fit naturally within existing British institutions; they were, in a sense, a small revolution within the British context. Instead, political parties, individual politicians, and politically connected pressure groups were the primary forces behind passage of the 1965 act.

In keeping with the hypotheses of the problem-solving and power-interest perspectives on policymaking, race rose to the top of the agenda because of a combination of problem indicators, partisan interests, and power shifts. The factor that finally brought race into Parliament was the arrival in office of the Labour government of 1964. Their pledge to legislate on race was first made in 1958, but they were hamstrung in their actions by a long sojourn in opposition between 1951 and 1964. Their interest in enacting race protections was not, ironically, in gaining new voters among the ethnic minority community. This was too thin an electoral vein to mine, and any attempt to do so risked the ire of working class supporters wary of immigrant competition for jobs and housing. Rather, their interest was twofold. First, to appease progressive elements of the party (and to ease the guilt of the leadership) in light of the recent about-face on immigration policy. Bowing to the electoral necessity of backing the Commonwealth Immigrants Act of 1962 had triggered a reaction among many who wanted a progressive counter-measure to balance these restrictions. In addition, Labour recognized race as a potentially explosive issue. Without an accord with the Conservatives to take race out of politics, Labour leaders feared that they (and the country) would suffer.

Problem indicators such as the 1958 riots in Nottingham and Notting Hill, and the 1964 election of Peter Griffiths in the district of Smethwick helped Labour to understand the extent of race-based tensions in British society. Yet, underlying these problem indicators were frames that prompted people to interpret these tensions as based on race. Riots in which young white British natives attacked black nonnative-born residents could have been understood in a number of ways. They might have been seen as the result of cultural differences between immigrants and natives, as a consequence of poverty and joblessness in British society (affecting both groups), or as a product of the anomie of teenagers growing up in a modern, urban, capitalist system. The interpretation of the riots as racial events resonated because of a frame of reference that made race meaningful to observers (and perhaps to participants). Similarly, the derogatory slogan associated with the Smethwick campaign – "if you want a nigger neighbor, vote Liberal or Labour" – generated votes among an electorate attuned to racial differences and to thinking in terms of racial competition. Although race frames were not a primary force in getting race on the agenda in 1965, they underlie central aspects of interpreting problems and political interests.

This chapter has also sought to explain the precise form of the 1965 act, accounting not just for the agenda setting phase of the policy process, but also for alternative selection. At this stage of the Race Relations Act, frames and party political considerations were the critical explanatory factors; more so, for example, than concerns about institutional fit. The government's "traditional" policy of criminalizing access racism was overturned mid-way through the Parliamentary process. This highly irregular event occurred in part due to the interests of the opposition and the government (for a "softer" policy, and for consensus, respectively) and in part due to the introduction of North American ideas about race relations policies. Viewing British problems through the North American lens and focusing first and foremost on access racism can be traced back to the mid-1950s when Labour Party representatives began to address issues of race. In the early 1960s, key actors who had spent time in the United States and studied North American policies brought ideas about administrative conciliation and civil court penalties into British debates. These proposals found purchase among Labour liberals who felt them to be the most efficient responses to the societal problem of racism; for the Conservatives they were useful political tools with which to attack the government. These frame elements became a focal point for powerful opposition to government policy proposals. In this particular case, therefore, a set of frames adopted by several powerful groups and bargaining between these groups and the Labour government shaped the ultimate policy chosen.

The 1965 British Race Relations Act was truly a whimper of a law, limited in its coverage and weak in its enforcement. Nevertheless, it had important ramifications for future institutions, debates, and policies. It established an administrative agency that became a strong voice in further rounds of race legislation. It encoded civil rather than criminal punishment for access racism into British law, a formula that exists to this day. Finally, it created and implanted perceptions among actors that British problems were close parallels to American problems of race and racism. By bringing in policy ideas about race from the North American context, the passage of the 1965 Race Relations Act established a pattern which reverberated through future rounds of British race legislation.

Although the 1965 Race Relations Act marked the birth of the first domestic race institutions in postwar Western Europe, it was clearly not intended to establish race as a major arena of domestic policymaking. Few people foresaw further action in this domain. The government had resisted expanding the act during its passage and had publicly expressed hope that no future antidiscrimination provisions would be needed. The Conservatives – whose compliance on race policies the government was anxious to secure – had demonstrated little enthusiasm for such laws. Bucking the odds, however, the issue of race resurfaced quickly in British political life and the 1965 act was very shortly given significantly more breadth.

3

Round Two

1965 to the 1968 Race Relations Act

The Labour government intended to remove race from the political agenda in 1965. For many, it had done just that. The electorate, the cabinet, the opposition Conservatives, and the unions each seemed content with the status quo. The state's new law served as a public proclamation against racism, and institutions acceptable to both ends of the political spectrum had been established to cope with concrete cases of racism. There was pervasive indifference or hostility to further race policies in the public and the political elite in the late 1960s as reflected in opinion polls and in public statements of most politicians. Three short years after Parliament brokered its legislative compromise, however, Britain's domestic race institutions were – against all odds – significantly expanded and strengthened.

The 1968 Race Relations Act struck out in two directions. It widened protection against access racism to the fields of employment, housing, and provision of a broader range of goods and services. Even after passage of the 1965 act, it had remained permissible in Britain to refuse a job, an apartment, or insurance to an individual because of the color of his or her skin. The 1968 law provided safeguards against this kind of discrimination. The 1968 legislation also shored up enforcement, providing (a few) additional teeth to the race relations bureaucracies. Under the new law, the Race Relations Board could investigate instances of racism even when no complaint had been filed, and it could bypass the Attorney General and take cases before courts on its own initiative.

The 1968 law was therefore a significant extension of Britain's race institutions. Given the overwhelming desire to damp down race as a political issue, how did it come about so soon after the 1965 act? To answer this question, this chapter focuses on the activism and activities of a small group of British "progressive learners."[1] They were progressive in the sense of being advocates for the strongest form of the Race Relations Act. They were learners in the Hecloian (1974) sense of being primarily concerned with gathering information and crafting solutions to perceived problems. This group, strengthened by their positions in the newly established race institutions, shared a frame that consisted of a belief in the importance and invidiousness of access racism and a strong identification with the North American analogy. Their strategy was to highlight "problems of race" within Britain, arguing that employment and housing discrimination (key concerns in the United States in the late 1960s) could generate riots and social disorder visible in places like Los Angeles and Detroit. From their perspective, North American-style legislation – if enacted in time – could help resolve racial tensions before they escalated to U.S. levels.

The politics of race policymaking did not end once race relations returned to the Parliamentary agenda. The 1968 act expanded the scope and increased the enforcement powers of Britain's race institutions in keeping with the aims of the progressive learners. Yet the final version of the law was not a simple function of the progressives' arguments about procedural effectiveness. Rather, loopholes and weaknesses were built into the institutions as the result of bargaining with legislative skeptics, who feared that the law created a disincentive to minority integration, that it allocated substantial power to minorities, or that it risked provoking backlash within the majority community. The institutions established by the 1968 Race Relations Act can best be understood as the product of bartering between groups arranged on a continuum from progressive learners to skeptical populists. Although many elements of the law were influenced by the predominant framing of race issues in North American terms, bargains struck among powerful actors helped to temper the transfer of policy ideas.

This chapter outlines Britain's path from 1965 to the 1968 Race Relations Act. To provide a complete picture of British race institutions, the first section describes race policies and organizations existing in the 1960s that were established outside of the aegis of the 1965 act. It then

[1] The term progressive learners is not a normative judgment about this group. It is meant to capture a certain idealism held by these individuals, who were motivated by goals of equality, influenced by an understanding of U.S. civil rights developments, and believed in the seriousness of the problems of racism faced by Britain's minority citizens.

demonstrates that, taking into account the legislative and nonlegislative actions in the sphere of race in the mid-1960s, most observers felt that the issue had been settled and were hostile to renewed race legislation. Race returned to the agenda, as the following section demonstrates, through the activism of the progressive learners. This group included (most centrally) the Labour Home Secretary Roy Jenkins, as well as a host of race professionals and minority activists; together, they argued forcefully that substantial societal problems remained unresolved within the current institutions – problems that could be resolved through a further round of legislation. The path from the political agenda to the final version of the law was not without battles between progressives and skeptics, however. In the end, the 1968 Race Relations Act embodied important continuities as well as significant changes. It was inspired by and consistent with prevailing race frames, but did not go as far as progressives hoped.

The 1965 White Paper, Integration, and Local Race Organizations

Although many of the basic British institutions for managing racism were established by legislation, others emerged outside the walls of Westminster. Local volunteer organizations – designed to welcome and assist incoming immigrants – had sprouted in several communities prior to the first Race Relations Act (see Messina 1989; Patterson 1969; Rose 1969).[2] These groups performed a wide variety of functions, putting new arrivals in touch with state agencies, dealing with housing concerns, providing personal counseling, and assisting with employment advice (Rose 1969: 380–93).[3] The prevalence of these groups across Britain is difficult to gauge. Although there were fifteen formal committees founded by 1964, there were others that had unofficial roots stretching back to earlier years (Messina 1989: 54–5).

As the 1964 Labour government restricted immigration and turned its attention to integration, it looked to these local organizations to perform some of the race relations heavy lifting. In its August 1965 White Paper entitled *Immigration from the Commonwealth*, the government set out its policies, stating that flows would have to be limited, but that assistance

[2] Rose (1969: 382) states that as of 1965 there were three main types of local organizations in this field: immigrant organizations, antidiscrimination "campaign" committees, and local voluntary liaison committees.

[3] Although they did not have much impact on the course of legislation, some groups also became centers for antiracism campaigns, particularly following the 1958 disturbances in Nottingham and Notting Hill (Rose 1969: 380–393).

would be made available to immigrant-populated local areas to deal with problems of integration (Great Britain: Home Office 1965). The White Paper (Great Britain: Home Office 1965: 10) argued:

> The United Kingdom is already a multi-racial society and Commonwealth immigrants make a most valuable contribution to our economy. Most of them will stay and bring up their families here and there can be no question of allowing any of them to be regarded as second-class citizens. At the same time it must be recognised that the presence in this country of nearly one million immigrants from the Commonwealth with different social and cultural backgrounds raises a number of problems and creates various social tensions in those areas where they have concentrated. If we are to avoid the evil of racial strife and if harmonious relations between the different races who now form our community are to develop, these problems and tensions must be resolved and removed so that individual members of every racial group can mingle freely with all other citizens at school, at work and during their leisure time without any form of discrimination being exercised against them.

In addition to the recently passed Race Relations Act, two strategies aimed to mitigate these tensions. First, the government pledged to provide funding for extra staff in local authorities to cope with cross-cultural or multilingual issues. It intended to encourage integration by providing extra resources to classrooms with substantial numbers of nonnative English speakers. The fruits of this promise were borne in the form of the 1966 Local Government Act which by 1978/79 had distributed £50 million to various regional governments in the UK (Young 1983: 294).[4] The second prong of the White Paper's attack on social problems involved mobilizing and energizing the voluntary organizations. It praised their role in providing information, education, and welfare, and in helping to dispel tensions between groups. It argued, however, that there was a need for national coordination of these groups, for sponsoring of groups in areas which did not possess a voluntary group, and for tangible evidence of government support of such efforts (Great Britain: Home Office 1965: 17).

As a result, it launched a National Committee for Commonwealth Immigrants (NCCI).[5] The NCCI was a national body of specialists in race relations who were to be autonomous from the government, but with whom the government could maintain close ties (Great Britain: Home

[4] For an overview as well as a critique of this scheme, see Young (1983).

[5] Somewhat confusingly, there had already existed an NCCI prior to the Labour Party's initiative. It was sponsored by the Commonwealth Immigrants Advisory Committee (CIAC), a group established in 1962 to advise the government on immigration issues. Labour's NCCI thus subsumed the work of the previous NCCI and the CIAC (Great Britain: Home Office 1965; Patterson 1969: 114–28).

Office 1965: 17–18).[6] The government funded the NCCI, which in turn paid for the salary of one permanent race specialist for each local voluntary group.[7] The purpose of the volunteer groups was to be distinguished from that of the local conciliation committees established by the Race Relations Act. The NCCI groups' function, according the White Paper (Great Britain: Home Office 1965: 17), was "essentially the co-ordination of local effort and the positive promotion of goodwill, not the implementation of the statutory requirements of the Race Relations Bill." Under the financial lead outlined in the White Paper, the number of NCCI-sponsored local committees rose to seventy-eight by 1969 and became "semipermanent, quasiofficial institutions," which were "universally recognized as the principal race organization[s] at the local level" (Messina 1989: 55, 59). As of the mid-1960s, therefore, Britain had two parallel institutional structures for managing different aspects of race relations.

Race Off the Agenda?

According to Katznelson (1976: 126), by 1965 Britain had entered into its third phase of race politics: a political consensus to depoliticize race (see also Messina 1989). The package deal hammered out within the Labour Party between 1963 and 1965 had been fulfilled. Continued immigration restrictions had been balanced against integration measures such as passage of an antidiscrimination law, provision of funding for local authorities to deal with immigrant problems, establishment of a nationwide locally based network for facilitating integration, and appointment

[6] As the White Paper (Great Britain: Home Office 1965: 17–18) argued, "The Government take the view that the work of the National Committee should not be directly under Government control since its main stimulus must come from the harnessing of voluntary effort, and a degree of autonomy is necessary if the Committee is to remain free from party political influence and other partisan pressures; but the Government propose to maintain close liaison with the work of the Committee and to associate itself fully with the Committee's efforts."

[7] Although one knowledgeable observer has argued that the intent of creating the NCCI was to establish "buffer institutions" to keep local race relations under a watchful eye and to dissipate minority activism (Katznelson 1976: 175–88), this conclusion can be contested. Had it wished, the government undoubtedly could have chosen institutions which mandated much more oversight of local groups. Moreover, members of the NCCI were far from puppets in the government's hand. As Martin Ennals, an active participant during the era, wrote in the *Tribune*: "Certainly, whatever its motives, the Government has appointed a Committee which opposes its policies and has said so to the Prime Minister" (quoted in Rose 1969: 524).

of a new Ministerial Coordinator of Policy on Integration.[8] Race was a sleeping political dog that few wished to rouse.

Between 1965 and much of 1967 there was no reason to believe that Britain would pass new race legislation. The Labour Party had no further mandate to legislate on race. It had not hinted at action in its 1966 election platform (Craig 1975), nor was such legislation widely desired by voters. The climate toward immigrants (strongly associated in the public eye with minorities) was clearly hostile, and pushing for prominority legislation was therefore not electorally popular (see Bonham Carter 1987: 4–5, Kushnick 1971: 235, Lester and Bindman 1972: 148–9). Surveys taken between 1963 and 1970 show that over 80 percent of those questioned in each of the five polls thought that "too many immigrants [had] been let into this country" (Messina 1989: 12). Attitudes toward race legislation were more moderate than those toward immigrants: In all polls taken before Powell's infamous "rivers of blood" speech in April 1968, at least a plurality of respondents approved of legislation against discrimination. Nevertheless, in a majority of polls, a thin plurality also felt that antidiscrimination legislation should not cover jobs or housing, the fundamental thrust of the proposals to extend the existing law (Rose 1969: 597). All in all, the government could hope at best for neutrality among the voters, and had significant reasons for fearing hostility to any actions on race.

Within Parliament itself, there was little enthusiasm for renewed legislation. As the Institute of Race Relations' project director E. J. B. Rose (1969: 535) stated, "in the period after the [1966] Election interest in race relations among ordinary politicians diminished sharply." Since the 1967 proposals for a new Race Relations Act were meant to extend protection to areas of employment and housing, the attitudes of the government ministers holding these portfolios would prove critical. If there had been strong cabinet support from these corners, an additional round of legislation would perhaps seem natural. Yet, Rose describes the Housing Minister in this era (Richard Crossman) as "a sceptic on legislation" and "complacent and even negative on broader issues" (1969: 518–19).[9] His

[8] Maurice Foley MP was appointed to this post by the Prime Minister in March 1965. Saggar (1993: 260) characterizes him as "the first de facto race relations government officer." In January 1966, Foley and his staff were transferred from the Department of Economic Affairs to the Home Office (Saggar 1993: 266).

[9] Crossman's diaries (1975; 1976) give little indication of this penchant. Roy Jenkins (1991: 210), however, also suggested that Crossman's "heart was never in race relations."

TABLE 5. *Do you think that too many immigrants have been let into this country or not?*

	1963	1964	1966	1969	1970
Yes	83	81	81	87	85
No	12	13	14	10	10
Don't know	5	6	5	3	5

Source: Messina (1989: 12).

TABLE 6. *Attitudes toward Legislation Against Discrimination*

		1967	Early April 1968	1968	Late April 1968	May 1968
Do you approve of legislation against discrimination?*	Yes	58	42	53	30	44
	No	31	29	36	46	44
	D/k	10	29	11	24	12
Should it affect jobs?	Yes	48	40	44		58
	No	44	47	51		34
	D/k	8	13	5		8
Should it affect housing?	Yes	44	34	39		
	No	45	49	53		
	D/k	10	17	8		

Note: *After April 1968: Do you approve of the Race Relations Bill?
Source: Rose (1969: 597)

counterpart in the Ministry of Labour (Ray Gunter) submitted a memo to the Home Affairs Committee in the summer of 1967 in which he wrote bluntly "I do not agree with the proposals in the memorandum by the Secretary of State for the Home Department for legislation on racial discrimination in employment," expressing his preference for industry and unions to adopt voluntary measures of their own (PRO CAB 134/2856, H[67] 75). Furthermore, Labour had to be wary of a bumpy ride in Parliament over race initiatives. In a time when cross-party consensus on race was a priority, moving to put discrimination on the Parliamentary agenda was a risky proposition given many Conservatives' track record of hostility to antiracism measures. When it came time to legislate, the cabinet miscalculated that the opposition would support its initiative. This put a number of constituencies at risk when the Conservatives opposed the 1968 bill during Parliamentary debate (see Crossman 1976: 784–5, Hansard 763: 53–174).[10]

While lack of enthusiasm accurately described the position of the cabinet, the Labour Party, the electorate, and the opposition, outright hostility better summarized the stance of organized labor (see Lester and Bindman 1972: esp. 126–7, Rose 1969: 529). The Trades Union Congress (TUC) – normally among Labour's strongest supporters – spearheaded the opposition to protections against employment discrimination, even ahead of the equally reluctant Congress of British Industry (CBI) (see Patterson 1969: 102–5, Rose 1969: 529). The unions feared outside involvement (derided with the tag "interventionism") in industrial matters, and the general attitude was consequently one of "alarm and suspicion" at the possibility of employment related provisions in any new legislation (Rose 1969: 530, Trades Union Congress 1967: 267–73). Because employment was the crux of the matter for Jenkins and most other supporters of legislation, reforms would have to come at the expense and without the backing of Labour's most powerful interest group ally.

In sum, as Lester and Bindman (1972: 122) state:

> The Government had only recently tackled the subject, and it had no mandate to legislate in the field of employment or housing. Any extension of the Act might well be electorally unpopular, and would be better made long before a General Election;... there was a scant support in the Government, the Labour Party, or the trade union movement for such a bold and rapid action.

Nevertheless, the plan for new legislation became a reality with the 1968 Race Relations Act, and with it, Britain took another significant step in developing antiracism institutions. Viewed from today's perspective, the passage of this legislation seems wholly natural. Viewed from the perspective of the late 1960s, the passage of this legislation was anything but assured.

Getting Race on the Agenda

Given widespread misgivings about further race legislation, how did it return to the Parliamentary agenda so quickly? In 1968, the initiative for legislation was taken not by the Labour Party, but by a progressive coalition of newly appointed race bureaucrats and a key cabinet minister, backed by the support of the ethnic minority community. These groups

[10] The Conservatives tabled a reasoned amendment to the bill, seeking to derail its progress.

were motivated primarily by concerns about the inefficiencies or the insufficiencies of existing legislation. Their collective strategy for muscling race back to the foreground of public and political attention contained three elements: highlighting actual or potential societal problems; arguing that the current institutions were not capable of solving these problems; and making the case that new legislation (and therefore new institutions) provided a viable solution.

Race Activists: The Progressive Learners

When the Race Relations Board and the NCCI were created in 1965, they were designed to be weak. No government official anticipated that either organization in its appointed form was going to be a powerful force for change. Rather, they were meant to work at the margins to resolve race disputes and help integrate immigrants without ruffling too many native feathers. Political actors, however, cannot always foresee the effects of the institutions they create. While they did not revolutionize British society, these organizations did punch above their weight and helped to generate momentum toward further legislative action on racial discrimination. The race bureaucracies (the RRB and the NCCI) worked closely with Home Secretary Roy Jenkins and in conjunction with the Campaign Against Racial Discrimination (CARD); together, these actors orchestrated the push for the 1968 Race Relations Act.

An important element of its charter allowed the Race Relations Board to require periodical reports from its local conciliation committees and "at such times as the Secretary of State may direct, make annual reports to the Secretary of State with respect to the exercise of their functions" (Race Relations Act 1965, s. 2, para. 4). Moreover, the board and the NCCI undertook initiatives such as organizing a conference and sponsoring research on the extent of discrimination in Britain. These factors eventually helped build a critical mass of supporters for new legislation. So, while both the NCCI and the board on paper (and in fact) had little power, in practice they were resources for information about problems in the field, which could then be used to pressure for further legislative changes. They were also institutionalized specialists on race relations issues in Britain, giving more weight to their input than to that of a simple pressure group. They were to become instruments for the new Home Secretary to use in pressing for further legislation.

With the December 1965 arrival of Roy Jenkins in the Home Office came possibilities for extending the scope and provisions of the Race

Relations Act.[11] As Saggar notes, the liberal race lobby saw Jenkins as "*their* man in government" (Saggar 1993: 265). Jenkins set out almost immediately to extend the scope of the legislation and to give it greater powers of enforcement (Jenkins 1991: 211, Lester and Bindman 1972: 122, Rose 1969: 515). One of his first decisions in office was to select the chair for the new Race Relations Board. Jenkins sought out a proactive ally with political clout in former Liberal MP Mark Bonham Carter,[12] who made a condition of accepting the position that he be allowed to argue for extending the act after a year of operating the board (Rose 1969: 520).

Although many in Britain at the time were still working within a conceptual paradigm of immigration, the progressive learners framed issues much more in terms of domestic race relations. Activists highlighted the twin issues of British-born minorities and color-based discrimination in contradistinction to questions of migrant numbers or border crossings (see Race Relations Board 1967: 16, Rose 1969: 515–16). Jenkins, in particular, viewed employment discrimination as a problem of the first order, because it was linked to "the whole future success of our integration policy." For Jenkins, the problem was especially sensitive because Britain was "beginning to move from the era of the first generation immigrant to that of the second generation immigrant."[13] In a speech delivered to the Institute of Race Relations in October 1966, the Home Secretary stated that the aspirations of the next generation of immigrants must not be frustrated, or else "we shall irreparably damage the quality of life in our society by creating an American type situation in which an indigenous minority which is no longer an immigrant group feels itself discriminated

[11] In his autobiography, Jenkins (1991: 376) says that he saw his task in this era as one of "opening the windows of freedom and innovation into the fusty and restrictive atmosphere of the Home Office." Rose (1969: 515) suggests that for Jenkins, "the selection of the extension of legislation as the key issue offered an escape from the blind alley of immigration policy which the new Home Secretary clearly found extremely distasteful."

[12] A close personal friend.

[13] See the NCCI pamphlet, "Address given by the Home Secretary the Rt Hon Roy Jenkins MP on the 23rd May 1966 at the Commonwealth Institute to a meeting of Voluntary Liaison Committees," in LPA, File 331.61. The automatic British institutional conferring of citizenship on second-generation immigrants made Home Secretary Jenkins especially sensitive to how these children, born and raised on British soil, were being treated as they went through the school system and reached adulthood.

against on the grounds of colour alone."[14] If the 1965 act was passed in part because of political bargains over immigration issues (both within the Labour Party and between Labour and the Conservatives), the 1968 act marked the birth of race as an autonomous policy sphere.

Race Problems: Social Order

In order to carry their message to a wider audience, the progressives struck a public chord by emphasizing issues of social order. The Race Relations Board argued that discrimination resulted in "racial tension" and "major social problems" and that a new law would maintain "the peaceful and orderly adjustment of grievances and the release of tensions" (Race Relations Board 1967: 22, 16). Debates in this era took place against the backdrop of the U.S. civil rights movement and particularly against the riotous turn of events there in the late 1960s. Images of American cities in flames were pervasive in Britain, and because so many framed race issues as analogous to those in the United States, the specter of American events haunted discussions of Britain's future (Heineman 1972: x; Rose 1969: 11).[15] In presenting its influential first annual report, the Race Relations Board (1967: 21) asserted: "Nor should we neglect the experience of others, and in particular the U.S.A., which indicates quite clearly that, where colour is an element, race relations if left to themselves deteriorate, that inertia and inaction in this field solve no problems and merely create greater problems in the future."

These greater problems were not far in Britain's future. On April 20, 1968, three days before the high-profile Second Reading Debate on the government's Race Relations Bill, Enoch Powell (a member of the Conservative shadow cabinet) pronounced his famous "rivers of blood"

[14] See PRO HO 376/13, "Full Text of Speech given by the Secretary of State to the Institute for Race Relations, Goldsmith's Hall, 10th October 1966."

[15] Virtually every major actor or observer of this era made frequent and explicit references to the United States' racial problems (Cosgrave 1990; Heineman 1972; Lester and Bindman 1972; Race Relations Board 1967; Rose 1969). See also editorials in venues like *The Times* ("What Britain can learn from America," April 22, 1968), Parliamentary debates on the Race Relations Bill (Hansard 763, 768), and memos by Home Office bureaucrats who made trips to North America (report by J. T. A Howard-Drake of visit to America and Canada with Mr. Ennals, July 13, 1967. PRO T 227/2535). While most saw important differences between Britain and the United States, many concluded that the best way to avoid American problems was to learn from America's mistakes. As Conservative MP St. John-Stevas pleaded in the House of Commons, "Let us not be Bourbons and let us learn cheaply and vicariously from the experience of others" (quoted in Saggar 1993: 272).

speech in Birmingham in which he articulated in inflammatory rhetoric a doomsday scenario for Britain's multiracial future (see Cosgrave 1990: 245–53, Shepherd 1996: 434–69). Powell believed that the Commonwealth immigrants would not integrate into British society, and that the Race Relations Bill would entrench this problem. He concluded his speech with the memorable classical allusion:

> As I look ahead, I am filled with foreboding. Like the Roman, I seem to see, 'the River Tiber foaming with much blood.' That tragic and intractable phenomenon which we watch with horror on the other side of the Atlantic but which there is interwoven with the history and existence of the States itself, is coming upon us here by our own volition and our own neglect (Cosgrave 1990: 250).

The speech made headlines across the nation. Although widely supported by public opinion,[16] Powell was dismissed from the Conservative shadow front bench (Cosgrave 1990: 251). Perhaps due to the tone set by Powell, the ensuing Parliamentary debate was marked by repeated references to the bill's public order implications. On introducing the bill during the Second Reading Debate, the Home Secretary[17] argued that its purpose was "to protect society as a whole against actions which will lead to social disruption, and to prevent the emergence of a class of second-grade citizens" (Hansard 763: 55). And David Ennals, a Labour government junior minister, declared dramatically: "Those who suggest that we ought to delay before bringing in our legislation are playing with fire and danger. There need not be a flash point in this country, but it can happen if we dither.... I say with absolute conviction that we may have a flashpoint [sic] in this country if we do not extend the field of legislation" (Hansard 763: 163, 166).

Race Problems: Pervasive Discrimination

In addition to sounding warnings about public disorder, the progressive learners set out to prove that discrimination was still a major social problem even in the wake of the government's 1965 initiatives. Whereas Labour and the Conservatives were willing to pass limited legislation in 1965 without much hard proof of discrimination, in 1967 there could be no legislation without clear evidence of a serious problem.[18] Those who felt

[16] Powell received thousands of letters, most favorable, and polls showed between 67% and 82% of respondents expressing support for him (Cosgrave 1990: 252–3).

[17] James Callaghan, as of November 1967.

[18] Speaking for the opposition during the Second Reading Debate of 1965, Shadow Home Secretary Peter Thorneycroft asked: "Are these potential crimes

there was still a "race relations problem" in Britain needed to convince others that its magnitude merited further Parliamentary efforts.

They did so in two ways. First, the progressives used the very weakness of existing race institutions as leverage in their push to widen the legislative provisions (Rose 1969: 520). The Race Relations Board exposed and emphasized its own inability to deal with the complaints that filtered up through the new institutional structures. In the summer of 1966, the Campaign Against Racial Discrimination organized a project to test discrimination and to make complaints to the RRB, regardless of whether the complaint came within the scope of the 1965 act (see Heineman 1972: 130, Lester and Bindman 1972: 124). The Race Relations Board therefore fielded numerous complaints that it could not legally process within its current mandate. In its report the board stated plainly that: "70 per cent. of the complaints are about matters which fall outside the scope of the Act and the two largest categories have been employment and housing.... We were left in no doubt, especially by immigrant groups, that... it was in employment and housing that discrimination most seriously affected the day to day existence of coloured people" (Race Relations Board 1967: 15). By demonstrating the limits of the existing institutional structures, advocates of further action turned a potentially lame-duck organization into a body whose own limitations argued for extension of race institutions.

The evidence which ultimately won over many fence-sitters and even some skeptics was the publication of the April 1967 Political and Economic Planning (PEP) report on the extent of discrimination in Britain.[19] It concluded unequivocally that there was "substantial discrimination" against minorities (as defined by color) in employment, housing, and the provision of services (Political and Economic Planning 1967: 8). Its impact was undeniable. One author argues that the PEP report was the British equivalent to the U.S. civil rights movement as a catalyst for reform (Heineman 1972: vii), while another – the former Director of

so widespread? The right hon. and learned Gentleman produced little evidence of them. If one studies the kindly, sensible British people as a whole, one will find instances... but [the Home Secretary] produced precious little evidence to the House that the instances were so widespread as to justify an important change in the criminal law" (Hansard 711: 946).

[19] The report was sponsored by the RRB and the NCCI and was morally if not materially or officially supported by the Home Secretary (Heineman 1972: 137; Pinder 1981: 141). It was funded by the Joseph Rowntree Memorial Trust (Political and Economic Planning 1967).

PEP – asserts that "seldom can research have had such a direct and immediate effect on legislation" (Pinder 1981: 142).[20]

The substantial influence of the report was due not only to the clarity of its results, but also to the dramatic build-up it was given throughout the year preceding its publication. In the months leading up to the report's April 1967 unveiling, reform-minded groups pinned their future course of action on the results of this document. When in December 1966, two private members' bills on racism were introduced in Parliament, the government argued that action in this arena was premature until the results of the PEP report were known, and that these results would be decisive in terms of the government's attitude toward further legislation (Lester and Bindman 1972: 125, Rose 1969: 529).

Publication of the report had the desired effect for advocates of a new law. Even the Conservative opposition's shadow Home Secretary was impressed by the evidence (Pinder 1981: 142, CPA ACP[67]38). During the Second Reading Debate in April 1968, Quintin Hogg expressly mentioned the PEP report's evidence as a factor which encouraged him to rethink his initial reluctance for fresh legislation (Hansard 763: 78, 160). One MP, Sir Dingle Foot, summed up the impact of the PEP report by saying that "no one can have any doubt that in many parts of the country there is widespread discrimination in housing and employment" (Hansard 763: 82–3).

The PEP report, however, did not fully sway the Trades Union Congress General Council.[21] The TUC was fearful of including employment provisions in the new law; even proof of widespread discrimination did not allay its fears that such legislation would be the first step down the slippery slope towards government interference in independent industrial

[20] The PEP survey was powerful because of its credibility and its methodology. The PEP was seen to be an objective, rigorous, and independent research organization. Methodologically, it relied on interviews with immigrants and with people in a position to discriminate (those who controlled access to jobs, housing, or services), and crucially, on a series of 'situation tests' where the conditions of potential discrimination were reproduced (see Political and Economic Planning 1967: 2). These tests were conducted with three categories of individuals: a non-white immigrant; a white immigrant; and a white Englishman; each of which independently sought access to employment, accommodation, or a rental car. The situation tests allowed PEP to conclude unequivocally that discrimination was based primarily on color (Political and Economic Planning 1967: 8).

[21] The TUC Annual Report (Trades Union Congress 1967: 269) asserted that "neither the proceedings at a conference organised by the National Committee for Commonwealth Immigrants nor the P.E.P. report gave grounds for modifying the attitude of the General Council."

relations structures (Lester and Bindman 1972: 128–9, Rose 1969: 535, Trades Union Congress 1967: esp. 267–70). The General Council did, however, make adjustments in the wake of the report, agreeing in April 1967 to discuss the Congress of British Industry's proposal to establish additional voluntary machinery to deal with problems of discrimination (Lester and Bindman 1972: 129, Trades Union Congress 1967: 269). By June 1967, TUC representatives had moved another grudging step towards accepting reforms when they stated that they "did not altogether rule out the possibility that legislation might ultimately play some residual part in the process" (quoted in Lester and Bindman 1972: 129). In addition, the PEP report reaped a harvest of backers amongst union members, some of whom tabled a motion during the September 1967 annual conference to support the government's plans for legislation. The General Council fended off this proposal on a procedural point enforced rather testily by the president (see Trades Union Congress 1967: 583–90).[22]

Elsewhere, particularly in the nonpolitical world, the PEP report had a weighty impact. It received widespread press coverage, and all major newspapers – including the staunchly Tory and previously hostile *Daily Telegraph* – argued editorially that urgent action was required to address such an intolerable situation (Rose 1969: 534). *The Times* shifted its position on legislation as a consequence of the report, and *The Sunday Times* argued that dealing with discrimination was a moral issue, stating forcefully that "the gradualist myth was exploded by the facts" (see Bonham Carter 1987: 5, Kushnick 1971: 253). The Home Secretary, the Chairman of the Race Relations Board, and other prolegislation advocates had staked much on the PEP report. The results argued strongly for renewed legislation and became a critical element in getting race back on the Parliamentary agenda.

The Legislation Solution

Concurrent to articulating the problems within British society and the weaknesses of its race relations institutions, progressive learners adopted a strategy of advancing antidiscrimination legislation as a viable solution. The race bureaucracies took the lead in this effort through two initiatives. First, they argued that the institutions established by the 1965 act were

[22] In a voice-vote asking for support for the General Council's policy, the President declared that the "ayes" had it, which was loudly contested by many members, who demanded a card vote. The President responded: "The Congress has agreed to remit, and I am going on [to the next issue]. (Cries of "*No.*") Well, I am. I have given the ruling" (Trades Union Congress 1967: 590).

valuable, but too limited. The law only sanctioned acts of access racism in a limited range of public places and by voiding discriminatory housing covenants. In its first annual report, the Race Relations Board attested that the act worked well in these spheres, and that "the same principles might successfully be applied to other areas where discrimination occurs" (Race Relations Board 1967: 12). In addition to portraying current British laws as useful, the board asserted the general value of race law for resolving a host of problems. In its conclusions, the board (1967: 22) lobbied for extension of the Race Relations Act by stating that:

1. A law is an unequivocal declaration of public policy.
2. A law gives support to those who do not wish to discriminate, but who feel compelled to do so by social pressure.
3. A law gives protection and redress to minority groups.
4. A law thus provides for the peaceful and orderly adjustment of grievances and the release of tensions.
5. A law reduces prejudice by discouraging the behaviour in which prejudice finds expression.

It bolstered its conclusions about the usefulness of the law for punishing access racism in employment, housing, and other areas by focusing on the North American analogy.[23] Once again, it advanced the core argument that Britain had an "American future" full of trouble and strife unless it eliminated discrimination and promoted successful integration at an early stage (Race Relations Board 1967: esp. 16). Behind Labour Party doors, activists like Anthony Lester also promoted lessons from the law in North America in an effort to mobilize support among Members of Parliament. In an April 1967 confidential paper presented to the Labour Party Race Relations Working Party, Lester argued that "The recent experience of the United States and Canada indicates that law can have a powerful and benign effect in discouraging discrimination and promoting racial equality."[24]

[23] The report (Race Relations Board 1967: 21) argues that "our own experience of legislation against discrimination is supplemented by what we have learned of such legislation in the United States and Canada. There, despite initial doubts, the law is now regarded as essential to the success of other government policies and is a powerful stimulus to voluntary action. A combination of all these, to ensure equal opportunities for all, is the only sound basis for successful action against discrimination."

[24] LPA, Folder: Race Relations Working Party 1967.

Interest in North American policies flourished in the late 1960s. The Chairman of the Race Relations Board went to the United States to gather evidence and information of race relations practices.[25] British newspapers publicized and explained U.S. civil rights laws, "suggesting a positive and beneficial role for this approach at home" (Saggar 1993: 272). And the race bureaucracies (the RRB and the NCCI) sponsored events which sought to draw on lessons from across the Atlantic. The NCCI organized a conference in February 1967 designed to bring together employment experts from Britain and North America to discuss the usefulness of antidiscrimination policies in that field.[26] More important, however, for legitimizing the 1968 law was the October 1967 Street Report on antidiscrimination legislation.[27] It examined laws around the world, focusing the vast majority of its attention on the North American experience (Street, Howe, and Bindman 1967). Like others, the report concluded that the U.S. and Canadian experience proved that "the law is an acceptable and appropriate instrument for handling the problem" (Street, Howe, and Bindman 1967: 62), legitimizing the legislation solution and helping to place race back on the Parliamentary agenda.[28]

Rather than being the product of electoral calculations or influential interest group lobbying, race returned to the political agenda through the

[25] Bonham Carter's report of his trip to North America influenced Conservative Party shadow cabinet members. In a July 1967 internal memo Quintin Hogg wrote "the three documents I have read (the annual report of the RRB, the PEP report, and Mr. Bonham Carter's account of his personal Odyssey in the U.S.A.) make impressive reading. Discrimination in housing and employment is almost inevitable if there isn't legislation against it. My conclusion is that we should play this issue coolly, and cautiously, but liberally. We should not shut the door against extension. We should take the credit for the conciliation machinery. We should, on the other hand, sound a warning against excessive precipitancy. We must lead public opinion, not drag behind it, or bulldoze it" (CPA ACP[67]38).

[26] Although there were high hopes that this conference would win British industry support, it failed to do so (Lester and Bindman 1972: 127). It offered a forum for the CBI to express its strong reservations about new legislation, and the general secretary of the TUC (George Woodcock) declined to attend, claiming that he had been invited in a personal, not a professional capacity (see Lester and Bindman 1972: 127).

[27] Professor Harry Street, Geoffrey Howe, and Geoffrey Bindman were the authors of this RRB and NCCI instigated report. It was funded by Marks and Spencer, Ltd.

[28] The Street Report also argued that a law was not enough to solve the problems of discrimination. Furthermore, its authors made detailed suggestions for the exact shape of the law, some of which were incorporated into the 1968 act, but many of which were not.

coordinated efforts of a cabinet member and the specialized bureaucracies, with the aid of the minority communities. These groups worked to convince other cabinet members, the opposition, the media and important interest groups such as the TUC and CBI of the value of renewed race legislation. They used a conscious strategy of highlighting social problems, of arguing that they could not be solved by existing institutions, and of offering legislation as a viable solution. Their identification of relevant problems and their proposed solutions rested to a large extent on their race frames. Yet, opening the path for action was not the only aim of the progressive learners. Once the obstacles to passing a new law were overcome, debates over the shape of the new institutions moved to the political front burner.

From the Agenda to the Law

On July 26, 1967, less than two years after the Race Relations Act of 1965 became law, Home Secretary Roy Jenkins announced to the House of Commons that the government had decided to legislate on race. Although the negotiations over the shape of the forthcoming law were intense in several respects, there was one element that was off the bargaining table – the enforcement mechanism for punishing access racism. Hard fought but settled in 1965, a reliance on conciliation through administrative machinery and enforcement through civil courts (as opposed to criminal punishment) remained the fundamental principle of the 1968 act. This basic continuity across time responded to the political and bureaucratic viability evoked by conciliation in 1965.[29] Favored by progressives and skeptics alike, seemingly proved effective by the experiences of the 1965 act, and viewed as particularly applicable to access racism complaints made in employment and housing (given the North American analogy), there was simply no reason to challenge administrative conciliation in 1968.[30]

Several other aspects of the legislation were, however, the object of significant debate and dispute. The negotiations that shaped up between late 1967 and passage of the act in 1968 can best be analyzed in terms

[29] For an argument about viability in a different setting, see the conclusion of Hall (1989).

[30] Although some institutionalists may argue that continuity can be reduced to path dependence and institutional lock-in, in fact it had more to do with dominant ideas. All British actors believed by 1968 that conciliation was either effective or appropriate, thus it was not challenged.

of tensions between four groups.[31] The first group consisted of the progressive learners, led by members of the race bureaucracies and by Home Secretary Jenkins, and backed by liberal Labour MPs within the House of Commons and by members of CARD. At the opposite pole (forcefully symbolized by Enoch Powell, but finding sympathizers in the Conservative party ranks) were a small group of skeptical populists, who asserted that passing race legislation in any form would be detrimental to non-minority interests or to the integration of minorities into British society.[32] Between these groups were the government and opposition front benches, united by a belief that a new law could serve a useful purpose, but divided over the optimal contents of the law.[33] These mainstream Labour and Conservative groups sought to strike a balance between the positions of the progressive learners and the skeptical populists.

The tussles between these camps were organized around two core issues: breadth of coverage and strength of enforcement. The progressive learners argued for a wide scope of the law (see esp. Lester and Bindman 1972, Street, Howe, and Bindman 1967). They advocated a law that would prohibit access racism in the spheres of employment, housing, insurance, and credit facilities and argued that coverage should apply to all individuals and groups, excepting only a few cases in which the nature of the interpersonal relationships was deemed too intimate to regulate.[34] Some even desired extending coverage to bar discrimination on religious grounds,[35] and many sought to close loopholes opened by the

[31] Lester and Bindman (1972: 136–46) also describe the negotiations as a function of bargaining between four groups, although they limit their analysis to the committee stage of the process and do not describe the groups in the terms I use. Nevertheless, I am significantly indebted to their observations.

[32] By populists here, I do not simply mean that they were concerned about electoral considerations (although this was certainly a key issue). They were also concerned about popular backlash against any law that was seen to give too much power to minorities. Some MPs who sided with this position, such as Iain Macleod, were not particularly populist by nature.

[33] Not all Conservative front bench members felt that a new law was necessary (see, for example, CPA LCC[68]231).

[34] In his memo to the Labour Party Race Relations Working Party, Lester lists the exceptions as an employer with fewer than ten employees (though he recognized this as a substantial exception) or a landlord sharing facilities with a tenant. He also argued for an exception to be made when race was a bona fide requirement for employment, giving as an example the case of hiring a Chinese cook for a Chinese restaurant (LPA Folder: Race Relations Working Party 1967).

[35] In internal discussions, in the Second Reading Debate, and in committee, not only the progressive learners, but also the opposition suggested extending the scope of the bill to cover other forms of discrimination (notably based on religion). While

government's April 1968 bill (Lester and Bindman 1972: 135). In addition, this group argued for changes in enforcement procedures. They wanted more power for the Race Relations Board to issue subpoenas and to collect evidence in its conciliation efforts, to obtain damages on behalf of victims, and to invoke the courts without the approval of the Attorney General (see Lester and Bindman 1972: 143–5, Street, Howe, and Bindman 1967).

As part of a difficult internal party compromise that sought to balance the positions of skeptical populists and skeptical supporters of the bill (see CPA LCC[68]231), the Conservatives tabled a reasoned amendment to the government's Race Relations Bill. It read: "This House, reaffirming its condemnation of racial discrimination and accepting the need for steps designed to improve the situation, nevertheless declines to give a Second Reading to a Bill which, on balance, will not in its practical application contribute to the achievement of racial harmony" (Hansard 763: 81).[36] The opposition wanted the scope of the bill limited to employment and housing (exempting insurance and credit facilities), and argued that it should not apply to businesses with fewer than twenty-five employees (which constituted one fifth of the total workforce) (CPA LCC[68]231, Lester and Bindman 1972: 139).[37] In addition, they argued against permitting the board to compel people to produce evidence in the conciliation stage and against the right of the victim to seek damages (Lester and Bindman 1972: 146–7).

In the months preceding passage of the law, the progressives hand was weakened in a number of ways. A November 1967 currency crisis prompted Prime Minister Wilson to shuffle his cabinet and to replace Roy Jenkins with James Callaghan in the Home Office. Through a quirk of historical fate, the progressive learners lost the critical post of Home Secretary to a cabinet member more skeptical of legislation. Jenkins later argued in his memoirs that Callaghan was carried along purely by the

many in the Conservative Party lacked enthusiasm for race relations legislation, it appears that portions of the party sincerely favored protection against religious discrimination, and that such a position was not simply a tactical argument designed to make the government uncomfortable (see, eg, CPA LCC[68]232).

[36] As Quintin Hogg argued in the House of Commons (Hansard 763: 70), the Conservatives were pressing the bill to a division, not because they did not like eggs; on the contrary, he said, "We like eggs, but we would like a fresher one rather lightly done. Please take this one away and give us another nearer to our specification."

[37] The opposition did, however, team up with the progressive learners during the committee stage to extend the scope of the bill to make the Crown legally liable for discrimination (see Lester and Bindman 1972: 145–6).

momentum of the legislative procedure and had little enthusiasm for the bill (Jenkins 1991: 211).[38] Then in early 1968, the Kenyan Asians crisis led to the sudden imposition of the February Commonwealth Immigrants Act, severely restricting immigration of ethnic minority British passport holders from Africa (Hansen 1999). Although this turn of events had no direct impact on the passage of the 1968 Race Relations Act, it did serve to reawaken the tensions around race issues just as the bill was being prepared for publication. Adding to the overall atmosphere of the Parliamentary discussion in April 1968 were Enoch Powell's inflammatory speech and the assassination of Martin Luther King Jr.[39]

In this context, whether motivated by fears of a majority backlash in the face of too-strong antidiscrimination enforcement or by the desire not to break with the Conservatives over an electorally volatile issue, the government pursued consensus and compromise on its bill. Home Secretary Callaghan clearly thought that the major impact of the law would come from its declaratory nature and therefore was much less concerned that the particular details respond to the progressive learners' specifications.[40] He argued strongly that the enforcement procedures would focus on conciliation and would therefore not be too heavy-handed (Hansard 763: 53–67). In another nod toward a bipartisan and depoliticized approach to race, the Home Secretary announced the establishment of an all-party Parliamentary Select Committee on race relations "so that the House as a whole might be involved in coping with the problem" (Hansard 763: 67).

In keeping with the spirit of skepticism and of compromise, the government and the opposition front benches allied on many issues in committee and out-voted both the progressives and the populists who wanted to expand or retract the breadth of coverage or strength of enforcement.

[38] Callaghan himself suggested that he generally supported the bill, but that he was careful not to incorporate overly ambitious elements into the final version (Callaghan 1987: 268–9).

[39] Although not explicitly mentioned in official documents, the U.S. passage of its 1968 Civil Rights Act in mid-April would certainly have been noticed by many in Britain. For more information on the American context, see Weisbrot (1990).

[40] In opening the Parliamentary debate, Callaghan stated: "I attach great importance to the declaratory nature of the first part of the Bill" (Hansard 763: 55). Notes from cabinet discussions in December 1967 and January 1968 spelled out Callaghan's perspective on race legislation: "He recognized that these provisions would be difficult to enforce, but enforcement was not their prime object. The purpose of the Bill was to establish the principle that discrimination was contrary to the public interest; to educate public opinion; to encourage people of goodwill to stand out against discrimination; and to provide machinery for conciliation" (PRO CAB 128/42, CC[67]74:7). See also PRO CAB 128/43, CC(4)68.

Although the government by no means ignored its back bench, it sided with the opposition on at least as many occasions as it did with its own Labour Party members (Lester and Bindman 1972: 136–46). The result of the wranglings was a bill little changed in substance from its initial form. The new act extended the law against access racism to cover the spheres of employment, housing, unions and employers organizations, banking, insurance, and goods and services. Moreover, the act created the Community Relations Commission to supersede the NCCI, to "encourage the establishment of . . . harmonious community relations," and to advise and make recommendations to the Home Secretary on any matter it considered appropriate (Race Relations Act, s. 25, para. 3). It also moderately strengthened the role of the Race Relations Board by allowing it to investigate discrimination even when no complaint had been received, and by giving the board the power to bypass the Attorney General and to bring legal proceedings when conciliation failed.

The 1968 Race Relations Act thus expanded existing British race institutions, using the established framework of administrative conciliation backed by the civil law. Yet the act remained riddled with loopholes, quirks, and residual weaknesses.[41] These can be seen largely as the product of political compromise between progressive learners and skeptics. In the Third Reading Debate, Callaghan again stressed his commitment to a bipartisan policy, and the Conservative front bench allowed a free vote on the bill, which passed easily by 182 to 44. Against many expectations and great odds, a new Race Relations Act came into effect on November 25, 1968.

Conclusion

By 1968, British race policies were no longer simply dictated by concerns about immigration and integration.[42] Race relations began to take shape

[41] Acts not considered unlawful included discrimination: (1) by small employers (with twenty-five or fewer employees for the first two years and with ten or fewer in subsequent years); (2) by landlords sharing accommodations with tenants; and (3) in provision of sleeping cabins on passenger ships. There was also a separate institutional mechanism established to investigate employment related discrimination complaints, whereby the complaint would be handled first by the Secretary of State for Employment, rather than by local conciliation committees or the Race Relations Board. For a complete list of the exceptions and provisions, see the text of the act, cited in Lester and Bindman (1972: Appendix 3).

[42] This is not to say that immigration had ceased to be an important issue in this era. Enoch Powell and others continued to drum up concern about immigrant numbers, an issue that leapt to the public eye during the Kenyan Asians crisis and passage

as a policy sphere in its own right. Progressives framed race issues in North American terms, highlighting problems of access racism in employment, housing, and a variety of other areas, and drawing attention to images of U.S. cities in flames. Britain was commonly viewed as an "early-stage" America with potentially troubling domestic race relations requiring immediate action to diffuse lurking tensions. North American laws against access racism provided compelling evidence to Britons of the value of further legislation. As Rose (1969: 538) notes, race relations issues "ceased to be local American concerns and had taken on a relevance to the British situation." Moreover, the rise of the second generation of minorities in Britain and the evidence of pervasive discrimination on the basis of color persuaded important segments of the polity and the elite that Britain's problems could not be viewed purely in immigration terms.

The 1968 Race Relations Act owed its inception to the impetus of a small group of progressive learners, led in Parliament by an activist Home Secretary, and composed of race bureaucrats in quasigovernmental organizations, policy experts, and minorities themselves supporting the coalition. It did not come about because of straightforward electoral calculations of political parties, nor because of strong and sustained pressure from societal groups such as unions or highly organized immigrant organizations.[43] Moreover, although the activists used the newly minted race institutions as a home base from which to launch their campaign offensive, it was not the institutions themselves that gave them the power to get new legislation on the agenda. The Race Relations Board and the NCCI were deliberately established as weak institutions. The timing and the existence of the 1968 act instead depended largely on a well-orchestrated campaign by the progressive coalition of politicians, bureaucrats, activists, and minorities to highlight British race problems and to argue that legislation was the most effective solution to these problems. Turning the weaknesses of existing institutions into a strength must therefore be seen as a product of the coalition's strategizing more than as a result of the institutions themselves.

The rise of race onto the legislative agenda cannot, however, be portrayed as a classic example of problem-solving politics. It is not the case,

of the 1968 Commonwealth Immigrants Act. Immigrant integration was also a central political and policy concern in this era, as institutions such as the NCCI and funding sources like the 1966 Local Government Act were set up to deal with problems related to immigrants.

[43] Minorities played an important role in passage of the 1968 act, but it was a supporting role rather than a leading role.

for example, that feedback from previous policies raised a new set of problems that were subsequently tackled by policymakers (see Heclo 1974, Pierson 1993). Rather, prevailing race frames played a significant role in shaping actors' understandings of the existing problems and the available and appropriate solutions.[44] By the mid-1960s, enough activists in the area of race had come to view discrimination in areas not covered under British law not only as troublesome, but also as tractable given the North American analogy. Extensive studies of foreign legislation by Jowell (1965) and Street, et al. (1967) demonstrated that countries such as the United States and Canada took access racism in these domains seriously and developed laws to stop it. Why couldn't and shouldn't Great Britain do the same? The progressives therefore set out to "prove the problems" to a wider audience. When the problems were set in stark relief (especially due to the 1967 PEP report) and legislation was seen as a viable solution, race arrived on the Parliamentary agenda.

Although the explanation of the agenda-setting stage owes much to the progressive learners, the final form of the law was not directly determined by their proposals. The 1968 act did extend coverage to the spheres of employment, housing, insurance, and credit facilities, and it modestly strengthened the enforcement mechanisms. Nevertheless, it left many progressives unsatisfied. Weaknesses remained, principally due to political compromises that had to be made with skeptics who argued either that the law was itself dangerous or that the law would be damaging if seen to be too strong. In keeping with actors framing their concerns in terms of the North American analogy, however, the new law focused exclusively on access racism, and it exhibited much continuity with respect to the 1965 provisions in that it relied on administrative conciliation as the principle of enforcement. That it did so can be seen not primarily as an example of institutional path dependence, but more accurately as a case of ideational path dependence. Once the debate over the enforcement mechanism was decided in 1965, there was no reason to call its justification into question when dealing with parallel issues. All agreed that administrative conciliation was either the most appropriate or most effective way to counter access racism.

The 1968 Race Relations Act thus maintained a level of continuity with its elder sibling. However, it also moved beyond a primarily symbolic law designed to offset restrictions to nonwhite immigration. By expanding

[44] The problems of the 1965 act were known by the progressive learners well before feedback information was available, as were the preferred legislative solutions.

into the terrain of employment and housing, it addressed core areas of the British economy and society, and established race relations as an independent policy arena. In spite of progressives' disappointment with aspects of the 1968 act, much had been accomplished with this piece of legislation, and all in the face of initial indifference or hostility of a host of powerful groups in the country. Once again, many saw this law as the final step on the road to establishing race institutions. Unlike the previous act, this one held sway for eight years. By the mid-1970s, however, the drums of the progressives began to beat again for a new round of race legislation that would carry the country well beyond where it was prepared to go at the end of the 1960s.

4

From 1968 to the 1976 Race Relations Act and Beyond

Although the progressive learners succeeded in placing race on the Parliamentary agenda in 1968, their ambitions for the shape of British institutions were not realized in the eventual legislation. From their perspective, political compromises negotiated with skeptics had spawned relatively inefficient and unsatisfactory race institutions. Yet, the anti-immigrant tenor of the late 1960s and early 1970s undercut any steps toward more activist race policies. It took the return of Roy Jenkins to the Home Office under the new 1974 Labour government to jump-start the efforts of progressives. Once the Home Secretary announced the government's openness to revising race policies, progressives threw their weight into the political arena, building momentum towards new institutions of the type they favored.

If the shape of the 1965 and 1968 laws was determined in large part by a political balancing act, negotiations over the 1976 legislation were dominated by the progressive learners. They made significant changes on the basis of "feedback" learning from the problems that arose through the functioning of the 1968 act. In particular, British institutions turned away from a pure conciliation model in the realm of access racism. Although administrative bodies remained a central element of British institutions (and were in fact strengthened), individuals were no longer obliged to undergo administrative conciliation procedures that many deemed slow and inefficient. Instead, the 1976 act permitted victims of discrimination direct access to civil courts or industrial tribunals. In this, British policy experts struck out in a direction that differed from the one they charted in 1965 under the influence of the American model.

At the same time, however, the progressives also recast British institutions in a North American direction, demonstrating the continuing influence of prevailing race frames. Drawing directly on the American analogy, two race-conscious elements – indirect discrimination protections and positive action – were introduced into British legislation following the Home Secretary's visit to the United States in the winter of 1974. These developments inaugurated a new, although tentative, British concern with overcoming societal inequalities based on racial group membership. Such a concern has also been reflected in policy developments since 1976. Although through the late 1990s there were no Parliamentary initiatives equivalent to passage of the 1976 Race Relations Act, British race institutions did not cease to evolve. One critical aspect of British policies – ethnic monitoring – came about gradually in the quarter century following the 1976 act and is now a regular aspect of British life, as evidenced by the first-time inclusion of an ethnic question in the 1991 national census. The collection of racial and ethnic statistics has become natural within the context of British institutions concerned with group equality. These sorts of policies are absent in France where racial group equality and identification with a North American analogy are not part of the country's race frames.

To bring out the trajectory of race policy developments in Britain from 1968 to the end of the century, this chapter first reviews the race and immigration context between 1968 and passage of the 1976 Race Relations Act. It then argues that the actions of the progressive learners were the critical factors accounting for the renewed legislative action in the field of race. Section three examines the shape of the 1976 law, demonstrating that the outcomes responded to feedback from existing British institutions and to the lessons about race policies drawn from the other side of the Atlantic. Section four illuminates the most important institutional developments that took place between the 1976 act and the end of the century, focusing most centrally on the growth of ethnic monitoring in Britain.

Beyond the Liberal Hour: 1968–1976

The 1968 race legislation has frequently been characterized as one of the capstone achievements of a brief "liberal hour" in late 1960s British politics (Bonham Carter 1987, Rose 1969: 10–26, Saggar 1993).[1] This era and its immediate aftermath saw the burgeoning of government policies

[1] The liberal hour is typically measured between 1966 and 1968.

and nongovernmental organizations in the field of race. Parliament initiated its Select Committee on Race Relations following Home Secretary Callaghan's suggestion during the 1968 debates, and in addition it passed the 1969 Local Government Grants (Social Need) Act, designed to fulfill Prime Minister Harold Wilson's promise to aid communities with ethnic minority immigrants (Young 1983: 289–93).[2] Outside of Westminster, advocates of minority rights founded private groups such as the Runnymede Trust to carry on research and activities relating to race; in 1969, the Institute of Race Relations published its landmark study *Colour and Citizenship* on the state of race relations in Britain (Rose 1969); and Political and Economic Planning began a series of studies on racial disadvantage and discrimination in 1972 (see McIntosh and Smith 1974, Smith 1974, Smith 1976, Smith 1977, Smith and Whalley 1975). In short, race became well established as an issue of public concern.

It is safe to say, nevertheless, that race did not trouble the British political elite between 1968 and 1976. There were no mass protest movements or significant electoral pressure for further action on race issues. The Conservative Party continued to demonstrate limited enthusiasm for existing measures and the Labour Party made few references to race policies, omitting mention of the issue in its February 1974 election manifesto (Craig 1975).[3] Race relations was not a hot-button issue during the two general elections of 1974 (Layton-Henry 1984: 145). Even Roy Jenkins, returned to the Home Office under the new Labour government, was not as inspired an advocate of prominority legislation as he had been in the 1960s, admitting that "odd as it may seem to those who regard me as a frenzied promoter of liberal laws in the 1960s, by the 1970s these instincts required a little stimulation" (Jenkins 1991: 376). If domestic race relations had become an institutionalized policy sphere both inside and outside of government by the late 1960s, it remained for most a distant cloud on the political horizon.

Immigration, by contrast, continued to rumble closer to home, with Enoch Powell always a potential storm in the making. Powell's public

[2] Young (1983: 289–93) argues that Wilson's plans for an Urban Programme were related to Powell's April 1968 'rivers of blood' speech. Moreover, he shows that although the language of the legislation had to be race neutral to avoid anti-immigrant backlash, the program was clearly aimed to benefit minorities and communities with high proportions of minorities.

[3] Labour's subsequent October 1974 manifesto, which devoted a half page to women's rights, stated briefly that the party would "strengthen legislation protecting minorities" (Craig 1975: 464).

presence during the 1970 election served to keep issues of immigration alive in national debates (Hansen 2000: 191–2). In 1971, the Conservative government passed its Immigration Act, fulfilling its election promise to the restrictionist wing of the party. Coming into full force with supplementary immigration rules in 1973, the act limited rights of permanent residence and rights of entry for dependents, and established the concept of patriality as a criterion for facilitating access to rights of entry and residence (Freeman 1979: 61–8, Hansen 2000: 194–6, Layton-Henry 1992: 83–5).[4] In a more liberal vein, the government chose to accept some 27,000 British passport-holding Ugandan Asians expelled by Idi Amin in the early 1970s (Layton-Henry 1992: 85–7, Sked and Cook 1990: 269). As with Labour's 1976 acceptance of a smaller number of Asians expelled from Malawi, this act provoked a *cris de coeur* among the right and provided grist for the mill of the budding far-right National Front (Layton-Henry 1992: 89–97; see also Messina 1989: 109–25). Although Powell's electoral significance declined after 1974, the National Front and the Conservative Party took up the mantle of anti-immigrant rhetoric, ensuring that immigration remained a prominent concern throughout the decade.[5]

Although it was logical to assume that the predominance of immigration as a political issue in this era meant that race legislation responded to concerns about migrant intake (as was largely true in 1965), this is not the case. It is true that race relations and immigration remained intimately intertwined in the minds and politics of many British leaders, particularly those on the right. During the 1976 debates over the Race Relations Bill, for example, Conservative Members of Parliament regularly stressed control of immigration as the best guarantor of peaceful race relations (Hansard 906: 1547–1670). On the other side of the aisle, by contrast, race was understood largely as an autonomous policy sphere. Race legislation was placed on the agenda within a context of antidiscrimination concerns, not within a context of immigration concerns, even if

[4] British subjects living abroad with at least one grandparent born in the UK were considered patrials (see Freeman 1979: 62, f. 42). They were granted rights to entry and abode in the UK denied to nonpatrial subjects. Although the term patrial was introduced in the early 1970s, a similar concept of a "qualifying connection" originated with the Labour-sponsored 1968 Commonwealth Immigrants Act (see Hansen 2000: 163).

[5] Founded in 1967, National Front membership peaked between 1972 and 1974, with its electoral returns strongest in 1976 and 1977 (Messina 1989: 109–25). On the Conservative Party's anti-immigrant posture after 1975 see Messina (1989: ch. 6).

Labour leaders debated immigration issues in Parliament when prompted by Conservatives. By 1976, passage of race legislation had little to do with questions of cross-border flows.

Race to the Agenda

With the end of the liberal hour, with the onset of the economic recession following the 1973 oil shock, and with Conservatives' focus on themes of immigration, the years leading up to the 1976 Race Relations Act were not overly promising ones for proponents of new race legislation (Freeman 1979, Hollifield 1992, Money 1999).[6] In such a context, electoral concerns per se understandably had a minimal influence on Labour's decision to legislate against racism. Although parties began to seek black votes in the late 1970s (see FitzGerald 1987, Geiger 1989, Messina 1989: 144–9), there was little attempt to appeal to minorities directly or to respond to minority pressures in the 1974 elections (Sooben 1990: 48–54). By the time the Community Relations Commission published its 1975 report arguing that minorities had played a significant role in Labour's 1974 victory,[7] Roy Jenkins had already announced Labour's intention to pass the 1976 act.[8] There is, however, evidence that the electorate at large and Labour supporters in particular were more aware of discrimination and moderately better disposed toward race relations policies by the mid-1970s. Although the issue was not salient enough to rally significant electoral support, within the party there was a tendency among some to blame "Powellism" for what they viewed as Britain's distasteful immigration and race policies (Labour Party 1970: 205–9). Segments of Labour thus attempted to rethink the party's strategy and to develop an alternative to the prevailing anti-immigrant rhetoric. This new philosophy was reflected in policy documents such as Labour's 1972 Green Paper on Citizenship,

[6] Hollifield (1992) notes that the post-oil shock 1970s were years of attempted restrictions on immigrants across Europe. He also points out, however, that the most restrictive measures were unsuccessful.

[7] It has since been shown that the report exaggerated the effect of the minority vote. See Crewe (1979).

[8] There is a debate over the effects of this report on the Labour Party. Sooben (1990: 51) argues that there is no evidence that this report influenced government policies, since Labour had long known of its support among minorities; moreover, he argues, this report may have made them complacent. By contrast, FitzGerald (1987: 30–1) asserts that as Labour saw its traditional base dwindle, it looked to consolidate its loyal black vote. It is possible that the 1974 report had little short-term effect on Labour's policies, but that it contributed to its longer term strategic shift toward more active recruitment of black voters.

Immigration and Integration and in their 1973 Party Programme (Sooben 1990: 49–50). In spite of this activism, the party chose first to omit and then to marginalize promises to legislate on race in its February and October 1974 manifestos (Craig 1975), suggesting that proreform members lacked the clout to parlay changing attitudes into a Labour commitment to act.

Not electoral stimuli, but a combination of perceived problems, a shift in the party in power, and the use of an analogical argument served to place race on the Parliamentary agenda. Three types of problems manifested themselves in this time period. Based on accumulated experience under the 1968 Race Relations Act, experts and practitioners were beginning to receive feedback that highlighted flaws in the existing legislation. In its 1972 annual report, the Race Relations Board called for amending the act in order to facilitate enforcement of the law (Race Relations Board 1972). It maintained that whatever the declaratory effect of the legislation in deterring discrimination, it did not provide sufficient means to resolve many actual cases of racism.[9] Moreover, the institutional division of power between the two branches of the race bureaucracy (the Race Relations Board and the Community Relations Commission) left many observers feeling that each was inefficient or simply ineffective, and prompted calls for reform (see *The Times,* June 24,1970; *The Times,* November 21, 1970, and esp. Great Britain: Select Committee on Race Relations and Immigration 1975a: 11–12). Finally, beyond learning about the problems in the functioning of the 1968 act, British commentators began to realize that the very definition of discrimination enshrined in British law was too narrow. The law defined discrimination as less favorable treatment on grounds of race,[10] but it did not ban acts which were discriminatory in effect without being discriminatory in intent. It permitted, for example, employer policies against wearing beards, which had the effect of discriminating against Sikhs for whom wearing a beard is a religious duty (Lester and Bindman 1972: 23, Smith and Whalley 1975).

In addition to these feedback problems, there were persistent, low-level concerns about social order. In 1972 and 1974, racial tensions flared in industrial disputes (Sooben 1990: 44–6). Asian workers at the Mansfield Hosiery Mills struck in 1972, arguing that they were systematically

[9] Specifically, it asserted that the complaints procedure discouraged valid complaints, that the board's investigative powers were insufficient, that the board should have the power to ignore frivolous complaints, and that certain loopholes of the 1968 law should be closed (Race Relations Board 1972: esp. 20–4).

[10] Or color, or ethnic or national origins.

denied the best-paid jobs. At one point in the stand-off, more than one hundred Asian picketers chanted "management racialist," and police had to separate them from white workers who did not support the strike (*The Times*, December 7, 1972). In 1974, approximately 400 of the 1500 manual workers at Imperial Typewriters in Leicester struck over allegations that the company was cheating on its bonus system and that unions would not allow Asians to elect their own stewards (*The Times*, May 31, 1974). The disputes resulted in several rounds of fighting and arrests (*The Times*, June 3, 1974). In 1973, the Race Relations Board reflected on the Mansfield case, intoning that "the frustration of legitimate expectations, particularly if this applies to a significant proportion of the work force, carries a heavy risk of conflict" (Race Relations Board 1973: 10). During the 1976 Parliamentary process, several Members echoed the concern about potential social disorder as a strong motivating force behind their actions.[11]

Finally, Political and Economic Planning began presenting research in the summer of 1974 that demonstrated the continued prevalence of discrimination in British industries, perhaps reinforcing fears of social upheaval. David Smith, the PEP's lead researcher, found that of the fourteen plants he examined in depth, eight clearly practiced some form of discrimination, a conclusion that was soon confirmed by further PEP studies (McIntosh and Smith 1974, Smith 1974: 5).[12] These reports, coupled with the CRC's 1974 report on employment and homelessness among minorities, generated media commentary about the weaknesses of the current act as well as speculation about the timing of a new round of antidiscrimination legislation (*The Times*, June 17, 1974; *The Economist*, June 22, 1974).

[11] Somewhat out of the public eye (in Parliamentary committee) one MP revealed these fears in the starkest manner when he stated that "the object of this legislation is to prevent American-type race riots and race hatred which poisons society" (Standing Committee A, Race Relations Bill; 15th Sitting, June 22, 1976, c. 730).

[12] This study followed in the footsteps of earlier work on discrimination (Political and Economic Planning 1967) by using "situation tests" to gauge the respective receptiveness of employers and landlords to white versus nonwhite applicants. The authors (McIntosh and Smith 1974: 35–36) argued that "The results of our tests demonstrate that there is still substantial discrimination against members of the minority groups when seeking jobs and housing.... Asian and West Indians applying for unskilled jobs faced discrimination in 46 per cent of cases. This finding implies that there are tens of thousands of acts of discrimination of this kind in a year.... [T]he general conclusion from these findings must be that the number of cases of discrimination that are dealt with by the law ... forms a very small proportion of the number of acts of discrimination that actually occur."

Although feedback, concerns about social order, and additional research on discrimination had generated some attention to the weaknesses of the 1968 institutions among the specialist community, the Conservative government of 1970 to 1974 had not responded to arguments for remaking British race institutions. It took the return of the Labour Party to power and of Roy Jenkins to the Home Office for the tide to turn in favor of renewed legislation. Jenkins took immediate steps upon arriving in office to ensure that discrimination would be granted significant consideration. By the first election in 1974, gender equality had become a beacon for social progressives as well as an issue that politicians calculated could win them support. In May 1974, Jenkins appointed long-time liberal activist Anthony Lester as his special adviser, signaling his commitment to legislate not only on sex discrimination, but also on the politically less popular theme of race (*The Times*, June 17, 1974; interview with Lord Lester, July 23, 1997; Jenkins 1991: 375–6). Lester had played an important advocacy role in earlier rounds of race legislation and would serve that function again, this time from within the government itself.

On July 23, 1974, the Home Secretary announced in the House of Commons that "sex and race discrimination will be dealt with separately at this stage, but my ultimate aim is to harmonise, and possibly to amalgamate, the powers and procedures for dealing with both forms of discrimination" (Hansard 877: 1,298). Jenkins and others in the Labour Party were clearly sympathetic to passing a fresh round of race legislation, yet as this roundabout statement indicates, they had to proceed with caution. In its October election manifesto, the party therefore tucked a half-sentence pledge to legislate on race in the shadow of bold and prominent promises for gender equality. Once again, although advocating race legislation met with a certain amount of popularity in the party, it was not likely to be rewarded with many swing votes in an era of continuing anti-immigrant sentiment and it put at risk the support of working class groups that sympathized with Enoch Powell.

Jenkins' 1974 statement prompted race professionals to move into high gear in their efforts to build momentum and consensus for new legislation. The three governmental and quasigovernmental bodies (the Parliamentary Select Committee, the Race Relations Board, and the Community Relations Commission) challenged the viability of the 1968 institutions and proposed alternatives. They presented a relatively unified front for new legislation in their respective reports of 1975 (Community Relations Commission 1975a; Community Relations Commission 1975b; Great Britain: Select Committee on Race Relations and Immigration 1975a-c

Race Relations Board 1975), providing crucial channels for the government, Members of Parliament, the media, and the public to learn about the weaknesses of the current legislation. In addition, the series of PEP reports issued between 1974 and 1976 continued to demonstrate persistent discrimination in Britain, buttressing the antiracism efforts (McIntosh and Smith 1974, Smith 1974, Smith 1976, Smith and Whalley 1975). During the months between July 1974 – when Jenkins announced his desire to pass race legislation – and November 1975 – when the Queen's Speech announced forthcoming Parliamentary action – the sustained pressure for institutional reform by the statutory bodies and the select committee (and by private groups and minority communities) and the on-going research reports drawing attention to discrimination problems prevented race from dropping off the agenda and persuaded a wider audience of the need for new legislation.

Even within a context of sustained pressure from race professionals and a sympathetic Home Secretary, however, the 1976 Race Relations Act could not have emerged absent one other critical factor: passage of the 1975 Sex Discrimination Act. The momentum toward women's rights legislation began in 1970, when the Labour government passed the modest Equal Pay Act, requiring employers to harmonize pay to men and women performing the same or similar jobs (Lester 1987: 24).[13] By 1973, the Conservatives had introduced their own Sex Discrimination Bill[14] and once in opposition they supported Labour's 1975 Sex Discrimination Act.[15] But if women's rights had steamed on to the Parliamentary agenda largely for electoral reasons, race provisions merely trailed in the wake of the gender juggernaut.[16] From the earliest stages, both the race professionals and the Home Secretary strongly argued that the areas of sex and race discrimination were exact analogs and that reform of race institutions would be logically necessary in light of new gender equality provisions.[17]

[13] See Meehan (1985: esp. 78–85) for a discussion of the causes of the Equal Pay Act.

[14] Though it covered discrimination only in a limited number of areas.

[15] Note that although race and gender equality legislation were closely intertwined, the religious discrimination law (the Northern Ireland Fair Employment Act of 1976) that passed through Parliament concurrently was intentionally distanced from both gender and race legislation (see Lester 1994: 226).

[16] Lester (1987: 24) argues that the two issues were not dealt with in one act because women and minorities did not see themselves as part of a common movement.

[17] As early as 1973, in response to the Conservative government's proposals, the Race Relations Board asserted that the "two forms of discrimination being dealt with in entirely different ways is in itself considered unacceptable" (reproduced in Great Britain: Select Committee on Race Relations and Immigration 1975b: 41).

Jenkins' July 1974 announcement in the House of Commons struck this chord, and the Labour Party annual report from 1974 showed others to be equally concerned "that protection against racial discrimination should not lag behind that appended to women" (Labour Party 1974: 115). The Parliamentary Select Committee and the CRC also made this point forcefully (Community Relations Commission 1975b, Great Britain: Select Committee on Race Relations and Immigration 1975a: 7), and it was well taken by many in the media. Reflecting on Jenkins' strategy, *The Economist* (November 2, 1974) argued that once the Sex Discrimination Act was on the statute book, "it will then seem illogical that powers against racial discrimination should lag behind, and the RRB will, its members hope, be quietly allowed to catch up."

The gender issue thus plowed the road for the politically weaker race initiative, with advocates using analogical arguments to defuse challenges to its legitimacy.[18] Yet the precise effect of sex discrimination legislation on passage of race provisions is easy to overstate. Sooben (1990: 33) asserts, for example, that "it would have been difficult to justify the denial to victims of one form of discrimination... opportunities for redress... given to victims of another." British policymakers, however, have proven willing and able to avoid logical consistency on any number of occasions, most notably by creating protections against racial discrimination in Britain but not in Northern Ireland, while granting provisions against religious discrimination to Northern Ireland yet studiously avoiding them in Britain. The power of the analogy is most significant at the margin where important actors use it to enlist support among fence-sitters and the public at large, and to undercut challenges by political opponents. In the case of returning race to the Parliamentary agenda, the gender analogy fulfilled precisely this role, and was therefore of critical political importance.

Negotiating New Institutions

If the final version of the 1968 Race Relations Act reflected compromises between progressive learners and skeptical populists, the balance of power during the 1970s negotiations had tilted substantially toward the progressives. With Jenkins as Home Secretary and Lester as an official advisor,

[18] As Gregory (1987: 3) argues, "the introduction of the Sex Discrimination Act in 1975 provided an ideal opportunity to test the climate of opinion and rehearse the arguments before introducing an almost identical set of measures on racial discrimination the following year."

progressives had priority in shaping the final version of the law. Skeptical populists continued to mount a vocal campaign within the House of Commons attacking the bill as counterproductive to good race relations (which they felt would be better managed by even stricter immigration policies) and as likely to create a protected class of citizens who would foist unlimited grievances upon the body politic (Hansard 906: 1547–1670). These voices remained relatively marginal, however, and in the final vote of the Second Reading Debate, only eight members opposed the bill, with abstention being the official Conservative Party line.[19]

In the end, the 1976 act was seen to remedy virtually all of the problems that were at the heart of the reform effort. One expert observer, for example, noted that the government's proposals provided "precisely the powers which the Race Relations Board asked for" and that "the Bill has gone further still" (Rendel and Bindman 1975: 13). The principal innovations of the legislation were of two orders: stronger enforcement mechanisms, and the introduction of new elements to the British institutional repertoire. If feedback lessons from the functioning of previous British Race Relations Acts encouraged the drive for stronger enforcement, developments in North America inspired many of the new institutional elements. As in earlier rounds of legislation, however, North American policies were not adopted lock, stock, and barrel; rather, they were adapted and molded to fit British needs.

Many of the American innovations incorporated into race legislation were first instituted in the preceding year's law on gender equality, which itself was also influenced by the 1960s' Race Relations Acts. Jenkins learned both positive and negative lessons from the field of race discrimination when crafting the 1975 Sex Discrimination Bill. The 1974 White Paper on sex discrimination referred explicitly to the 1968 Race Relations Act, acknowledging that in many important respects, "the principle of nondiscrimination contained in the proposed bill is identical to the principle of nondiscrimination contained in the race relations legislation" (Great Britain: Home Office 1974: 9). In addition, Jenkins argued in July 1974 that in fashioning the government's proposals to legislate against sex discrimination he "tried to avoid a number of the weaknesses which have been revealed in the enforcement provisions of the race relations legislation" (Hansard 877: 1298). He thus wrote the Sex Discrimination

[19] According to Trevor Russel (1978: 119), only a threatened revolt by senior Tory "left-wingers" prevented the new Conservative leader (Margaret Thatcher) from ordering party opposition to the bill.

Bill informed by past race experience and with future race institutions in mind. When the Race Relations Bill was drafted in 1975, it incorporated virtually the same language as that of the final version of Sex Discrimination Act. Therefore, tracing the path to race legislation must be done with an eye toward Parliamentary provisions on gender equality.

Lessons of Weakness: Stronger Enforcement

The Sex Discrimination Act of 1975 and the Race Relations Act of 1976 vastly strengthened the enforcement mechanisms of antidiscrimination institutions. Legislative initiatives of the 1960s had placed significant emphasis on the declaratory function of race law. Like a school-teacher's tut-tut and wagging finger, race laws were meant to set a tone of disapproval without inflicting pain on wrongdoers. Many considered this a more effective way to promote good race relations than summarily rapping the knuckles of those who may not know better. Race professionals disagreed, however, and their pleas for stronger enforcement were codified in the 1967 Street Report, a document that resurfaced in preparation for the new legislation (Great Britain: Home Office 1974: 5, Lester 1994: 224–7, Race Relations Board 1974: 16). The Street Report revolved around the principle of administrative conciliation that animated the British model from 1965 to 1976. The major innovation in enforcement introduced by the 1976 Race Relations Act, however, marked an important departure from a pure administrative conciliation model. Since the 1976 law, complainants have been able to take their cases of access racism directly to civil courts.[20] This new principle therefore tilted the balance within the administrative/civil model toward the civil courts and away from administrative procedures. It arose primarily due to endemic frustration with the perceived weaknesses of the 1968 act,[21] although it was also in keeping with the principle of direct court access enshrined in the Equal Pay Act of 1970.[22]

[20] Or to the equivalent of civil courts – industrial tribunals – in employment related cases. There is an optional conciliation procedure which precedes industrial tribunal hearings. See Mankes (1994) for a detailed comparison of the U.S. and British employment discrimination provisions.

[21] Lester (1987: 23) argues that "the compulsory conciliation procedures embodied in our law had resulted in soft settlements which did not remedy the wrong, and in unacceptable delays within the administrative agencies responsible for attempting to settle a dispute by means of conciliation."

[22] The government's White Paper discusses in detail the balance struck between the Equal Pay Act model of individual complaints and the Race Relations Act model of a representative public body (Great Britain: Home Office 1974: 6–7). It is interesting

In spite of this significant change, British institutions were not altogether revolutionized. The administrative agency remained – consolidated from two bureaucracies into one – and was given a new mandate with extended powers. The Commission for Racial Equality (CRE) currently performs the public relations, local funding, and antidiscrimination watchdog functions of the previous bureaucracies. It assists individual victims of discrimination by providing them with information about seeking remedies,[23] or by acting as an advocate in cases where a special consideration applies.[24] It advises the government on the functioning of the act,[25] publishes an annual report, runs antidiscrimination advertising and public campaigns, and issues codes of practice informing employers and industries of preferred rules of conduct which may then be invoked in court cases involving discrimination. Furthermore, the CRE's mandate continues to include funding for organizations that promote equality of opportunity or "good relations between persons of different racial groups" (Great Britain: Home Office undated: 11.30).[26]

The 1976 Race Relations Act (again, paralleling the 1975 Sex Discrimination Act) also provided additional powers to the CRE to conduct "race-relations audits."[27] If the commission suspects discrimination, it may begin a formal investigation of a company, of an industry as a whole, or of divisions of the public sector, such as universities, government departments, or local authorities. If the CRE finds that the Race Relations Act is being contravened, it may issue a non-discrimination notice, which may then be followed by a court order requiring compliance with the act

to note that the Labour government's 1970 Equal Pay Act (introduced by Barbara Castle) was modeled on the "stillborn" U.S. Equal Pay Act of 1960, just as Britain's choice of the administrative model for race was inspired by North American state and provincial laws (Lester 1997: 168).

[23] Typically referring them in employment cases to the Advisory, Conciliation and Arbitration Service or to the Race Relations Employment Advisory Service of the Department of Employment.

[24] Such as when the case raises a question of principle or where it unreasonable to expect the complainant to deal with the case unaided (Great Britain: Home Office undated: 11.26). In addition, the commission has sole responsibility for pursuing cases involving discrimination in advertising or pressure or instructions to discriminate (Great Britain: Home Office undated: 11.21).

[25] In 1992, the Commission for Racial Equality issued its Second Review of the Race Relations Act, calling for changes to the law (Commission for Racial Equality 1992).

[26] In the year 1995/96, the CRE disbursed £4,412,791 in payments to local Race Equality Councils and to other organizations for project aid (Commission for Racial Equality 1996: 43–5).

[27] See Rendel and Bindman (1975) for early commentary on these provisions in the Sex Discrimination Bill.

(Great Britain: Home Office undated: 11.3–11.20). Although there are a series of (usually lengthy) steps between initiating a formal investigation and securing a court order in cases of pervasive discrimination, the threat of the administrative and legal headaches and bad public relations image associated with a formal investigation can provide the commission useful leverage in their push for reforms.[28] These tools have therefore substantially expanded the power of British institutions to tackle access racism.

Lessons from America: Indirect Discrimination and Positive Action

In addition to providing for stronger enforcement, the antidiscrimination legislation of 1975 and 1976 introduced two tentative steps toward group-based, rather than individual-based, equality.[29] This shift was in keeping with British leaders' framing their problems of racism in North American terms and in terms of color discrimination. Tremendously influenced by developments in United States civil rights law, British policymakers created new tools for combating access racism, punishing not only wrongs perpetrated against individuals, but also harms to groups defined by race or gender. First, Parliament expanded the definition of discrimination from direct, intentional discrimination to indirect discrimination, whether intentional or not.[30] Second, it explicitly permitted a soft form

[28] Before moving to a formal investigation, the CRE can undertake a preliminary inquiry. Because a formal investigation is viewed by organizations as onerous, as Barbara Cohen of the CRE says, "It's been a very useful stick in the background" (interview with Cohen, July 24, 1997). At the beginning of 1995, there were nine formal investigations in progress, of which five were concluded during the year and one nondiscrimination notice was issued. By year's end, terms of reference had been drawn up or proposed for an additional three formal investigations and preliminary inquiries were being conducted regarding another four. Furthermore, ten previous investigations which had resulted in a nondiscrimination notice or in voluntary agreements continued to be monitored by the CRE (Commission for Racial Equality 1996: 13–14).

[29] Gregory (1987: 5–7) discusses the new provisions in terms of substantive rather than formal equality. Formal equality is sex and color blind, whereas substantive equality recognizes and compensates for material inequalities suffered by certain groups.

[30] The first Parliamentary concern with this issue was raised fleetingly and not resolved during the 1968 deliberations. Joan Lestor complained that Sikhs were barred from jobs in public transport because their religious beliefs required them to wear beards and turbans, which employers prohibited. The government (represented by David Ennals) responded that the issue was not one of racial (or religious) discrimination, but rather one of discrimination against beards, which was not unlawful (see Lester and Bindman 1972: 139).

of affirmative action, known in Britain as positive action. Although these developments did not mark a sea change in British institutional principles, together they introduced an element of group-equality logic into British policy not found in France or in most other European countries.

Indirect discrimination and positive action provisions were not originally slated to be part of the antidiscrimination program as it was developing in 1974. When the White Paper *Equality for Women* appeared in September 1974 outlining the government's proposals for the law,[31] no mention was made of either new ingredient, and British commentators did not draw attention to their absence (Great Britain: Home Office 1974, Lester 1994: 227). Then in late 1974, Jenkins and Lester traveled to the United States where they held meetings with a range of American experts who alerted them to these omissions (Lester 1994: 227). Contacts between Britain and the United States were flourishing during this period, and looking to North American policies had become virtually a reflex among race relations elites.[32] One of the insights gained from tracking policy developments across the Atlantic was that there was more to discrimination than just direct intentional acts. The landmark 1971 U.S. Supreme Court case Griggs v. Duke Power Co.[33] had identified and rendered illegal disparate impact discrimination. The Griggs decision prohibited rules which applied equally to all but which had unequal and unfair effect on members of a particular racial group, such as a requirement for workers to have a high school diploma or to pass an intelligence test (Skrentny 1996: 166–71). Griggs was the "original intellectual inspiration" (Lester 1987: 23) for Britain's indirect discrimination provisions, seen by many as a major departure in British legal ideology (Gregory 1987: 35) . In addition, U.S. experts also emphasized the value of special aid aimed at historically or structurally disadvantaged groups such as women and minorities, even if such aid did not include the quotas and targets of American affirmative action policies (Lester 1987: 23). Accordingly, the government revised its 1974 White Paper proposals to include both indirect discrimination and positive action provisions in the Sex Discrimination and Race Relations Bills of 1975 and 1976.

Drafted with the Griggs decision in mind, British law defines indirect racial discrimination as treatment that is equal in a formal sense, but

[31] Lester drafted the White Paper, with support from Jenkins (Jenkins 1991: 376).

[32] In 1975, members of the Parliamentary Select Committee also traveled to the United States (and the Netherlands) to gather information for their report (Great Britain: Select Committee on Race Relations and Immigration 1975c: 267).

[33] 401 U.S. 424 (1971).

discriminatory in its effect on one particular racial group (Great Britain: Home Office undated: 2.4, Lester 1994: 227).[34] It involves the imposition of a condition or requirement to obtain a benefit (such as a job), where the condition is applied equally to everybody; where it is such that "the proportion of persons of the victim's racial group who can comply with it is considerably smaller than the proportion of persons not of that group who can comply with it;" where it hurts the individual who cannot comply; and where "it cannot be shown by the discriminator to be justifiable" irrespective of race (Great Britain: Home Office undated: 2.4).

Although as a general rule, the race and gender legislation of the 1970s was not hotly contested by the opposition, there were some exceptions over particular points. Indirect discrimination was not seriously challenged on the House of Commons floor, yet it came under heavy Conservative fire during Sex Discrimination Bill committee hearings. One MP moved to delete the clause, arguing that "we do not know what it means. Secondly, we do not think the Government know what it means; and, thirdly, if we did know what it meant we do not think we would like it, but we cannot be sure."[35] The topic was intensely debated in committee over the course of one and a half sittings during which time its eventual survival was in doubt. By a one-vote margin the proposal to delete the clause failed, and indirect discrimination survived this most serious Parliamentary hurdle and went on to be incorporated into both the gender and race discrimination legislation.[36]

To the disappointment of many progressives, it has not had as prominent an impact on British race institutions as the Griggs decision across the Atlantic (see Commission for Racial Equality 1992: 28–9, Gregory 1987: ch. 2; McCrudden 1983). Indirect discrimination cases made up only 2.5 percent of the total discrimination cases in the CRE database between January 1994 and September 1996,[37] and the scope of the provisions has

[34] The 1976 act continues, of course, to prohibit direct racial discrimination, where an individual is treated less favorably than another on racial grounds.

[35] Standing Committee B, Sex Discrimination Bill; 1st Sitting, May 22, 1975, c. 36.

[36] It was also challenged at the committee stage of the Race Relations Bill, although somewhat less successfully, at least in part because of the 1975 publication of the PEP report demonstrating the effects of indirect discrimination in the housing market (Standing Committee A, Race Relations Bill; 1st Sitting, April 27, 1976, cc. 5–41; Smith and Whalley 1975).

[37] Information provided from CRE database (interview with Bandopadhyay, October 21, 1996). This percentage seems variable, however, as McCrudden (1983: 57) notes that in 1979–80, 7.7% of allegations were of indirect discrimination, and in 1980–1 the percentage rose to 20.5% of allegations. Gregory (1987: 45) states

been narrowly interpreted by the courts (Commission for Racial Equality 1992: 28–9, Gregory 1987: ch. 2). Nevertheless, indirect discrimination can be used in creative ways to skirt the limits of the existing law. For example, a case of discrimination against Muslims in Sheffield was held to be indirect racial discrimination.[38] Unequal treatment on the basis of religion – not a punishable offense in Britain – can thus be ruled indirect discrimination if its targets are disproportionately members of a particular ethnic group or have the same country of origin (Commission for Racial Equality 1992: 80). In spite of their seeming underuse, indirect discrimination provisions have proven important in Britain because, as Christian Joppke (1999: 230) has argued, they "created a space for the language of group rights and for the result-oriented logic of achieving statistical parity between the races."

The Home Secretary's 1974 visit to the United States also tempered his opposition to positive discrimination, which he had previously explicitly ruled out (Gregory 1987: 48, Meehan 1985: 52–3). British progressives had long-standing reservations about policies that involved uneven treatment by race; they unsuccessfully opposed a clause in the 1968 act permitting certain industries to limit the number of immigrant workers in the interest of preserving a "racial balance" (Lester and Bindman 1972: 140–1).[39] This intellectual commitment to race neutrality and rejection of affirmative action-inspired quotas are reflected in a Home Office publication emphasizing that "the [1976 Race Relations] Act does not permit 'reverse discrimination'" (Great Britain: Home Office undated: 7.7). Nevertheless, after returning from North America in 1974, Jenkins had softened his stance on recognizing race for the purpose of remedying inequalities. He argued in the House of Commons debate on the Sex Discrimination Bill that "we should not be so blindly loyal to the principle of formal legal equality as to ignore the actual and practical inequalities

that an average of 15% of industrial tribunal cases are concerned with indirect discrimination.

[38] Most Muslims in Britain are ethnic or racial minorities from South Asia, or, less numerously, from the Middle East. Using the current law to punish discrimination against Catholics or Protestants in Britain would be more difficult.

[39] The reinstatement of this clause was denied by a close vote in the committee stage of the 1976 Race Relations Bill (Standing Committee A, Race Relations Bill; 3rd and 4th Sittings, cc. 139–53). It should be noted that the progressive learners also opposed provisions in the 1968 law designed to benefit minorities, on the grounds that they were superfluous and possibly dangerous in that they might be interpreted as justifying segregated facilities (Lester and Bindman 1972: 138).

between the sexes, still less to prohibit positive action to help men and women to compete on genuinely equal terms and to overcome an undesirable historical link" (Hansard 889: 514).[40]

Surprisingly, positive action was virtually unchallenged during the Parliamentary process. Even in committee, where the most contentious discussion of indirect discrimination had occurred, opposition MPs mounted no serious challenge to positive action. The issue was not raised at all in the committee stage of the Sex Discrimination Bill. During discussion of the Race Relations Bill, one member voiced the concern that it might cause resentment at the grassroots level. The government spokesman countered that the provisions would most likely not be used frequently, but that they were indeed about "positive discrimination" and that "that is what this legislation is all about."[41] Numerous were the Members who spoke in favor of the provision on the House of Commons floor, and some argued more radically for the use of quotas under special circumstances (Hansard 899: 552–69).[42] Although Parliament proved unwilling to institute hard quotas, it quietly incorporated positive action into Britain's antidiscrimination institutional repertoire, thereby taking a clear step toward American-style affirmative action.[43]

Britain's positive action provisions allow training bodies, employers, or unions to allocate training resources to underrepresented racial groups, or to take steps to encourage members of those racial groups to take advantage of employment opportunities (Great Britain: Home Office undated). The underlying goal of the policies is to increase the pool of qualified candidates from underrepresented groups who compete for valued jobs. The method is to expand recruitment efforts in targeted communities (through advertising signals such as "equal opportunity employer" and the use of ethnic minority press, for example), and to help provide skills that enable those individuals to compete effectively. Britain's positive action does not, however, permit racial criteria to play any role at the point of hiring or promotion. On the whole, British observers tended to be disappointed by

[40] For the parallel Parliamentary statement about positive action in the Race Relations Bill, see Hansard (906: 1558).

[41] Standing Committee A, Race Relations Bill; 10th Sitting, May 27, 1976, cc. 466–7.

[42] Roderick MacFarquar and Maureen Colquhoun, for example, urged that the Equal Opportunities Commission have 50 percent female staff, even though it contradicted the spirit of the bill (Hansard 899: 562; 599–601).

[43] This argument is in direct contrast to the perspective of authors such as Joppke (1999: 225), who writes that "Britain has firmly stood back from granting affirmative action privileges" and of Teles (1998), whose 1998 article is entitled "Why is There No Affirmative Action in Britain?"

the implementation of positive action provisions during the first decade following legislation. They noted, for example, that although employers were *permitted* to act positively, no incentives were offered to *induce* action (Gregory 1987: 52–3, 63). Although there is no composite data on the number of positive action schemes in Britain or on their overall effectiveness, more recent case study data imply that their use is visible in a wide array of employment sectors, even if their impact remains less than revolutionary (Race Relations Employment Advisory Service 1994, Taylor 2000; Welsh, Knox, and Brett 1994).[44]

Beyond strengthening enforcement mechanisms and introducing American-inspired group equality measures, the 1976 Race Relations Act embodied several other innovations. It closed a number of access racism loopholes, including one opened by the widely publicized 1974 case of the Preston Dockers club. The House of Lords decision put over 4,000 Working Men's clubs beyond the reach of the 1968 law, creating a media stir and eliciting vocal protests from the race relations community (see Sooben 1990: 8).[45] The 1976 act also added new provisions for punishing instructions or pressures to discriminate, for protection against victimization, and for exceptions to the race neutral rule where race is a "genuine occupational qualification" for employment.[46] In addition, it made minor revisions to the expressive racism clauses in light of recommendations that the law was not operating effectively.[47] Finally, inserted almost as an afterthought and containing no specific statutory requirements, the 1976 act assigned to local authorities a particular duty of vigilance with respect to eliminating discrimination and promoting equality

[44] On equal opportunities policies and practices more generally, see also Commission for Racial Equality (1985) and Jewson et al. (1995).

[45] It should be noted that there are still exemptions for certain types of clubs (see Great Britain: Home Office undated: 5.11–5.13).

[46] For the full list of provisions and exceptions, see Great Britain: Home Office (undated) and the text of the Race Relations Act 1976.

[47] Recommendations came from prosecutors and from Lord Justice Scarman in the wake of the 1974 disturbances in Red Lion Square. The Criminal Justice Act of 1967 had made prosecution of incitement more difficult, and the 1976 amendments were designed to bring the Race Relations Act provisions into line with those of the Public Order Act of 1936 (Hansard 906: 1563–7; *The Times*, September 12, 1975). The 1976 revisions made prosecution possible in cases where oral or written expressions were *likely* to stir up hate. Previously, successful prosecution had to demonstrate an *intent* to stir up hate. The number of prosecutions following the revisions remained low, but climbed from twenty prosecutions between 1965 and 1976 to approximately fifty-four between 1976 and 1984. For an overview of defamation law in Britain, see Jones (1995).

of opportunity and good relations between people of different races. In sum, British institutions emerged from the 1970s legislative rounds much wider in scope and much stronger than they had been in the 1960s.[48] Yet, the development of the British race policy structure did not end in 1976. Most centrally, one key piece of the institutional puzzle remained absent: ethnic monitoring.

Institutional Developments: 1976–2000

Between 1976 and the race laws of the past few years (discussed in Chapter 8), the source of British institutional developments shifted away from Parliament to three other locations: the judiciary, local jurisdictions, and the bureaucracy.[49] Judicial decisions have served to define more precisely several potentially ambiguous elements of the 1976 law, in many instances limiting their scope. Case law has, for example, impeded the Commission for Racial Equality from dealing with certain forms of governmental activity, limited the commission's power to carry out formal investigations, and undermined the definition of indirect discrimination (Commission for Racial Equality 1992: 82, Gregory 1987: 37–45, Lester 1994: 178).[50] On the expansive side of the ledger, it has increased the level of compensation available to victims, limited some of the circumstances under which forms of discrimination are justifiable, and officially categorized Sikhs as a protected group for the purposes of the act (Commission for Racial Equality 1992: 80–1).[51] In contrast to that of the United States, the British judiciary has not, however, exhibited extensive judicial activism

[48] Nonetheless, many progressives argued throughout the 1980s and 1990s that there remain substantial weaknesses in the 1976 act (Commission for Racial Equality 1992; Gregory 1987; Lester 1987; McCrudden 1983; Sanders 1983).

[49] This does not mean, however, that no Parliamentary initiatives have impacted race policies in this time period. See Commission for Racial Equality (1992: 81) for a list of the minor changes since 1976. Additionally, in 1986 expressive racism provisions were altered in the context of changes to the Public Order Act (Jones 1995). Furthermore, the 1994 Criminal Justice and Public Order Act created a new offense of intentional harassment, which may be applied in cases of racial harassment (Great Britain: Home Office 1996b: 8). The most significant legislative action has been the 1988 Local Government Act, which outlawed the use of contract compliance by public authorities (with a limited exception with respect to racial discrimination) (Lester 1994: 179, Solomos 1986: 215–17).

[50] For more information on early case law, see also McCrudden (1983).

[51] It has thus classified this primarily religious group as an ethnic group. Jews are also protected as an ethnic group.

in expanding race institutions. Rather, British courts have shown a penchant for narrow interpretations of antidiscrimination law.

Since the early days of British race institutions, local governments have played an important role in funding and coordinating race relations groups. Following the 1976 act, and especially through the end of the 1980s, local authorities in minority-populated areas have taken a special interest in race policies, frequently adopting a vanguard role in the realms of equal opportunities policies, contract compliance, and multicultural education initiatives (see Ball and Solomos 1990, Ben-Tovim et al. 1986, Bleich 1998, Saggar 1991).[52] By the late 1980s, however, the proactive edge of local authorities had been blunted by a conservative backlash (see esp. Gordon 1990, Smith 1994). The right and the media mocked "loony left" authorities that engaged in measures such as banning candy bars from schools because their producers refused to supply information about compliance with gender and race equality legislation (Solomos and Ball 1990: 216). Such public relations fiascos undermined public support for progressive race policies and encouraged the Conservative Thatcher government to prohibit the use of contract compliance except under limited circumstances, thereby restricting local jurisdictions' scope for racial equality initiatives (Solomos and Ball 1990: 216–17).

The most significant step taken by many local authorities was also taken more prominently by the bureaucracy: ethnic monitoring. Monitoring is a critical element of British race institutions, yet it was not mandated by the 1976 legislation. Instead it has picked up momentum and been implemented incrementally between the 1960s and today. By the mid-1970s, the Race Relations Board (1975: 9), the Community Relations Commission (1975b: 10) and the Parliamentary Select Committee (Great Britain: Select Committee on Race Relations and Immigration 1975a: 20–2) were arguing that ethnic monitoring was essential to government policy, even though they recognized that there was "strong and widespread opposition to the keeping of such records" (Race Relations Board 1975: 9). Under the pen of Lester and Jenkins, the Home Office's White Paper on Race Relations (Great Britain: Home Office 1975: 5) offered that "the Government considers that a vital ingredient of an equal opportunities policy is

[52] Local authorities were responding both to increased ethnic minority voting power and mobilization and to the increasingly leftist and progressive tendencies of Labour politicians and bureaucrats in positions of power (Bleich 1998, FitzGerald 1987, Geiger 1989).

a regular system of monitoring," but included no statutory requirement to collect race statistics.

Opposition to monitoring is still strong in several pockets of British society, and ethnic monitoring is pursued with nowhere near the vigor in Britain as it is in the United States. However, there has been a marked burgeoning in the locations and extent of data collection in Britain since the 1970s. In 1981, following the Home Affairs Sub-Committee on Race Relations and Immigration's report on "Racial Disadvantage," the civil service began to implement ethnic monitoring within its ranks on an experimental basis (Ollerearnshaw 1983: 158, Sanders 1983: 75), and in 1989 it started comprehensive collection of ethnic data (see Great Britain: Cabinet Office 1995). Other bureaucracies that collect ethnic data include the education department, the prison service, and the health service (Beishon, Virdee, and Hagell 1995; Great Britain: Department for Education 1995; Great Britain: Home Office 1994; Great Britain: Home Office 1996a).[53] Ethnic monitoring has also been adopted at the local policy level, especially in urban areas with high concentrations of ethnic minorities (Ollerearnshaw 1983: 156). For one inner London education authority policymaker, the "mountains of data" demanded from each school are "absolutely incredibly useful, essential" (interview with Williams, June 26, 1996). Ethnic monitoring and studies of social differences between racial and ethnic groups are spreading in Britain. Data from the 1960s and 1970s on "racial disadvantage" was collected primarily by private sources such as the Institute of Race Relations, the Runnymede Trust, and Political and Economic Planning[54] (Brown 1984, Lomas 1973, Modood and Berthoud 1997, Rose 1969, Smith 1977). Since that time, official bodies have increasingly amassed ethnic information, beginning with the national Labour Force Surveys and General Household Surveys, and culminating in the implementation of the first ethnic question in the 1991 British census (Coleman and Salt 1996b, Peach 1996, Ratcliffe 1996).[55]

[53] The Education Department argued that monitoring was needed to understand "the national scale of needs of different ethnic groups and the extent to which the education system is meeting them," to gather "evidence of those strategies which are successful in reducing under-achievement among some minority ethnic pupils," and finally, "to enable the Home Office to obtain a national picture of the relative levels of educational attainment by different ethnic groups, in the context of its overall responsibility for race relations" (Great Britain: Department for Education 1995: 1–2).

[54] Later renamed the Policy Studies Institute.

[55] See Bulmer (1996) for an exploration of the politics of the census question on ethnicity.

Although it may seem possible to attribute the birth of ethnic monitoring to demographic changes in the population (see, for example, Coleman and Salt 1996b: 1), equally diverse countries such as France have refused to undertake systematic collection of ethnic data. Ethnic monitoring came about in Britain primarily because of the perceived importance of group inequalities between whites and non-whites, commonly called "racial disadvantage." Although the definition of the term has fluctuated, Smith (1976: 1) summarized it as "the extent to which racial minority groups tend to suffer disadvantages (compared with the white majority), whether or not these disadvantages are the result of unlawful discrimination against them." In order to identify and to remedy such group inequalities, British advocates asserted, statistics were essential. An observer argued in *The Guardian* (October 11, 1976), for example, that since black and white were not equal, there was a need for monitoring: "If coloured people are to be helped, governments need more information, not less." As awareness of group inequalities has increased, progressive policymakers wishing to promote substantive equality have become strong advocates of ethnic monitoring (interviews with Williams, and Robinson and King, June 26, 1996; Coleman and Salt 1996b: 9; Bulmer 1996: 35).

The influence of the American model is also observable in the growth of ethnic monitoring, although it has not been as important as in the cases of indirect discrimination or positive action. In part, themes of racial disadvantage and group inequalities can be seen as inspired by the civil rights movement in the United States and as following logically from debates occurring in 1960s and 1970s North America. Referring to Britain's use of an ethnic census question in 1991, the editors of the Office of Population Censuses and Surveys' first volume on the results reveal that "Britain's approaches to the development of a multicultural society, which underlie the census question, however, do have something in common with policy in the US and the Old Commonwealth, through ethnic monitoring, targets and the legal recognition of group rights and privileges, much of which need ethnic statistics" (Coleman and Salt 1996a: 26–7). Less prominently and more sporadically, attention to the benefits of ethnic monitoring (particularly in the early years of British institutions in the 1960s and 1970s) originated directly from observation of North American policies. As early as 1964, Home Office civil servants were questioning British attitudes toward ethnic monitoring. As one civil servant wrote to another, "it has seemed to me for some time that our assertion that the collection of statistics 'by race' was objectionable in principle was curiously at variance with American practices. You might like to think about this!"[56] As with Jenkins' position on positive action versus affirmative action, however, British observers discussed how to apply less radical measures in the UK. The Parliamentary Select Committee wrote in 1975:

> The Committee during their visit to the United States were greatly impressed by the importance of an effective monitoring system to race relations policy. Nevertheless we emphasise that we are not recommending that we should follow the American precedent. It is too bureaucratic and legalistic and on a scale inappropriate to the circumstances obtaining in this country (Great Britain: Select Committee on Race Relations and Immigration 1975a: 22).

In line with this logic, British experts exploring the possibility of a census question on race in the mid-1970s examined the U.S. and West Indian censuses – but merely to demonstrate the feasibility of such a question (Bulmer 1996: 46). The decisions to begin ethnic monitoring taken in subsequent years by a host of government and non-government organizations alike were undoubtedly not directly dependent upon North American influences; nevertheless, the political culture that softened early entrenched opposition to collecting race statistics was certainly affected by race professionals' understandings of North American policies, practices, and attitudes.

Conclusion

The institutions established by the 1976 Race Relations Act and by subsequent policy choices mark a significant development from the race structures of the 1960s. Some ideas and policies – such as a preference for an administrative agency and civil sanctions for punishing access racism – have remained from 1965 until today. Substantial changes were introduced in 1976 and after, however, when the administrative agency was consolidated and strengthened, when the priority placed on administrative conciliation gave way to individuals' direct access to civil courts, and when elements of group equality were incorporated into British institutions in the form of indirect discrimination, positive action, and ethnic monitoring provisions. The British race relations model has come a long way from its inception in the mid-1960s debates about immigration. Race relations now stands as an independent policy sphere in Great Britain with a well-developed set of organizations and rules.

[56] See PRO HO 376/3, letter from W. N. Hyde to Mr. R. M. Morris, dated August 14, 1964.

The impetus for and ultimate shape of present-day British institutions owes much to relatively small groups of policy experts working at the interstices of bureaucracies, research organizations, interest groups, and political parties. Lessons from policies in North America and from the failures of extant domestic structures strongly shaped developments in Britain throughout the 1960s, 1970s, and beyond. In this, we see the usefulness of the problem-solving model of policymaking for illuminating processes of political learning. The issue of direct court access enshrined by the 1976 act responded to the problem of slow and seemingly ineffective conciliation mandated by the previous legislation. Race-conscious elements in the British model reflected state-of-the-art policy innovations across the Atlantic, although the push for monitoring also originated in bureaucrats' desire to assess and to rectify racial disadvantage. These goals, of course, were influenced not only by objective societal stimuli, but also by actors' race frames and their consequent interpretation of such stimuli. Over time, progressive learners increasingly drove forward the process of policymaking and molded the institutional outputs closer to their specifications. By contrast, race policies have not been determined principally by electoral politics, party competition, or social movements. Politicians did not pass race legislation in an attempt to maximize their votes or to distinguish their party "product" from opponents' in order to secure office, nor were they pressured into action by a broad-based civil rights movement, as was the case in the United States.

Building British race institutions has not, however, been a politics without bargaining, conflict, and partisan effects. The political compromises between progressives and skeptics in the 1965 and 1968 Parliamentary rounds, for example, significantly affected the final shape of race institutions. Moreover, Labour leaders have traditionally been much more receptive to developing race institutions than their Conservative counterparts; in fact, having a Labour government in power appears to be a necessary condition for the passage of race legislation. Having a sympathetic ally within the cabinet also seems to be an element that can clinch the progress of race policies.

The politics of race policymaking in Britain has resulted in institutions which can be identified by their state-led, if tentative, pressures for group-based equality. Although comparing British policies with those in the United States (which far exceed in scope and structure any in Europe) must be done with care, the North American influence on British institutions cannot be ignored. Indirect discrimination provisions, positive action, ethnic monitoring, the activism of the administrative agency, and the use of civil rather than criminal law to punish access racism each derive from lessons learned across the Atlantic, and collectively imbue British race policies with a distinct American flavor. In this, we see the clear effect of British race frames. Since the 1960s, progressives in particular have shared a view that British race concerns were broadly analogous to those in the United States. Race was defined by color, and access racism and concerns about social order were raised high on the agenda. Over the past three decades, British policymakers moved away from certain aspects of the American model (such as relying on administrative conciliation in the first instance), but they also continued to examine North America for policy innovations and philosophical orientations. Britain's race frames differ sharply from those that have prevailed in France; as a result, race policies have developed along significantly different lines in the two countries.

5

The Origins of French Antiracism Institutions

1945 to the 1972 Law

The 1972 French law against racism stands as the cornerstone of the nation's antiracist institutions. Although it was enacted in the same era as the three British Race Relations Acts (of 1965, 1968, and 1976), the similarities between the two countries' race policies are surprisingly limited. Rather than proceeding in a series of small steps toward comprehensive antiracism structures, for example, France took one giant leap. It covered in a single bound most of the territory it took Britain three rounds of legislation and over a decade to traverse. Moreover, in contrast to British legislation, France's 1972 law generated relatively little political controversy at the time of passage, having been adopted by a unanimous vote in both the National Assembly and the Senate.

On the other hand, much as in Britain, passing the law was not an easy task for its supporters. Proposals for comprehensive antiracist legislation were first developed in the 1950s by the human rights interest group MRAP (Movement Against Racism, Anti-Semitism and for Peace).[1] It was not until over a decade after they were introduced into Parliament, however, that they were enacted into law. Once on the agenda, the MRAP's formula for legislation remained largely intact and strikingly different from that of its cross-Channel neighbor. In its final form, the French law of 1972 established criminal rather than civil penalties for access racism, contained no race-conscious elements, and promoted the role of private groups – rather than an administrative agency – in leading the fight against racism. Why did France craft its laws so differently from British and North

[1] Founded in 1949, the MRAP changed its name (but not its acronym) in 1977 when it became the Movement against Racism and for Amity among Peoples.

American provisions? And what finally led the government to enact legislation over a decade after it was first proposed?

The shape of French legislation was influenced by a postwar, post-Vichy framing of race and racism. Unlike in Britain, where race laws were forged in the heat of a public anti-immigrant controversy, antiracism provisions in France were less affected by worries about immigration than might be expected. For the MRAP and for many in France, racism was framed not in North American terms (with a focus on color-based discrimination), but rather in terms of their memory of Nazism, anti-Semitic newspapers and public speeches by far-right spokespersons. These problems leapt most prominently to the eye and demanded primary attention in the years following France's experience with the Vichy regime.

Between the 1950s and 1970s, the MRAP's proposals gathered increasing support in Parliament. Deputies and parties from disparate corners of the political spectrum signed on to the project of passing antiracism legislation. Intensified lobbying in 1971 and 1972 eventually convinced the relatively liberal Chaban-Delmas government to support passage of the law, even though the electoral payoff to the party in power was slim and the bureaucracy was not necessarily convinced that the laws served a useful purpose. In the end, the combination of this increased pressure and the symbolic benefits of action persuaded the government to relent in its opposition to antiracist legislation.

This chapter retraces the development of the 1972 French law against racism to uncover the reasons for its passage and for its final form. To place these issues in a broader context, section one examines the history and relevance of immigration concerns to antiracism debates, concluding that they played only a tangential role in the process. Because the human rights group MRAP was responsible for much of the final shape of the French institutions, section two concentrates in detail on how its framing of race and racism effected its motives and arguments for enacting antiracist legislation. Parts three and four recount the history of the proposals through the 1960s. Although the conservative government was initially well-disposed to the MRAP initiative, by the early 1960s it had shelved plans to pass race laws. The ensuing decade saw slow but low pressure on the government to place race back on the Parliamentary agenda. The breakthrough of 1971 and 1972 is the focus of section five, which highlights the new political context and details the increase in lobbying for legislation. Section six demonstrates that the bills, once accepted in principle by the government, encountered few challenges or revisions and were written into the law books in essentially the same form as drafted in the late 1950s.

The Immigration Context: 1945–1972

The post-World War II French state focused much of its political energies on economic considerations during the "thirty glorious years" between 1945 and 1975. Promoting and maintaining growth, as in Germany and many other European countries, required the recruitment of foreign workers (Freeman 1979, Hollifield 1992, Weil 1995a). Between the end of the war and the mid-1970s, millions of foreigners gravitated toward the flourishing French economy, encouraged in their journeys by the state and by employers eager for able bodies. By 1975, there were over two and a half million immigrants living in France, of which almost one and a quarter million originated from non-European Community countries (Weil 1995a: annex 6).[2] It is reasonable to assume that, as in Britain, race policies served the integrative function of offsetting restrictive, anti-immigrant border policies.

Circumstantial evidence lends some support to this hypothesis. There were early hints of racialization in 1945, when administrative elites briefly debated whether to select postwar immigrants on the basis of their ethnicity. This option was immediately rejected by the Council of State, however, and was never seriously reconsidered (Weil 1995b). Ethnic considerations clearly played a role in French immigration policy, yet they were markedly less conspicuous than in British public debates of the late 1950s and early 1960s. The French state's organization of recruitment centers abroad, for example, favored the influx of migrants from Italy, Spain, and Portugal over those from Turkey and North Africa, but the state did not formally restrict access to French soil on the basis of ethnic considerations (Weil 1995a: 90–1).

Moreover, during the painful process of decolonization from North Africa in the late 1950s and early 1960s (which brought down the French Fourth Republic in 1958) anti-Algerian sentiment ran high in metropolitan France. It culminated in the violent October 1961 Paris marches that resulted in thousands of arrests and scores of dead and wounded (Levine 1985). Anti-Algerian feelings, policies, and attacks were not limited to the era of decolonization. In the late 1960s, the French government attempted

[2] For these purposes, the European Community includes Spain, Portugal, and Greece, even though they became members only in the 1980s.

to curtail the flow of Algerian migrants to France, imposing a brief quota of 1,000 per month in 1968 and introducing a host of policies designed to restrict immigration (Blatt 1996: 76–8, Silverman 1992: 48–9, Weil 1995a: 93–100). In part, this appeared to be a response to fears of an "unassimilable island" of ethnic Algerians that might lead to "tensions between communities" (see Blatt 1996: 75–6, Silverman 1991: 73–8, Wihtol de Wenden 1988: 147–8). Such tensions were arguably manifested in a spate of attacks on Algerians beginning in the early 1970s and peaking in 1973, which prompted the Algerian government to announce in September of that year that it was suspending further emigration to France (Benoît 1980: annex 1, Silverman 1992: 52).[3]

Political leaders could not fail to notice the tensions generated by immigration in this era. Gary Freeman (1979: 85–98) dates the incipient shift away from France's open door policy to the aftermath of the events of May 1968. At that tumultuous moment, well over one hundred immigrants were summarily expelled from French territory for their political activism in support of French workers (Freeman 1979: 85). Not only judged as potential troublemakers, immigrants were also portrayed in this era as victims of injustices and serious disadvantages. Concerns about housing conditions had been voiced since the early 1960s when thousands of newcomers were revealed to be living in shantytowns (*bidonvilles*) on the outskirts of major industrial cities (Money 1999: 123–4). The tragic death of five African workers one 1970 winter's night in an unheated building renewed attention to these issues and generated a visit to the premises by Prime Minister Chaban-Delmas, who vowed to solve the problem by building more quality housing (Freeman 1979: 91–2). In addition, as Money (1999: 140) points out, local politicians in areas with many immigrants campaigned on such issues in the lead up to the 1973 Parliamentary elections.

The French state began to react to this changing context in the late 1960s and early 1970s by formulating plans for limiting new immigration and strategies for stricter regulation of migrants already on the national territory. In January and February 1972, some of these proposals came to fruition in the form of the Marcellin and Fontanet circulars, which sought to restrict clandestine immigration and to link regularization of current immigrants to availability of jobs and housing (Freeman 1979:

[3] Weil (1995a: 112–15) argues, however, that racism was only part of Algeria's motivation for stopping emigration; other motives included concerns about the country's international image and its control over emigrant workers in France.

93, Money 1999: 111). Later that same year, the law of July 5, 1972 (72–617) increased penalties to employers who violated immigration laws. The state also began to reject requests for regularization, an unusual step given the expanding economy (Money 1999: 111–12).

As noteworthy as these policies proved, immigration was not truly problematized in France until *after* passage of the first antidiscrimination law in 1972. As Blatt (1996: 77) notes, for most of the 1960s and early 1970s the government was "unable or unwilling to resist the pressures from labor-hungry employers and governments of developing countries to keep the migratory taps flowing." The numbers of permanent immigrant aliens arriving in France fluctuated year by year, but rose on the whole from the immediate postwar era through 1973 (Money 1999: 109–113). It was not until the oil crisis and economic downturn of 1973 that immigration policy arrived squarely on the political cutting board, with France placing a ban on all permanent worker immigration only in 1974 (Hollifield 1992: 80).[4] If British race relations laws were passed in the context of heated public battles over immigrants and integration, the first French antiracism law was passed prior to the 1974 migration restrictions, and with only modest and sporadic soul-searching about racism in French society. In spite of the government's burgeoning will to attend to immigration issues, the 1972 antiracism legislation was not crafted as part of its overall immigration or integration strategy. In fact, the 1972 law was passed due to a substantially different set of pressures.

The MRAP's Antiracism Proposals: 1949–1958

Plans for comprehensive French antidiscrimination legislation originated in the early 1950s among a small group of human rights activists in the Movement against Racism, Anti-Semitism and for Peace (MRAP). As an organization, the MRAP had its roots in resistance to the Vichy regime and although not officially favoring any political perspective, it was seen by many as sympathetic to the French Communist Party.[5] As one prominent

[4] Of course, as Hollifield (1992) and others have shown, this ban was not close to fully effective. Nevertheless, it did succeeed in dramatically reducing the annual inflow of permanent worker immigration (see Money 1999: 113).

[5] There is a debate over whether the MRAP was itself a Communist organization. Former MRAP General Secretary Albert Lévy argues that this label was attached to the MRAP for political reasons, pointing out that MRAP Presidents Blumel, Lyon-Caen, and Paraf were not members of the Communist party (interview with Lévy, March 19, 1997).

member notes, the founders of the MRAP (in contrast to the members of the antiracist group LICA – International League Against Anti-Semitism), "belonged to the more popular milieus" (Lévy 1993: 2). In addition, many had either been deported or had family members deported during the war (Lévy 1993: 2). In spite of the left leanings and recent immigrant status of many activists, the MRAP also contained high-profile figures; the committee that developed the antidiscrimination legislative proposals, for example, consisted of several prominent members of the French legal establishment.[6]

Rather than responding to concerns about discrimination against postcolonial immigrant ethnic minorities, the MRAP leadership was much more sensitive in the 1940s and early 1950s to what it perceived as a post-Vichy rebirth of anti-Semitic sentiments. Albert Lévy, longtime General Secretary of the MRAP, has described the era until the middle of the 1950s as the period of the "aftermath of the war, where the dominant questions were neo-nazism, the revival of anti-Semitism and the Cold War" (Lévy 1993: 3). The MRAP was officially formed in 1949, when local committees mobilized against the film "The New Masters," the subject of which was summarized by the MRAP as "the Jews are once again masters of France." The MRAP also took notice of several prominent collaborationists, who, released from death sentences, took over editors' positions at racist newspapers (Lévy 1993: 4).[7] Within this broader context, the legal committee felt that existing French law was incapable of effectively sanctioning racism (MRAP 1984: 9–13). Prior to 1972, the 1939 Marchandeau decree-law[8] was the principal legal instrument used to call perpetrators of racist acts into the courts.[9] The Marchandeau decree, however, was both narrow in scope and rarely enforced. It punished racial or religious defamation in the press that was explicitly recognized as having the goal of stirring up hatred (MRAP 1984: 10). Although this law carried stiff penalties it was seldom invoked: MRAP lawyers catalogued only two successful prosecutions between 1945 and 1949 (MRAP 1984: 10).

[6] André Blumel had taken part in the Blum government of the 1930s; and Léon Lyon-Caen and Robert Attuly were both honorary presidents of the Cour de Cassation, one of the highest courts in the French legal system.

[7] One of the most prominent of these periodicals was *Aspects de la France*, which played symbolically upon the initials of the extreme right movement *Action Française*, and even counted the latter's former leader, Charles Maurras, among its writers (Lévy 1993: 4).

[8] Abrogated by the Vichy regime and then restored upon liberation.

[9] The Declaration of Human Rights of 1789 and the preambles to the constitutions of 1946 and 1958 inveighed against racism, but to no concrete legal effect.

Thus, with unpunished anti-Semitism in the media and perceived lacunae in sanctioning mechanisms, the MRAP drafted proposals for a new law in the early 1950s.[10] As with the Society of Labour Lawyers and the Lester group in Britain, the MRAP scanned the international horizon for foreign examples of relevant legislation. Although they noted use of antiracist laws in North America and Central America, in the Soviet Union and Eastern Europe, and in other West European countries (Paraf 1964: 198–200), the MRAP did not investigate any particular country with an eye to incorporating foreign lessons into domestic policies. Rather, it used foreign examples (drawing rather more heavily on those from the Soviet bloc than their British counterparts) to justify and to legitimate its pressure for French laws. In arguing for Parliamentary action on MRAP proposals, President Léon Lyon-Caen (1959) cited other countries' laws to combat "the after-effects of Hitlerian racism" in order to show that French law had been "surpassed." The article mentions a German bill dated January 1959 as well as decrees or laws in Poland, the USSR, Albania, Bulgaria, and Romania, Czechoslovakia, and Yugoslavia which date for the most part to the early 1950s.

By late 1958, the MRAP had codified its ideas into three critical elements (Lyon-Caen 1959; MRAP 1984: 117–22). First, it proposed extending the reach of the 1939 Marchandeau decree to encompass more forms of expressive racism than those already sanctioned. As with the Marchandeau decree, this necessitated a revision to the 1881 press law on freedom of expression.[11] Second, the MRAP lobbied for protection against access racism in employment and in furnishing of goods and services.[12] This proposition was motivated primarily by concerns about racism facing immigrant minorities. Issues of decolonization and nonwhite, non-Christian immigration came to occupy the MRAP leadership in increasing proportions throughout the 1950s, 1960s, and 1970s (Lévy 1993: 3, Lloyd 1998: 130–3, Paraf 1964); but at the time the MRAP submitted its legal proposals in 1959, these were clearly recessive counterparts to the dominant concern with anti-Semitic expressive racism.[13]

[10] Because this process took place in a very young organization, no records exist of the early proposals in the MRAP archives.

[11] Another effect of the press law can be seen throughout France on buildings stamped with "*défense d'afficher: la loi du 29 juillet 1881*."

[12] Including discrimination by public authorities.

[13] As Lloyd (1998: 130) notes, the MRAP paid relatively little attention to issues of colonialism and immigration in the early postwar years. Even when they did turn

Finally, the MRAP advocated a procedural change to the law that would permit antidiscrimination groups to participate as "civil parties"[14] in court cases involving racist crimes. Under French penal law – given certain circumstances – public interest groups can take part in or can even take a lead in instigating and arguing cases that relate to the interests of their group. Civil parties have the power to set a criminal case in motion if the public prosecutor refuses; they can collect and submit evidence to the court; and they can make additional legal or moral arguments in an effort to obtain a conviction. In sum, becoming a civil party to a criminal case can place the group in a pivotal and powerful position within French legal institutions.[15]

If perceived weaknesses in the positive law prompted the MRAP to submit proposals for change, what factors influenced their precise formulations? The race frames of the MRAP leaders account for many aspects of their suggestions for antiracist institutions. The wartime experiences of these actors encouraged them to focus their primary attention on expressive racism, the Marchandeau decree, and its weaknesses. In addition, the lack of identification with North American concepts of race and racism limited their analysis of developments taking place across the Atlantic (Freeman 1979: 94).[16] This helps explain their proposal to eschew the civil law for cases of access racism and their lack of suggesting an administrative agency as an effective tool in fighting racism, two elements central to American and British institutions. Moreover, by arguing that access racism be punishable by the criminal law, the MRAP responded not only to

to these concerns, they were prone to framing them in terms reminiscent of Vichy, such as the comparison between raids on Algerians with the infamous "*rafle du Vel d'Hiv*" against French Jews during the war (1998: 92, 141–2). It is also important to stress that the MRAP's focus when discussing colonialism and immigration was not often on "discrimination" (or access racism) as Lloyd argues (1998: 2–3), but rather on immigrant disadvantage or inequalities. See, for example, her discussion of housing issues (Lloyd 1998: 154).

[14] *Parties civiles.*

[15] In such cases the standards of proof conform to criminal law, but French courts are in effect dealing with both a criminal and civil case at the same time. If the defendant is found guilty, he is punished by the state according to the penal law, and may additionally have to compensate the victim financially as in a civil case (in the form of "*dommages et intérêts*").

[16] Lloyd mentions examples of the MRAP's contacts with Britain (1998: 167) and drawing on information from the United States (Lloyd 1998: 137). However, contacts with Britain and the U.S. were few and far between and cross-national learning was rare (Freeman 1979: 154).

considerations of legal effectiveness, but also to normative considerations of what was appropriate.[17] Following a Durkheimian logic, several French participants and observers have asserted that since the wrong of access racism concerned not just the individual victim, but implicated society as a whole in confronting racism, criminal sanctions were the appropriate method of punishment (Costa-Lascoux 1991: 128, Durkheim 1997, Paraf 1964: 197–8).[18]

Lessons learned from experience and a strategic concern with institutional fit account for other central aspects of the MRAP's decisions. Failure in court cases throughout the 1940s and 1950s not only convinced the MRAP that the Marchandeau law was insufficient, but also pointed out some of the precise problems with the provisions. For example, the law banned only the narrow offense of racial *defamation* and not instances of *provocation* to racial hatred or violence; and it only applied to expressions of racism leveled against groups and not targeted at particular individuals. The MRAP proposals therefore sought to redress these specific failings (Lyon-Caen 1959, MRAP 1984: 9–15, 117–22). Second, outlining the rationale for criminal sanctions against access racism, MRAP President Léon Lyon-Caen highlighted the weaknesses of French civil and administrative remedies, arguing that the mere threat of criminal sanctions would be "far more effective" than existing remedies (Lyon-Caen 1959, MRAP 1984: 121–2).[19] Finally, between 1945 and 1972, courts had systematically excluded antidiscrimination organizations from becoming civil parties in racism cases unless the associations themselves had suffered direct injury. The MRAP argued that this exclusion was a major weakness in the fight against racism – given the reluctance of the state to prosecute – and one which could only be rectified by a change in the law (MRAP 1984: 10).

Institutional fit also influenced the final shape of the proposals. In terms of punishing expressive racism, MRAP leaders explicitly chose to formulate their suggestions in line with the Marchandeau decree's precedent of using the 1881 press law. The committee strategically sought to fit

[17] On norms and logics of appropriateness, see Hall and Taylor (1996) and Powell and DiMaggio (1991).

[18] Interview with Sellami, January 28, 1997.

[19] To bolster the argument in favor of such a step, the president of the MRAP cited recent legal changes or proposals in the state of New York and in Great Britain along a similar vein (Lyon-Caen 1959, MRAP 1984: 121–2). This was, however, no more than a rhetorical flourish, since the British proposal was not made into law until 1965 and since the New York State procedures involved administrative conciliation rather than criminal sanctions (see Jowell 1965).

its proposals into the existing framework of French jurisprudence to the largest extent possible, in order to obtain the most favorable hearing from political leaders.[20] Finally, although obtaining civil party status in French law was a rare occurrence in the 1950s and was rightfully seen as a "fundamental innovation,"[21] in order to increase its political palatability, the MRAP downplayed the significance of such an innovation at the time, arguing that the status was perfectly compatible with existing institutions and emphasizing its conferral on analogous groups in similar domains, such as family associations, antialcohol leagues, and leagues for public morality (MRAP 1984: 120). They therefore used the rhetoric of institutional fit to undercut potential challenges to the significance of their proposed institutional change.

The Formal Campaign and the Government's Response: 1959–1961

In early 1959, the MRAP launched its formal campaign for legislative action by sending copies of its draft bills to the government and to deputies in the National Assembly, hoping to find allies to advance its agenda.[22] This initiative met with some success, prompting favorable reactions from members of several political groups (including the socialists and the more conservative MRP and UNR parties)[23] and receiving the formal backing of the Communist Party, which submitted the two bills virtually verbatim to the National Assembly.[24] Following the MRAP, the Communist deputies[25] argued that new provisions were necessary given the significant lacunae in the existing state of the law. Furthermore, they asserted somewhat dramatically that racism was on the rise in France and was poisoning public opinion. Such reforms, therefore, would help maintain social order and "prevent the formation of a climate of civil war."[26]

In the institutional context of the newly born Fifth Republic, however, nongovernmental Parliamentary initiatives – especially those emanating

[20] Interview with Lévy, March 19, 1997.
[21] As the MRAP itself later described it (MRAP 1984: 13).
[22] The MRAP began to make informal contact with government officials in the early 1950s, although never to any effect (interviews with Palant and Lévy, March 10 and March 19, 1997).
[23] See the MRAP newsletter *Droit et Liberté*, May 1961.
[24] AN 1: 37, 38.
[25] Robert Ballanger, Waldeck Rochet, Fernand Grenier, Pierre Villon, and Paul Cermolacce.
[26] AN 1: 37: 3.

from an opposition party – had virtually no chance of becoming law.[27] In many instances they served primarily as public relations tools for politicians to snatch brief media attention and to distribute to constituents during election campaigns. In this case, however, the official response was more favorable. Although the government addressed a brief missive to the MRAP dryly stating that there would be no follow-up to its petition,[28] it did not simply dismiss the Communists' bills. Instead, it took several concrete and significant steps in the direction of passing legislation between 1959 and 1961. However, unlike the MRAP and the Communist Party, the government was less concerned by the rise of post-Vichy anti-Semitism in the press, and more worried by colonial and postcolonial issues.

As early as the late 1940s, Parliamentarians had submitted legislative proposals to ban racial discrimination in the colonies.[29] By 1959, decolonization had taken on overwhelming importance in French public life, with the ongoing war in Algeria having toppled the Fourth Republic, effectively ending the multinational *Union Française* established by the 1946 constitution.[30] Arriving into power in 1958, De Gaulle had developed the alternative concept of a more federal Community (*Communauté*) uniting France's quickly evolving colonial empire. When the Communist proposals for antidiscrimination legislation landed in Parliament in April 1959, the government's immediate reaction was to assign responsibility for the propositions to the representative structures of the colonies. In late 1959 and early 1960, the Council of State and the Parliamentary committee sent the project on to the Senate of the Community.[31]

[27] The exception to this rule occurs when the government itself uses the Parliamentary route to enact its projects. It may choose this option if it does not wish to undergo the mandatory Council of State review process for government-origin bills.

[28] The letter to the MRAP was dated July 28, 1959 (MRAP 1984: 13).

[29] Fourth Republic, AN 1: 2167, 7713. See also the "*propositions de résolution*" from the Assembly of the French Union, 1948: 294 and 426, and 1949: 104. These proposals, however, were never enacted into law. Interestingly, the government at the time (in 1949–50) felt it necessary to develop a formal bill ("*projet de loi*") to ban discrimination in case the Parliamentary initiatives were pressed forward, even though it showed little enthusiasm for legislating against discrimination, arguing that existing provisions were sufficient and that new ones would likely lead to strife between the French and the "natives." Government action was thus a purely tactical move, which in the event proved unnecessary as the push for antidiscrimination law did not build enough momentum to get on the Parliamentary agenda. See MJA I.

[30] On decolonization, see Ageron (1991) and Pervillé (1991).

[31] AN 1: 358; ACE #278.492 (22 Oct 1959); and AN 1: 531, 552, 657. Some in the MRAP suspected that this may have been a stalling tactic (see *Droit et Liberté*,

However, in 1960, with decolonization proceeding apace, virtually all former French colonies became fully independent states, thus eviscerating the Community and ironically placing the antiracism bills in a political no-man's-land from which they could not emerge.

This historic turn of events did not signal the end of the Communist bills' progress. By late 1960 it had become clear that a separate path was needed to enact the laws. The Representative Council of French Jews (CRIF) and Deputy Ballanger had contacted the Ministry of Justice asking about the status of the 1959 propositions.[32] Minister of Justice Edmond Michelet took up the mantle, arguing that instead of trying to perfect the Parliamentary bills, it would be better for the government to develop and submit its own project.[33] The Justice Ministry bureaucrats drafted a bill, which the government submitted to the Council of State in March 1961.[34] Although the specialist committee of the Council of State (in its Interior section) approved the bill with certain modifications, the General Assembly issued a strongly negative opinion on April 20, 1961. It argued that there was no real need in France for such a law since there was not enough discrimination to justify legislative action. It added several additional points in opposing the bill, which included the argument that such a law would restrict personal freedoms and that it would hurt the international image of France by implying that racism was a serious domestic problem.[35] Indeed, in 1964 the French representative to the United Nations Security Council asserted: "There are few traditions which are so much a part of the history of my country as the concept of equality between the races.... Everywhere where French laws and mores are the rule,

June–July 1960). Internal archival memoranda show that Ministry of Justice bureaucrats had objections to the precise formulation of each of the proposals received from the Communist Party, but not that they were overwhelmingly hostile to them. In fact, they went so far as to redraft one proposition (AN 1: 38, on access racism), an act that revealed its political credibility. The bureaucrats argued, however, that passing such legislation in France was not necessary given the low level of domestic racism, but that in the Community there was a real problem to be addressed. Archival records show that forwarding the proposals to the Senate of the Community was thus a good-faith and logical step for the government to take given its immediate concerns and the overall historical context. See MJA I; MJA II, esp. letter dated Sept. 25, 1959, to: M. le Garde des Sceaux, Ministre de la Justice (attn. M. Baudoin, Conseiller Technique); from: M. Touren in the Service Législatif.

32 See letters dated May 13, and December 8, 1960, in MJA I.

33 MJA II. Note pour Monsieur le Directeur du Cabinet à l'attention de Monsieur Provansal, Conseiller Technique, 28 mars 1963.

34 This was in accordance with mandatory legislative procedure for governmental bills.

35 CEA #282.285 (March 31, 1961).

there is no racial discrimination. It has not even been forbidden because it is not necessary to do so" (cited in Cohen 1980: 114).

Although under normal circumstances such a hostile reaction from the Council of State might have been sufficient to terminate a government project, Michelet persisted. An internal Ministry of Justice memo countered the Council of State's objections vociferously, point by point. The memo listed the objections as follows: The bill does not respond to a real need; Article 1 is not useful given the rules and the discipline of the public administration; Article 3 risks repressing acts which belong in the realm of common personal freedoms; and the project might damage the international image of France. The memo responded by arguing: the government is better placed to decide the needs of France than the Council of State; the argument is confused: if an administrative sanction already exists, then a penal sanction will not apply; this logic ignores the preamble of the constitution; it is difficult to argue that refusing goods or a job based on race should be a right based on personal freedom; one could argue that the lack of laws in France may make others believe that racial discrimination flourishes in France.[36]

On June 23, 1961, Michelet wrote to Prime Minister Debré that although there had been opposition to the project: "I myself am inclined, nonetheless, to believe that the considerations developed in the bill retain their validity and that it would therefore be beneficial for the bill to be submitted to the Cabinet with the intention of forwarding it to the National Assembly."[37] The Prime Minister, however, indicated to Michelet that a decision on this project would not be taken immediately.[38] The momentum was lost. In August 1961, Bernard Chenot took over from Michelet at the Ministry of Justice. He showed little enthusiasm for the project when Ministry bureaucrats conveyed to him its history and wrote to the Prime Minister in March 1962 that it would not be "opportune" for the bill to be submitted to Parliament, thereby displacing it from the governmental agenda for the next ten years.[39]

[36] See MJA I; draft unsigned internal Ministry of Justice memo re: the April 20, 1961 Council of State decision.

[37] APM 780317 (F60 2444) extrait: projet de loi tendant à réprimer les actes de discrimination raciale ou religieuse, 1961. Letter dated June 23, 1961; From: Garde des Sceaux, Ministre de la Justice; To: Premier Ministre, Secrétariat du Gouvernement.

[38] MJA II. Note pour Monsieur le Directeur du Cabinet à l'attention de Monsieur Provansal, Conseiller Technique, 28 mars 1963.

[39] APM 780317 (F60 2444) extrait: projet de loi tendant à réprimer les actes de discrimination raciale ou religieuse, 1961.

Slow Pressure: 1962–1971

Throughout the 1960s, pressure for antiracism legislation rose marginally but steadily. Associations such as the MRAP and the LICA continued to lobby for a law and political parties and politicians began to take a moderate interest in Parliamentary action. With each new legislature,[40] additional groups within the National Assembly submitted antiracism bills, each modeled to a large extent on the early MRAP and Communist Party proposals. In response, however, the government continually – and with little political cost given low levels of pressure – blocked Parliamentary initiatives from being passed into law.

In the mean time, the MRAP legal committee participated in prominent cases of anti-Semitic or racist actions in an attempt to highlight domestic French racism and the weaknesses of existing legal structures (see MRAP 1984: 17–21).[41] A minor breakthrough occurred in 1966, when the owners of the *Paris-Londres* bar were convicted of refusing to serve black customers.[42] Because there were no laws explicitly banning segregated service or racial discrimination in provision of goods, MRAP lawyers turned to other precedents. They successfully argued that the ordinance of June 30, 1945 (initially designed to prevent shopkeepers from withholding goods to retain them for the black market) prohibited the refusal of sales on the basis of race (see MRAP 1984: 20). Ironically, however, the government later used this legal decision to argue that there was no need for an explicit antidiscrimination law.[43]

In Parliament, successive legislatures saw new and ever-more-conservative parties submit antiracism bills.[44] Whereas in 1959, the Communists were the only group to enter legislative proposals, in 1963, the socialist group and a group of independent deputies also submitted bills. By 1967, the moral and political osmosis of the antiracism initiatives spread even further to the right when the Christian Democratic party Progrès et Démocratie Moderne (PDM) advanced a proposal of its own. Finally, in the 1968 legislature, a deputy from the governing

[40] The duration of a legislature in France is marked by Parliamentary elections. 1958–62 was therefore the "first legislature" of the Fifth Republic. The second began in 1962; the third in 1967; and the fourth ran from 1968 until after passage of the antiracism law in 1972.

[41] The legal cases consisted primarily of anti-Semitic remarks in the press.

[42] The infraction took place in 1963.

[43] JODP AN, January 8, 1972: 38.

[44] Nongovernmental bills in the Fifth Republic are typically submitted by Parliamentary "groups" which usually correspond to political parties.

UDR party (Edouard Charret) added to the bills resubmitted by the other groups by including a bill of his own. Although putting forward legislative proposals was not in itself a strong form of political pressure,[45] the gradual formal acceptance of antiracism proposals by deputies further and further to the right provided the proposals with a broader base of political support and eventually with individual advocates within the governing Gaullist party.

The various political groups' bills were striking in their similarity.[46] Most followed closely the original MRAP proposals in seeking to ban expressive and access racism and to provide antiracist interest groups with increased institutional powers. Unlike the 1959 bills, however, each formulated its proposals for access racism in terms developed by the Council of State in 1961 when it formally reviewed the government's project. Moreover, in a significant new initiative, the Communist Party submitted a bill in December 1966 designed to ban domestic organizations that provoked racial hatred.[47] Communist deputies argued that such a step was justified given their perception of a "recent rise in racism" in France, which included the discovery of a camp in the south, where "those nostalgic for Nazism" went to train for combat and to study racist doctrines.[48] This proposal eventually evolved into a fourth element of the 1972 law. It became a staple of the Parliamentary diet, submitted again in the next two legislatures not only by the Communist Party, but also by the center-right PDM.[49]

Concurrent with pressure within Parliament was a modest level of media attention to racism. The MRAP took advantage of each year's "national day against racism" to argue that the existing legal propositions were languishing in Parliament (*Le Monde*, March 24, 1962, May 26, 1964, *Combat*, May 17, 1965). Moreover, the press would occasionally

[45] Former Minister of Justice and President of the Law Committee in the National Assembly Jean Foyer asserts that these propositions from Parliamentarians were virtually meaningless because rarely if ever followed up by lobbying (interview with Foyer, April 9, 1997). Lobbying by the CRIF in 1963 did prompt one last governmental eye toward legislation in March of that year (two months before a new set of legislative bills were presented by Parliamentarians), but action was never pursued. See MJA II. Note pour Monsieur le Directeur du Cabinet à l'attention de Monsieur Provansal, Conseiller Technique, mars 28, 1963.

[46] See AN 2: 320, 321, 322, 323, 332, 2338; AN 3: 252, 256, 257, 258, 298, 299; and AN 4: 93, 131, 308, 313, 344, 1662.

[47] AN 2: 2338. The bill called for amending the law of January 10, 1936 which allowed the state to dissolve private militias.

[48] See AN 2: 2338.

[49] AN 3: 252 and 258, AN 4: 131 and 344.

cover antiracist proposals when submitted in the National Assembly (*Le Populaire*, July 4, 1963, *Le Monde*, May 31, 1967). This publicity was accompanied by the gradual winning over of some high-profile supporters, such as the former Prime Minister Pierre Mendès-France, who argued in the LICA monthly newsletter *Droit de Vivre* (Nov.–Dec. 1966) that antiracist legislation was "indispensable in a democratic state." These isolated examples should not be taken, however, as evidence of overwhelming pressure. Many of the press articles covering the call for legislation contained minimal column inches. And with only one national day against racism per year, there was not much opportunity for the MRAP and others to generate consistent publicity.

In spite of the sporadic prolegislation pushes throughout the 1960s, the government's receptiveness to the legal propositions declined after its tentative actions between 1959 and 1961. From 1962 until early 1972, the official government line was well-rehearsed and quite firm: there was too little racism in France to merit legislation. This argument was advanced in 1963 in response to a Parliamentary question by Minister of Justice Jean Foyer,[50] and it was repeated in early 1971 by Prime Minister Chaban-Delmas, who argued that "we are undoubtedly one of the least racist countries in the world . . . there can be no question – it would be contrary to the goal aimed at – to campaign against what does not exist, in the sense of a systematic tendency and an organized movement."[51]

About Face – Getting Race on the Agenda: 1971–1972

Less than a year after Chaban-Delmas' statement, the French government agreed to pass antiracism legislation. Following ten years of formal opposition to such legislation, why did the government change its stance? A cluster of events between 1968 and 1972 help illuminate the evolution in the government's position. First, several broad societal trends served to nuance the context in which the bills were evaluated. The events of May 1968 contributed to President De Gaulle's resignation and the arrival of a new political team in 1969. Although part of the Gaullist party, Prime Minister Jacques Chaban-Delmas came into office with a more liberal outlook than his predecessors, promoting the idea of a "new society" (see Chapsal 1981: 437). His attentions did not immediately turn to antiracism legislation, yet the changed culture made a political impact,

[50] *Le Monde*, June 13, 1963.
[51] Interview given to the *Tribune Juive*, reported in *Le Monde*, February 6, 1971.

directly affecting Ministry of Justice gatekeepers. The day before finally approving legislation, one Ministry insider supported the decision with the argument that "it would not be bad for the 'liberal' image of the government."[52]

In addition to the political tenor of the era, there was a jump in the number, seriousness, and attention to racist crimes in the early 1970s. Benoît (1980: 363–4) counts nine serious racist incidents in 1970, a figure that increased to nineteen in 1971.[53] These crimes include drownings, firebombings, shootings, and a lynching. The *"affaire Djellali"* of October 1971 focused high-profile attention on racism. Following the shooting death of the fifteen-year-old Djellali Ben Ali in Paris, several thousand people marched against what was widely interpreted as a racist crime; moreover, celebrity intellectuals such as Jean-Paul Sartre, Michel Foucault, Gilles Deleuze, and Jean Genet threw their prestige into the public ring over this affair (Benoît 1980: 273–4). These crimes and the liberal attitude of the era also led to a rise in media and public attention to racism.[54] In early 1970, for example, *Le Monde* (March 20–3,) ran a three-day series entitled "Are the French Racist?", a question which was echoed in much of the left-wing and Catholic press.[55]

A new-found sensibility to racism, however, did not by itself force the issue on to the government's agenda. Throughout 1971 and even into the 1972 Parliamentary debates, the Ministry of Justice continued to assert that racism in France was not pervasive.[56] Although it responded to a variety of factors, the government's change of course depended to a large extent on the persistent lobbying of a host of actors. Prior to the January 1972 Ministry of Justice decision to legislate, there were increasing calls both from within and outside the political elite for passage of the laws. Antiracist human rights groups such as the MRAP continued to argue

[52] MJA III. Folder: Diffamation raciale, Réponse à M. Jean Foyer.

[53] This primarily includes attacks against Algerians. These numbers underestimate the attacks, given that some of what are listed as "single incidents" include cases such as those in Reims on July 14, 1971, where there were twenty attacks, four which included shots fired (Benoît 1980: 364). Evidence that the motive for these attacks was racism and whether the perpetrators were white is not provided.

[54] See the rising number of articles and the increase in column inches per article in the press archives of the Institut d'Etudes Politiques of Paris.

[55] See "Les Lacunes de la Loi" in *L'Humanité*, June 2/3/4, 1971, "Le racisme présent partout" in the *Tribune Socialiste*, June 10, 1971, "La France vit-elle une flambée raciste?" in *La Croix*, June 22, 1971, "Lyon à l'Eprueve du racisme" in *Combat*, December 6, 1971.

[56] JODP AN, June 8, 1972: 2290–92, JODP S, June 23, 1972: 1178–80.

for legislation, and were joined in July 1971 by the influential CGT and CFDT unions, which criticized the government for not acting on the existing Parliamentary proposals. These groups organized a series of activities in the fall designed to draw attention to the campaign for the law (Lloyd 1998: 168). Moreover, the press coverage of racism often included reference to the lack of government attention to the bills before the National Assembly.[57]

The most persuasive lobbying, however, came from within the political elite itself. The United Nations International Year Against Racism in 1971 provided a focal point for political action. When in April and May of that year the government ratified the UN International Convention on the Elimination of All Forms of Racial Discrimination (ICERD), Parliamentary critics of French legislative inaction stepped to the podium. The government responded that its existing legislation "largely conformed" to ICERD mandates for domestic antiracism laws and that there was therefore no necessity to enact further legislation.[58] Because the government had previously blocked discussion of the antiracism proposals, the ICERD ratification debates were seized on by proponents of domestic antiracism legislation to air their views in an official and public venue. Within the governing party itself, Alain Terrenoire openly questioned the government's position and stated that the National Assembly reserved the right to envision modifications to French law based on the legislative proposals already submitted to Parliament.[59]

Other deputies weighed in against the government line even more forcefully. Louis Odru of the Communist party, for example, asserted that "our group does not share at all the opinion of the government that French legislation is presently largely in conformity with this convention, and that, consequently, new legislative measures do not appear necessary for its application."[60] Another deputy (Paul Lacavé) remarked that "there is no real internal legislation against racial discrimination."[61] In the Senate, Gaston Monnerville, a leading member of the LICA, gave a long exposition on the weaknesses of internal antidiscrimination law, claiming that

[57] *Le Monde*, March 20–3, 1970.
[58] JODP AN, April 16, 1971: 1116–1117.
[59] JODP AN, April 16, 1971: 1116–1117. Terrenoire, the rapporteur of the bill, states that the Law Committee instigated its own report on the ICERD ratification in order to attract the government's attention to the weaknesses in domestic antiracist legislation. See AN 4: 2357: 5.
[60] JODP AN, April 16, 1971: 1117.
[61] JODP AN, April 16, 1971: 1119.

"French tribunals themselves, by the decisions they have rendered, have proclaimed the insufficiency of our legislation in this domain."[62] He went on to say that "if the Government thinks that French legislation is sufficient to protect . . . victims of racial discrimination, it is wrong."[63]

The deputies' and senators' use of this window of opportunity to chastise the state did not provoke an immediate policy retreat. The government remained firm in its domestic antireform line, ignoring its critics and reasserting that "our country counts, among its traditions, that of being considered as an antiracist country."[64] As late as January 8, 1972, Minister of Justice René Pleven responded to a Parliamentary question about three unpunished racist acts by stating that "it does not appear useful to instigate the adoption of new texts in the matter of racial discrimination because the facts reported here – and which remain out of the ordinary in France – can be punished by the texts in existence."[65]

Even by this time, however, the government's change of heart was beating under the public surface. In September 1971, President Pompidou spoke out publicly against racism before a joint session of Parliament (MRAP 1984: 27). In response to a MRAP letter directing Pompidou's attention to the National Assembly bills, Jacques Chirac – then responsible for coordinating relations between the Prime Minister and the Parliament – stated that he was "ready to examine with all the attention which this problem deserves the . . . dispositions which might be taken by the legislative path at the initiative of members of Parliament."[66] Chirac forwarded a copy of his letter to Achille Peretti, President of the National Assembly, demonstrating a heretofore unseen level of political will among key government elites.

Also in late 1971, Alain Terrenoire, member of the governing party and a critic of the government's position on domestic antiracism legislation, began internal lobbying for passage of the law.[67] He sought the party leadership's approval to prepare a report on the antiracism bills in the National Assembly,[68] writing to Law Committee president and key

[62] JODP S, May 19, 1971: 438.
[63] JODP S, May 19, 1971: 439.
[64] JODP AN, April 16, 1971: 1120.
[65] JODP AN, January 8, 1972: 38.
[66] MRAP archives. On the Pompidou and Chirac influence, see also Lloyd (1998: 168).
[67] Interview with Terrenoire, April 5, 1997. He states that he pushed for the law in private conversations with Prime Minister Chaban-Delmas and Minister of Justice Pleven.
[68] This was unusual because rapporteurs of nongovernmental bills in Parliament typically prepare a report only after the government has signaled its approval of the

legislative gatekeeper Jean Foyer. Foyer, in turn, requested guidance on the government's thinking from Minister of Justice Pleven.[69] Responding on January 6, 1972, Pleven reiterated that each of the rationales against legislation remained valid: that manifestations of racism are rare in France; that existing ones can be treated by the law in place; and that the Council of State in 1961 gave an unfavorable opinion on such texts, saying there was no real reason for them and that it might give credit to the false idea that racism was a danger, even though the state's representatives abroad had always argued that racism was not prevalent in France.[70] Yet at the same time, he seemed to open the door to passage of the law by relaxing official government hostility toward the Parliamentary bills, concluding:

> It is nevertheless true that racist-inspired acts are particularly odious and that it may therefore be useful to foresee a specific punishment against them. That is why, while reserving the right to include certain legal or technical amendments which might be brought to bear on them, the Ministry of Justice is not opposed to the legal proposals mentioned above.[71]

Although the decision had seemingly been taken, word of the impending legislation surfaced slowly and cautiously. There remained a six-month road to travel before passage of the law. Because the government exhibited little enthusiasm for the proposals and had not made a public commitment to them, there was lingering doubt among experts that they would indeed be acted upon (MRAP 1984: 28–30).[72] As in the 1959–61 period, the government could have shied away from final approval. The lobbying and the pressure therefore continued. On January 6, 1972, Edouard Charret – author of one of the Parliamentary bills – wrote to Jean Foyer inquiring about the fate of the proposals, to which Foyer replied on January 17, that they would be examined in the next Parliamentary session.[73] Also in early January, the MRAP helped to uncover the Latin-Musique bar's refusal of service to black customers, which was widely publicized in the press in the following days and weeks, prompting additional calls for new

prospective law. In this case, however, Terrenoire actively sought the party leadership's approval before the government had taken a decision.

[69] See MJA III. Folder: Diffamation raciale; Réponse à M. Jean Foyer; esp. Letter dated November 3, 1971 signed Jean Foyer; to M. René Pleven, Garde des Sceaux. Note that Foyer himself was not especially receptive to antiracism bills. As Minister of Justice during the 1960s he had blocked their progress, believing that there was not enough racism to merit legislative action (interview with Foyer, April 9, 1997).

[70] See MJA III. Folder: Diffamation raciale; Réponse à M. Jean Foyer.

[71] MJA III. Folder: Diffamation raciale; Réponse à M. Jean Foyer.

[72] See also MRAP *Droit et Liberté*, no. 310, February 1972, no. 311, March 1972.

[73] MRAP archives, letter dated January 17, 1972 from Jean Foyer to Edouard Charret.

laws (MRAP 1984: 28–30).[74] And on the occasion of the International Day Against Racism on March 21, 1972, the MRAP organized a press conference to publicize its campaign for the laws (MRAP 1984: 29).[75]

Finally, on April 15, 1972, the government publicly stated its intention to pass antiracism laws, although it did so in the subdued form of a written response to a Parliamentary question in the *Journal Officiel*.[76] Key observers mark this date as the definitive decision to legislate (MRAP 1984: 30), even though because of Parliamentary procedure the official placement of the bill on the formal agenda occurred a month and a half later. From his perspective, Terrenoire summarized the specific positions and pressures emanating from various corners in the push for legislation as follows: "Reluctance from the Ministry of Justice [bureaucrats]; good will from the Prime Minister's office... agreement by the Minister of Justice... insistence on my behalf and support of the MRAP: This was the process."[77]

It should be clear, however, that wearing the government down did not require a surge of overwhelming activity. The decision to allow antiracist initiatives on to the Parliamentary agenda in the face of truly moderate pressure must therefore be attributed in part to an additional factor: the government's calculation of the issue's salience. Although the law was immediately hailed among experts as a cornerstone of French antiracist institutions, it was not perceived as particularly significant by the press or by historians working during the era (L'Année Politique 1973).[78] To many in government and Parliament in 1972, passing antiracism legislation was

[74] See also the MRAP *Droit et Liberté*, no. 309, January 1972, *Le Monde*, January 14, 1972; *Le Nouvel Observateur*, January 17, 1972, *L'Unité*, January 28, 1972.

[75] See also MRAP *Droit et Liberté*, no. 312, April–May 1972; *Le Monde*, March 22, 72. The MRAP had also collected 15,000 signatures (including those of prominent politicians, writers, intellectuals, actors, and artists) on a petition calling in part for adoption of the Parliamentary bills (*Droit et Liberté*, no. 311, March 1972). The independent effect of such actions should not be overestimated, however. The government had proven capable of resisting such pressures, and it had already decided to allow the bills to proceed by early January. These actions were therefore supplementary pressure to ensure government action.

[76] JODP AN, April 15, 1972: 879.

[77] Interview with Terrenoire, April 5, 1997.

[78] For the immediate press coverage, see *Combat*, June 8, 1972; *Le Monde*, June 8, 1972, *L'Humanité*, June 9, 1972, *La Croix*, June 9, 1972, *L'Express*, June 12, 1972, *Le Figaro*, June 23, 1972. To place its relative impact in context, one short article on Parliamentary legislation in *Le Monde* (June 24, 1972) gave the antiracism law top but not exclusive billing. The other project deemed noteworthy was a law organizing the profession of automobile experts.

simply a symbolic act. There was no political contention and minimal government intervention during the process. The bills slipped through in a highly unusual fashion – as a Parliamentary initiative unanimously approved. As Jacques Foulon-Piganiol (1975: 160) mused three years later in the prestigious legal review *Receuil Dalloz*: "One must wonder about the law of 1 July 1972 if the unanimous voting of the text in Parliament did not simply translate the sentiment, among some at least, that such a text was in the end of little consequence, while at the same time permitting at low cost to reassure the Government, Parliament and citizens."[79]

With low political salience, therefore, even moderate pressure in the context of the post-1968 liberalism tilted the scales toward accepting the law. In spite of the perceived drawbacks of legislation, the possibility of even a minor public relations feather in the government's cap secured the initiative's access to the agenda. When the new Parliamentary session commenced in April 1972, the door opened to negotiations over the form of the laws.

From the Agenda to the Law

Whereas the first British Race Relations Act evoked intense and dramatic negotiations over its contents, in France, once the government publicly committed itself to legislation in April 1972, the law was passed speedily and with minimal substantive controversy. Because the antiracism bills emanated from the Parliament and not the government, the lead role in crafting the law was taken by the rapporteur of the National Assembly's Law Committee, Alain Terrenoire. By early May 1972, Terrenoire had met with a MRAP delegation[80] and, after discussion within the Law Committee on May 24, he submitted his initial report on May 25.[81] The report amalgamated the multiple proposals[82] into one blockbuster bill. Providing a rationale for the law, Terrenoire struck a chord similar to those struck by the MRAP and other Parliamentarians.[83] After briefly situating the current proposals in the context of the international fight

[79] A copy of this article was filed in MJA III.
[80] See the MRAP archives.
[81] AN 4: 2357.
[82] AN 4: 131, 293, 308, 313, 344, and 1662.
[83] This is not surprising, as he himself notes in the report (AN 4: 2357: 2), given that "despite the diversity of their political origins, the tenor of these propositions is in large part identical, for their authors, for the most part, were inspired by the suggestions of the Movement against Racism, Anti-Semitism and for Peace (MRAP)."

against racial discrimination, his report discussed at length the "insufficiencies of internal legislation," focusing in particular on the weaknesses of the 1939 Marchandeau law.[84]

Four essential elements were present in the various bills submitted, in Terrenoire's report, and in the final version of the law. The first aspect of the 1972 law amended the 1881 Press Law to ban a wider variety of expressive racism, criminalizing not only racial defamation, but also provocation to racial hatred or violence (against groups or individuals).[85] Second, it outlawed access racism for the first time by inserting two articles in the criminal code, punishing the use of race as a criterion in hiring, firing, or provision of goods and services, by either public employees or private citizens.[86] The third aspect amended the law of January 10, 1936 on private militias to enable the state to disband groups that seek to provoke or to promote expressive, access, or physical racism. Finally, the law took up the clarion call of the MRAP and of Parliamentarians for a stronger role for antiracist associations (such as the MRAP and the LICA) by according them the powerful "civil party" status.[87] Since 1972, these organizations have had the right to instigate and to participate in court cases of racism, a right that they exercise regularly.

Although there were few changes made to the spirit and the structure of the preexisting bills, there were important debates over specific points. It was generally agreed, for example, that antiracist associations should have the right to become civil parties, yet their exact status was only finalized at the last minute.[88] The associations' status as civil parties was in fact briefly jeopardized during the legislative process itself. While Terrenoire was preparing his report in early May, two senators

[84] AN 4: 2357: 7–12. The report also argued that rising racial tensions in France affected foreign workers and French citizens from overseas departments, reflecting the increasing concern with anti-immigrant and color-based racism (AN 4: 2357: 2).

[85] More technically expressed, the law forbade verbal or written defamation or provocation of hatred or violence against individuals or groups based on their belonging or non-belonging to an ethnicity, a nation, a race, or a religion.

[86] Articles 187-1 and 416 banned access racism against individuals or groups based on their ethnic, national, racial, or religious origin, group membership, or lack of group membership.

[87] For the details of the law, see JOLD, July 2, 1972: 6803–04; on post-1972 amendments see chapter 7 and Ahumada (1991). Another interesting element of the 1972 law is that punishment for access racism by private citizens may include publication of the verdict in newspapers at the guilty party's expense.

[88] In one significant alteration, Terrenoire expanded the scope of the associations' role to cases of access as well as expressive racism (AN 4: 2357: 18).

submitted an alternative bill in the upper house.[89] Although it was never pursued given the concurrent action in the lower house, one aspect of the bill was added to the official mix during the National Assembly's Law Committee meeting on May 24. The Senate bill proposed limiting the groups that could participate as civil parties to those officially recognized as having "public utility,"[90] a formal designation conferred by the French state which required five years to obtain from the date of application. After a lengthy discussion, the Law Committee adopted this wording in the hopes of preventing excessive and frivolous actions. However, since neither the MRAP nor the LICA had been formally granted public utility status, this provision would have ruled out their participation as civil parties for the next five years (MRAP 1984: 30–1).[91]

Another noteworthy discussion revolved around the types of racism to be punishable by law. The Marchandeau decree, the original MRAP proposals, and the majority of bills submitted by the Communist and Socialist groups envisaged outlawing acts based on *race* and *religion* (or *confession*). The bills on racist associations (submitted by the Communists, the centrist PDM, and Charret) sought to punish racism based on *religious*, *ethnic*, or *national* origin. The word "race" was omitted from these bills.[92] This latter formula was adopted in the Terrenoire report and by the first Law Committee meeting of late May 1972, in effect permitting racism based on race.[93] This was neither a mistake, nor an oversight. Terrenoire explained the motive for such a curious action:

> Speaking of races is always a delicate matter, for we run the risk of giving credibility to the idea that there are different distinctions [*qualitatives*] within the human species. That is why we must separate out the justified and necessary struggle against racism and its misdeeds from the factual recognition of differences between people according to their origins, their religions, and the color of their skin.[94]

[89] S 2, 1971–72: 192. The bill was submitted on May 9, 1972 by Gaston Monnerville and Pierre Giraud, leading members of the LICA.

[90] *Utilité publique.*

[91] AN 4: 2357: 18–20.

[92] AN 4: 93, 131, 344. The Senate bill of May 9, sought to ban racism based on race, ethnicity, religion or color. This is the only mention of color in French Parliamentary discussions leading up to the 1972 law.

[93] AN 4: 2357.

[94] Communication with Terrenoire, October 24, 1999. Note that the law as formulated does not explicitly protect or recognize racial or any other groups as such. Rather, it punishes racism based on certain objective or socially constructed criteria.

Following two weeks of heated discussion and active lobbying, the Law Committee met again, mere hours before the proposals went before the National Assembly. On the advice of the government, it reversed its decisions on both of the sticking points. The committee revised its clause on antiracist groups, allowing them to participate immediately as civil parties provided they had been established for at least five years (MRAP 1984: 31).[95] In addition, it accepted the government's advice to weave race into the law as an explicitly illegal ground for racism,[96] "in spite of the disadvantages" as Terrenoire later stated.[97] The government (in the form of Ministry of Justice bureaucrats) argued simply that race referenced "anatomical criteria" and was thus not the same as (and therefore would not be covered by clauses on) ethnicity or nationality. If it had not been for this last minute government intervention, there would ironically have been no mention of the word race in the French law against racism.[98] Interestingly in light of late 1990s debates and jurisprudence about anti-immigrant racism, the government also argued that punishing racist acts based on nonmembership in a group (as the 1972 law does) was vital and insightful. It asserted that "provoking discrimination, hatred or violence against people defined as non-French or nonwhite, for example, is as reprehensible as that which targets, for example, non-Catholics, or non-Christians."[99]

Once on the floor of the National Assembly on June 7, 1972, the bill received only accolades. Deputies participating in the debates reminded the audience of the existence of French racism, weaknesses in the existing law, and the necessity for new legislation. Many of these well-rehearsed themes dated back to the first Parliamentary bills of 1959.[100] Winding up the day's discussion for the government, Minister of Justice Pleven stated to applause that "this cannot be a partisan debate – and all the statements

[95] AN 4: 2394: 2–3. This enabled the MRAP, LICA, and other groups to participate in court cases from the date of the passage of the law.
[96] AN 4: 2394. The committee also accepted several technical suggestions from the government.
[97] Interview with Terrenoire, April 5, 1997.
[98] The government amendments also affected the final formulation of the third aspect of the French law: banning racist groups. It allowed them to be banned more easily and for a wider range of offenses, including notably for provoking or justifying physical racism. There was also agitation in committee and National Assembly debate about protection against discrimination against Corsicans and other regional groups. A "Corsican clause" was, however, not added to the law. See AN 4: 2357: 14, JODP AN, June 8, 1972: 2292.
[99] See MJA III. Folder: amendments presentés par le Gouvernement.
[100] JODP AN, June 8, 1972: 2280–95.

made by previous speakers in this tribune confirm this – because, by fighting racism, France is simply remaining faithful to herself."[101] After two small amendments, the text submitted on the morning of June 7, 1972 was unanimously approved by the National Assembly.[102] Following a handful of similarly favorable interventions and without amendment, the Senate unanimously supported the bill on June 22, clearing the way for official enactment of the "law no. 72–546 of 1 July 1972 relating to the struggle against racism."[103]

Conclusion

The 1972 law established the foundation of France's antiracism institutions. Unlike its British counterpart of 1965, the French law was broad and comprehensive, covering a relatively wide range of expressive and access racism.[104] It formally codified the partial privatization of enforcement mechanisms (by bestowing the power of civil party on human rights interest groups) and the use of the penal law to sanction discrimination. These decisions differed substantially from those taken by British political elites, and their legacy has been long lasting.

A glance back at the origins of the 1972 French law shows that it was not the immigrants or minorities themselves that were responsible for placing antiracism law on the state's agenda. Immigrants in France were relatively demobilized in 1972 and were preoccupied with securing the right to remain in France and obtaining better social conditions.[105] Nor did the law emerge from a government concerned with integrating immigrants into the national polity. Rather, the 1972 law was the hard-won fruit of the labors of the MRAP and its Parliamentary allies. In part, promoting the antiracism measures was useful to political groups like the Communist Party for burnishing an egalitarian image, and in part, passing the law corresponded to the Chaban-Delmas administration's desire to

[101] JODP AN, June 8, 1972: 2290.
[102] JODP AN, June 8, 1972: 2292–5.
[103] JODP S, June 23, 1972: 1172–81, JOLD, July 2, 1972: 6803–4.
[104] The law also banned provocation to physical racism and propagation of ideas which justified physical racism. It did not, however, specifically criminalize acts of violence underpinned by racist motives.
[105] Blatt (1996: ch. 4) dates the beginnings of immigrant and immigrant-sympathizer mobilization to the aftermath of the events of May 1968, yet most of the actions he points to take place in 1972 or 1973. Weil (1995a: 105–6) discusses several immigrant strikes and conflicts between 1968 and 1972, but allows that they hardly caught the eye of the public.

shore up its liberal credentials in the wake of the events of 1968. More important than these electoral motives, however, were the MRAP's and its associates' earnest desire to counter what they felt was the pressing social problem of racism.

Why did the government pass the law in 1972 and neither sooner nor later? There is no crisp answer to this question. In the context of decolonization and with the support of then Minister of Justice Michelet, the 1959 proposals made progress within the government. Following a change in personnel at the Justice Ministry and without the active support of the Prime Minister, however, the bills fell out of favor in 1962. All evidence demonstrates that the government continued to feel in 1972 as it had in the interim years: that there was no pressing need for such a law. Three broad factors, however, affected its calculation of the benefits attached to legislation. The post-1968 liberal tone of the Chaban-Delmas government provided more fertile ground for antiracism proposals, particularly in a context of increasingly visible hostility against North Africans in France. Second, the stepped-up lobbying by a few key Parliamentarians in 1971 played a central role in influencing the government's position. In particular, one of the governing party's own deputies leveled a proactive, public critique of government recalcitrance to legislate during the ratification debate of the UN ICERD in 1971. He subsequently actively pressured key gatekeepers (such as the Prime Minister, the Minister of Justice, and the President of the Law Committee), spurring the government to reexamine and to reverse – albeit hesitantly – its entrenched opposition. However, this reversal would not have happened with such moderate pressure if the bill had been judged to be of critical importance. The perceived low salience of the issue allowed the government to wave the bill through to a unanimous Parliamentary vote in a gesture of symbolic politics.

The when, why, and how of its passage also affected the form of the law. Concerns about immigration and integration of North Africans were enunciated in immigration policy circles beginning in 1968 (Silverman 1991: 73–8). Yet, immigration specialists played no role in drafting the 1972 law. Moreover, although immigration was rising on the political agenda in 1972, it only spread into the larger public arena as a topic of major concern after the 1973 oil shock and then again after the 1983 breakthrough of Le Pen's National Front. The shape of the 1972 law did not, therefore, respond to the political concerns of an active and engaged government and Parliament embroiled in an immigration imbroglio. Rather, the law's content responded primarily to the MRAP's framing of issues of racism in the post-Vichy years. The MRAP and their National Assembly allies tailored some aspects of their proposals to preexisting policies in order to enhance their credibility. Yet other aspects of their initiatives strayed far from institutional norms, demonstrating that institutional constraints had only a moderate impact on the final form of the law.

Virtually absent from discussions in the build-up to the 1972 law were references to North American or even to British antiracist laws and policies. French leaders simply did not frame their concerns with racism in terms that made these exemplars seem relevant. As a result, policymakers were unaware of the drawbacks of criminalizing access racism that formed such a visible part of the British debates of 1965. Although over time, actors paid increased attention to problems of discrimination targeted at people based on skin color, leading French activists operated with different race frames from their British counterparts. The very term race was seen as anathema by many in France, including the rapporteur of the law against racism. Problems of racial defamation and provocation to racial hatred reminiscent of the years preceding the Nazi and Vichy regimes were uppermost in the minds of MRAP leaders, especially in the years immediately following the war. These race frames had a tangible impact on the shape of French institutions.

Most government leaders during the first three postwar decades believed that racism and issues of interethnic tensions were not substantial problems in French society. Yet these issues have taken on heightened importance since passage of the law, particularly during the 1980s and 1990s given the dominance of immigration themes and the electoral impact of the National Front. The structures established in 1972 remain in place as the foundation of French institutions, continuing to influence how racism is managed today. They were not, however, the last word on fighting racism in France.

6

The Struggle Continued

Antiracism from 1972 to the 1990 Gayssot Law and Beyond

Over the course of the 1970s and 1980s, Parliament revisited antiracism provisions several times to refine and extend them. It was not until 1990, however, that the next major antiracism law arrived in France. The Gayssot law (as it is commonly known) comprised three substantial and new elements.[1] First and most symbolically, it punished those who deny the historical existence of the Holocaust. Although France is not unique in enacting provisions against revisionist history, prominent observers have argued that creating an "official" history is a dubious practice in an open society. Second, it created a new tool for punishing racists. Subject to the discretion of the judges, individuals found guilty of racist crimes can be stripped of certain civil rights – most provocatively the right to run for public office. Third, and least controversially, the law of 1990 mandated an annual report on the struggle against racism and xenophobia. This provision created institutionalized publicity for race policies and opened a yearly window of opportunity for antiracist activists to exploit.

[1] The Gayssot law was named after Jean-Claude Gayssot, a Communist deputy who lead the push for its passage in 1990. It is, however, somewhat of a misnomer. Gayssot's name did indeed figure at the top of the list of signatories on the Communist Party bill that formed part of the eventual legislation (AN 9: 43). However, the Communist proposal was not the only basis for the new law. Some of the most important elements of the 1990 law derived from a Socialist Party bill of 1988 (AN 8: 1247), resubmitted in 1989 (AN 9: 1004). Moreover, Gayssot did not draft the Communist Party document; instead he took up a bill which had been submitted in the previous legislature under the signature of Guy Ducoloné (see AN 8: 762).

The Gayssot law was passed in a significantly different era from that of the original French legislation. If the proposals for the 1972 law were initially formulated in the postwar years, those for the 1990 law were developed in the context of a rising far right party and of heightened concerns over immigration. By the mid-1980s, most of the French political elite and the public understood that immigrants were not merely temporary workers, but were a permanent part of French society. Immigration thus became a powerful electoral theme. The Socialist Party and the mainstream right seemed unable to contain the issue, and watched as the National Front (FN) steadily gained votes as of 1983 largely on the basis of anti-immigrant slogans. The presence of the FN and of the immigration theme served to shatter the cross-party consensus on race policies that had prevailed during the 1972 vote.

The Gayssot law arrived on the Parliamentary agenda due to the confluence of several events. Following a report on the state of racism in France, Prime Minister Michel Rocard launched an initiative designed to gather support for new legislation in early 1990. When the conservative parties balked at his overtures it looked as if the government was set to drop the proposals. Just at this time, however, an institutional change in the National Assembly allowed the Parliament a modicum of power in setting the official agenda by selecting bills to come up for debate. The National Assembly leadership chose the Communist Party's antiracism bill. As with the 1972 law, therefore, the 1990 legislation was introduced and pushed forward through the little-used method of Parliamentary rather than governmental leadership.

Negotiations over the final version of the law entailed several battles that pitted left against right, with the far right National Front influencing the entire process. Although the governing Socialists had wanted consensus on race legislation, the right opposed the project, decrying its potential restrictions on the freedom of the press and freedom of expression. The left negotiated amendments, but at the same time proclaimed that the right opposed the law primarily because the FN's leader Jean-Marie Le Pen had come out against it.

In spite of the shifting immigration context and the partisan tensions present in 1990, French race frames continued to play a significant role in shaping French race policies in the decades following its first law. The legal revisions between 1972 and 1990 tended to reinforce official color blindness as well as the role of nongovernmental groups as leaders in the fight against racism. Moreover, despite rising numbers of ethnic minority immigrants and their French citizen children, the political elite chose to direct its energies in the 1990 law[2] toward expressive racism – primarily in the form of anti-Semitism – rather than toward access racism against minorities in jobs, housing, and other domains. Partly, this responded to the attention generated by Jean-Marie Le Pen's public statements. But because parallel statements by Enoch Powell in Britain in the 1960s and 1970s did not generate the same results, this must also be seen as the product of French policy and political leaders' framing of the problem of racism in these terms.

Section one of this chapter discusses the institutional modifications made between the two major antiracism laws of 1972 and 1990. Although each was embedded within larger omnibus bills (not meriting a major legislative initiative in itself), each helped develop the French antiracism repertoire in important ways. This is especially true of the 1978 law on collection of racial or ethnic data. The increasingly important immigration context of the 1980s is the subject of section two. In contrast to the 1972 law, passage of the 1990 legislation was strongly affected by the rise of the National Front and by concerns about immigration. Sections three and four delve into party positions on race policies leading up to passage of the Gayssot law, displaying internal tensions within the right and consistent if not persistent activism within the left. Section five demonstrates that race arrived on the Parliamentary agenda because of the convergence of a high profile report on racism, an unrelated institutional change in the National Assembly, and an assumption that antiracist actions would prove consensual among all mainstream parties. Section six illustrates the miscalculation of this last assumption and focuses on the three key issues and how they were contested, amended, or (in part) excised from the antiracism bill. It also highlights the role of the National Front and of electoral and interest group politics in influencing party positions and in shaping the final version of the law and provides a capsule summary of the outcome of the 1990 Gayssot law.

Race Institutions in the 1970s and 1980s

The 1972 law has remained the centerpiece of France's antiracism institutions. Over the course of the 1970s and 1980s, however, it was extended in important if relatively low-profile directions. The first set of changes involved widening the coverage of antidiscrimination law from race to sex (in 1975 and 1983) and eventually to discrimination based on health

[2] As well as in the aborted governmental law project of 1996 (AN 10: 3045).

or handicap (1990).[3] The second direction of developments injected into the law were more effective tools for punishing racist actions. Although these alterations were usually seen as relatively minor and technical, they determined several very important legislative, practical, and philosophical issues.

If by the mid-1970s, British race policy experts were convinced of the usefulness of collecting ethnic data, their French counterparts held diametrically opposed views. Tucked away in a lengthy 1978 law (on "information storage and freedom") was a clause that all-but-banned race-based statistics. The 1978 provisions outlawed computerized storage of data on racial origins without the express consent of the individual or (in cases of public interest) of the state.[4] In practice, this has meant that no systematic data have been collected on race. There are no census estimates of French citizen populations as defined by race or ethnicity and no bureaucratic or private sector use of such data to estimate the positions of minorities relative to the majority. Moreover, there is little desire for such statistics. Although one influential researcher obtained hard-fought permission to conduct a study on immigrant integration which used an ethnic variable (Tribalat 1995), use of such data has since been roundly attacked (Le Bras 1998).[5] In the late 1970s, when the legal provisions were first discussed, antiracist groups such as the MRAP supported the drive to outlaw collection of ethnic data (interview with Palant, March 10, 1997). In Parliament, the debate turned not around whether to make race statistics legal or illegal, but around whether to permit exceptions to the ban or to outlaw collection of race data in every circumstance.[6] At the end of the day the exceptions remained; yet there has been a strong moral and legal bias against collection of race or ethnic statistics in France that continues to this day.

The question of physical racism was also addressed by the Parliament in the years following the 1972 law. Although there is no formal distinction in France between "racist murder" or "racist assault" and "murder" or

[3] See Ahumada (1991). These modifications, unlike in Britain, did not affect race policy outcomes and are thus not reviewed in detail here.

[4] It is also illegal to store data on political, philosophical, or religious opinions, or on union membership. However, churches and religious, philosophical, political, and union groups may legally keep a register of their own members. Minority groups may not legally keep records of their members, unless they obtain members' permission or the permission of the state (see JOLD 78-17, January 7, 1978: 229).

[5] See Blum (2002) for a review of the recent French debate over statistics.

[6] See AN 5: 3125: 25–26, JODP AN, October 6, 1977: 5878–79, S 1, 1977: 72, JODP S, November 18, 1977: 2799–2801.

"assault," the French state is not wholly neutral with respect to physical racism. As of 1985, antiracist groups such as the MRAP, the LICRA[7] and others have been permitted to participate in trials against certain crimes motivated by racism. This step represented a significant concession to the associations' pressure to extend their domain of action.[8] The government had been reluctant to confer these powers, arguing that French law examined the "motive" of the crime only in determining the punishment, not in defining the crime itself. In a letter to the MRAP, Minister of Justice Robert Badinter declared that making racist motives part of the definition of a crime "elicits the largest reservations on my behalf."[9] Nevertheless, a 1985 legal provision introduced a class of physical racism crimes by allowing antiracist associations to participate as civil parties in the prosecution of crimes of murder, death threats, battery and certain acts of destruction of property, provided that they were motivated by racist intent.[10]

The theme of revisionism also received attention prior to the Gayssot law of 1990. The 1986–1988 RPR government of Jacques Chirac rendered the *apology* of crimes against humanity illegal, stopping one (conscious) step short of outlawing the *denial* of crimes against humanity (Hannoun 1987).[11] In concrete terms, it was still legal to argue that the Holocaust never happened, but illegal to argue that it had happened and was a good thing. By passing a law against Holocaust apologists, race policy experts within the RPR and the government itself signaled their interest in these issues of expressive racism, even if their provision did not acquire the intense media profile of the left's more controversial 1990 law.

Although the legal revisions of the 1970s and 1980s often established important precedents or launched and codified new elements of the French institutional structures, none was viewed as sufficiently momentous to

[7] The International League Against Racism and Anti-Semitism (formerly the LICA).

[8] The MRAP had been lobbying the Ministry of Justice for such powers since at least 1983 (MRAP archives).

[9] Letter to Albert Lévy, Secretary General of the MRAP, February 4, 1983 (MRAP archives).

[10] Allowing associations to take part in such trials appears to have been a government compromise in order to avoid formally recognizing and institutionalizing specific "race crimes" (see AN 7: 2458: 83–4). The historically and politically conservative Senate voted to suppress the right of associations to take part in such trials, claiming that "the reform does indeed propose to institute 'specific racist infractions' " (S 1, 1984–5: 139: 34). The National Assembly, however, overruled the Senate (JOLD 85-10, January 4, 1985: 100).

[11] For the text of the law, see JOLD 87-1157, December 31, 1987.

merit an independent law.[12] Aside from the activity of the antiracist associations and their desire to widen the ambit of the 1972 law, two new and interrelated factors kept race on elites' radar screens: the presence of the National Front and the increased salience of immigration as a political issue.

The Political Context: Immigration and the National Front (FN)

If the law of 1972 was passed without political controversy and prior to any anti-immigrant maelstrom, the opposite was true of the 1990 law. During the 1980s, the rise of the far right National Front catapulted immigration, citizenship, and integration policies into the public eye. The FN redefined the electoral landscape and forced new issues onto the national agenda; its presence also sensitized politicians to neighboring themes of xenophobia and racism and instilled debates over these issues with heightened political, moral, and media significance. Although many politicians continued to demonstrate concern over the problems of racism, unanimity over race policies was no longer guaranteed in an era of elevated unemployment and of a new understanding that most immigrants in France were unlikely to return to their countries of origin. The electoral strength of the FN added heightened salience to all matters related to immigration, and had a strong impact on politicians' actions in the field of antiracism.

The growth of the National Front after 1983 has been one of the most important political events of the French Fifth Republic. Although the Front was founded in 1972, its electoral achievements were inconsequential for the first ten years of its existence.[13] Beginning with its surprise success in the municipal elections of 1983, however, it struck a chord with its themes of delinquency, criminality, and immigration (Raufer 1991). Between the mid-1980s and the late 1990s, the FN collected approximately 10 to 15 percent of the popular vote in national, regional, and European elections. Although France's electoral system has limited the

[12] Other changes made during this era include a 1977 amendment outlawing boycotts based on considerations of race, ethnicity, nationality or religion (see JOLD 77-574, June 7, 1977), a 1987 provision that excised the ability of actors to use a "legitimate motive" loophole as a justification for racial discrimination (JOLD 87-588, July 31, 1987), and another 1987 provision that permitted the Minister of the Interior to ban publications considered dangerous to youth because of their tone of discrimination or racial hate (JOLD 87-1157, December 31, 1987).

[13] Its leader, Jean-Marie Le Pen, received under 1 percent of the vote in the 1974 presidential elections and the FN got less than one half of 1 percent of the votes cast in the legislative elections of March 1978 (see Perrineau in Sirinelli 1995).

presence of National Front politicians in domestic institutions, a one-time use of proportional representation during the 1986 legislative elections permitted the Front to send thirty-five deputies to the National Assembly.[14]

The platform of the FN is openly anti-Semitic and anti-immigrant. Its leader, Jean-Marie Le Pen, has decried the "antinational role of the international Jewry" (Perrineau in Sirinelli 1995: 412) and has insisted on several occasions that "the gas-chambers are a detail of the history of the Second World War," declaring that "when you pick up a 1,000 page book on the Second World War, concentration camps take up two pages and gas chambers ten to fifteen lines; in other words, a detail" (*The Daily Telegraph*, December 27, 1997). In addition, given that the term "immigrant" is widely equated with ethnic minorities in popular perception (Silverman 1992: 3–5), National Front slogans such as "the French first" and "France to the French" attempt to evoke antiminority sentiment in the public at large. These slogans and the FN platform in general have made themes of immigration and integration (and racism by contagion) politically charged and electorally tricky.

The established parties have responded to the rise of the National Front with a grab bag of often contradictory signals.[15] In the early years after its breakthrough, President Mitterrand and the Socialist Party hoped to use the FN to create fissures within the traditional right (see Camus 1996: 50–1, 57).[16] The right, while never officially sanctioning the Front, has at times played to extreme-right themes of immigration, security, and nationalism in the hopes of winning back defecting voters. During a congress of the Gaullist RPR party at Vincennes, a leading politician (Charles Pasqua) received an ovation for calling for "the right of the French to remain French in their country."[17] Even a politician as powerful and as historically sympathetic to minority issues as Jacques Chirac has played to anti-immigrant crowds by expressing sympathy with those who deplore the "noise and smell" of immigrants (Hargreaves 1995: 115). Although

[14] Since 1988, the FN has had either one deputy or no deputies in the National Assembly.

[15] For a detailed discussion of the relationship between the FN and other parties, see Camus (1996).

[16] This logic was partly responsible for the introduction of proportional representation in 1986, which allowed the FN entry in numbers into the National Assembly. As then-First Secretary of the Socialist party Lionel Jospin said: "If there are votes for the National Front, there should be seats for the National Front" (Quoted in *Le Monde*, March 23, 1985).

[17] Quoted in *L'Unité*, June 21, 1985.

leaders on both sides of the aisle have also fought the National Front, no politician or party acting on immigration or integration themes has been able to duck the FN's initiatives in these domains (Schain 1996).

The rise of the FN led not only to mainstream party political maneuvering, it also spawned a plethora of private sphere mobilization and public policymaking. New groups such as SOS Racisme and established associations such as the MRAP, the LICRA, and the Human Rights League turned their attention to opposing the rise of anti-immigrant sentiment as expressed by the National Front (see Blatt 1996, Lloyd 1998). By the mid- to late 1980s the French government was generating highly publicized debates, laws and regulations relating to citizenship, immigration, and integration. The 1986–1988 government of the right commissioned a committee to hold public (and televised) discussions on how to reform French citizenship laws, and eventually restricted access to citizenship when it returned to office in 1993 (Commission de la Nationalité 1988, Feldblum 1999). Parties of both political stripes boasted of their restrictive immigration policies and claimed to be working toward the target of "zero immigration," which though impossible was a highly appealing goal for many voters (see Camus 1996: 70–1). On the integration front, the 1988–1993 government of the left established a prolific High Council on Integration to reflect on integrating immigrants into French life.[18] The French state also stepped up funding in the 1980s for the bureaucracy devoted to integrating immigrants (Weil 1995: 271)[19] and began to seek interlocutors in the Islamic community in order to minimize the risks of hostile antistate activities among domestic Muslim communities (Hargreaves 1995: 206–9, Kepel 1997, Roy 1994). Citizenship, immigration, integration, and the National Front thus left an indelible imprint on French politics of the 1980s and 1990s – an imprint which has carried over into the realm of race policies.

The Right and Race Policies

In spite of the mainstream right's periodic drift toward National Front policies on immigration and citizenship, it has not been historically opposed to antiracism laws. The French right passed the foundational antiracism law of 1972 and shepherded the 1977 and 1987 amendments through Parliament. This does not imply, however, that the RPR and

[18] See Haut Conseil à l'Intégration (1991, 1992, 1993, 1995, 1998).
[19] The Social Action Fund, or FAS.

UDF have been the most activist parties on race matters. Although all deputies and senators to the right of center voted for the law of 1972, the antiracist initiatives originated in a private association and first found Parliamentary purchase in the Communist Party. As with the reforms of 1977 and 1987, the impetus for the 1972 law came from a few committed activists within the governing party. As a whole, the right has been historically divided over antiracist policies, with progressive voices calling for action while many others see little or no need for further legislation.[20]

This fracture within the mainstream right was evident during the 1986–1988 RPR Government. On May 5, 1987, Philippe Séguin, Minister of Social Affairs, announced a proposal for a significant revision to the law of 1972.[21] Although Séguin's ministry had drafted a bill[22] and the Minister himself publicly pressured the Government in a proreform direction, the proposal was quickly shelved. The initiative did not gain wide support within the political right and was eventually sunk by the Ministry of Justice.[23] Such a high-profile action risked the displeasure of an anti-immigrant electorate; the few changes that were enacted in June of that year were therefore passed through the lower profile vehicle of an omnibus social order bill, downplaying the significance of race legislation and limiting its impact.

As if to compensate the progressive wing of the party, in June 1987 the government commissioned a report on racism and discrimination in France, seeking measures to promote tolerance and to "improve relations between the different components of the national community" (Hannoun 1987: 4).[24] Michel Hannoun was chosen for the task, a deputy representing the most multicultural-oriented section of the Gaullist (RPR) party.[25] Publication of his report in November 1987 caused a stir among leaders

[20] As in previous chapters, the term progressive is used as a value-free term to describe actors that favor more race legislation.

[21] *La Croix*, May 7, 1987, *Libération*, August 7, 1987. Among Séguin's ideas included establishing structures for mediating certain racism disputes rather than immediately invoking court action; expanding the associations' right of response in the press; sensitivity training for bureaucrats that deal with immigrants; and a rewording of the "legitimate motive" loophole for decisions about furnishing goods and services (see *Libération*, August 7, 1987).

[22] An *avant projet de loi.*

[23] *Libération*, August 7, 1987.

[24] The report was commissioned on June 30, 1987 by Dr. Claude Malhuret, Secretary of State for Human Rights in the Prime Minister's office. See *Le Monde*, July 2, 1987.

[25] Hannoun himself is a Jew of North African origin; on Hannoun's background see Safran (1989: 145); see also *La Croix*, July 2, 1987.

of the conservative RPR and UDF parties whose opinions divided over its recommendations.

The report offered fifty-three specific proposals for action. It argued for a public discussion of integration and immigration policies, which it felt should be linked to proposed changes in the law on racism.[26] Hannoun stressed the primary role of education in overcoming racism and argued for several modifications to the 1972 legislation, many of which were eventually instituted by the Socialists' 1990 law. His proposals included: giving a higher profile to the fight against racism by publicizing convictions, by creating a right of response for antiracist associations, and by creating a governmental obligation to present an annual report to Parliament on the application of the 1972 law; stiffening the penalties for racist actions, including limiting certain civil and political rights of individuals convicted of racist crimes;[27] and countering anti-Semitism by promoting the diffusion of uncontested historical works, by forbidding the wearing of Nazi paraphernalia, and by creating a punishment for apologies of crimes against humanity.[28]

Some in the RPR and the UDF viewed Hannoun's report as radical. According to *Libération* (November 23, 1987), future party leader and Prime Minister Alain Juppé (and others) thought the arguments and proposals were too ambitious. At the same time, those who evinced sympathy with the report claimed that the Hannoun suggestions could be put into action before the end of 1987. Philippe Séguin proceeded to push for adoption of the elements within his ministerial brief.[29] Antiracist groups such as SOS Racisme, France Plus, and the MRAP were also broadly favorable to the report.[30] Yet, even in the context of a late November march against racism and xenophobia that mobilized tens of thousands of supporters,[31]

[26] Apart from envisioning changes to the antidiscrimination law, the Hannoun report proposed the creation of a body called the High Council on Immigration, a structure designed for representation, advice and mediation between the government and private groups involved in immigration issues. "Representatives" of immigrant or minority groups were not on the proposed list of participants (Hannoun 1987: 167, 209–213).

[27] The report argued that it would be disproportionate to deprive guilty parties of the right to vote (Hannoun 1987: 111).

[28] The report also discussed at length the option of criminalizing revisionist history before rejecting it as too restrictive to freedom of expression and carrying the risk of validating some of the revisionists' claims about the existence of an "official history" (Hannoun 1987: 113–15).

[29] *Libération*, November 23, 1987, *Libération*, December 5/6, 1987.

[30] *Le Monde*, November 24, 1987.

[31] *Le Monde*, December 1, 1987.

the final word on the proposals from the government party was broadly negative. The RPR party spokesman (Franck Borotra) called the Hannoun report "a text which is unsuited to the French reality" and argued that putting a halt to immigration was the best way to fight racism.[32]

The Hannoun report therefore sent mixed messages about the position of the right on race policies. On the one hand, the RPR advanced concrete and substantial antiracism proposals. On the other hand, the official position of the government was not favorable to race legislation, presumably in light of pressures from the right of their own party and from the thirty-five sitting National Front deputies in Parliament. Although the government did not feel secure enough to enact high-profile or substantial policies or laws, it did snipe at smaller targets. Aside from the failed Séguin initiative and the Hannoun report, the 1986–1988 government undertook several small-scale antiracist projects that emerged from the Prime Minister's office and from the individual Ministries of Justice, Social Affairs, Interior, and Education.[33]

Immigration restrictions were, however, the order of the day. Any initiatives arguably favorable to immigrants were politically risky. Elements of the Hannoun proposals were nevertheless spirited into law in a December bill on drug trafficking,[34] suggesting that statements for public consumption did not necessarily have to mesh with low-profile policy changes.[35] The right was internally divided on race initiatives; it was willing to give a nod to antiracism through low-key channels but did not want to risk any large-scale undertakings. By the time the 1990 law against racism

[32] *Le Monde*, December 17, 1987.

[33] For example, the government issued a decree banning Nazi uniforms or insignia in public (see March 25, 1988, NOR: JUSD8830035C); the Minister of Justice sent out a circular calling for redoubled vigilance with respect to race crimes and asking for statistics on prosecutions (May 11, 1987, NOR: JUSD8730016C); the Ministry of Social Affairs sponsored a June 1987 joint MRAP/LICRA colloquium on the functioning of the 1972 law; on July 7, 1987, the Minister of the Interior (Charles Pasqua) organized a meeting with twenty-two antiracist and Jewish organizations for an exchange of views about the rise of anti-Semitism; Pasqua asked border police to block xenophobic and revisionist publications, and on August 10, of that same year, he asked the prefects to show "extreme rigor" with respect to discrimination in their departments or in their own services; finally, the teaching of human rights was to become a substantive part of high school education starting in 1988 (*L'Express*, August 28–September 3, 1987).

[34] In particular, as mentioned above, the provision that outlawed apologies of war crimes.

[35] The FN fought these amendments at the time, but the conflict did not balloon into a larger public debate.

came onto the Parliamentary table, however, the Séguin proposals, the Hannoun report, and the right's internal debate over race policies were soft-pedaled as the right united against the left's legislative proposals.

The Left and Law Proposals

Unlike the French political right which supported race legislation in fits and starts, the left supported it consistently but not necessarily energetically. Between 1972 and 1990, left party deputies submitted numerous legislative proposals to the National Assembly. As with the earlier proposals of the 1950s and 1960s, such initiatives marked Parliamentarians' acknowledgment of racism as an issue of public concern, without implying heavy pressure for state action. Both the Socialists and the Communists brought suggestions for legislation to the National Assembly. These were systematically ignored by the governments of both the right (1972–1981, 1986–1988) and the left (1981–1986), which made low-profile technical changes but had no intention of debating a race bill in Parliament.

Communist Party (PCF) deputies were the most persistent in drafting and submitting antiracist proposals to the National Assembly. Their tenacity on these issues was influenced by the twin motives of historical experiences and electoral incentives. Several of the deputies who led the crusade for antiracist laws had personally suffered at the hands of the Vichy and Nazi regimes, either having participated in the resistance (such as Robert Ballanger) or having survived deportation to Germany (in the case of Guy Ducoloné). Electorally, the legal proposals drafted by the PCF served as useful election campaign tools. They could be photocopied and distributed to voters to demonstrate the party's commitment to equality and to the protection of the underprivileged, and to reinforce the Communists' image as a leading force in resisting Nazi atrocities during the war.

The Communist Party opened its post-1972 antiracist activities by submitting a bill in 1979 calling for a ban on the apology of Nazism.[36] Although the PCF proposals were never seriously considered in the National Assembly, the 1987 law banning the apology of crimes against humanity eventually covered the Communists' principal concerns. In that same year, the Communist group penned a longer and more influential legislative bill.

[36] AN 6: 1005. The bill was resubmitted in 1981 in the new Socialist-led legislature (AN 7: 201).

Originally headlined by Ducoloné (who retired in 1988), it was resubmitted in the following legislature under Gayssot's name and eventually became the seed from which the 1990 law was to grow.[37] Under the conservative government of 1986–1988, the Communists realized that their bill had no chance of becoming law. However, one year later they held out hope that their proposals would be considered by a Socialist government which lacked an absolute Parliamentary majority (interview with Gayssot, July 4, 1997).

The party argued that a new law was needed given what they perceived as a rise in racism in France. Along with specific examples of expressive and physical racism,[38] it noted the generalized anti-immigrant tenor of the mid-1980s, a fact that it undoubtedly felt was compounded by the presence of thirty-five National Front members within the National Assembly at the time the bill was first submitted in 1987. Communist Party advocates suggested two essential types of remedies to the problems at hand.[39] First, their bill argued for more information and publicity relating to issues of racism and antiracism. In this vein, the Communist proposals called for a national day of antiracist information and action and for an annual government report on the fight against racism, to be presented to Parliament and followed by a nationally televised debate. Second, the bill proposed legal reforms to allow more private associations to initiate court action against perpetrators of racist acts[40] and to create stiffer penalties for crimes inspired by racist motives. This latter provision included the right to refuse certain civil rights to perpetrators of racist crimes. The PCF's suggested denial of civil rights to offenders revealed itself to be not a radical step, but merely a stronger version of the Hannoun proposals; nevertheless it was to be the source of heated debate during the passage of the 1990 law.

[37] There were, in fact, many Communist Party deputies' names on each bill. Nevertheless, bills tend to become associated with the first deputy on the list, as they usually bear primary responsibility for drafting and lobbying for the bill.

[38] Such as the existence of a "pseudo thesis" denying the Nazi gas chambers, cries of "Arabs in the oven" heard at an industrial conflict, the attack on a synagogue in the rue Copernic, and the murder of a young Algerian (Habib Grinzi), thrown from a train in the south of France (AN 8: 762: 5–6, AN 9: 43: 5–6).

[39] The bill also called for two general statements of principle: support for the 1965 United Nations International Convention to End all forms of Racial Discrimination, and an enjoinder to French schools to inculcate "the respect of the individual and of his origins and differences" (AN 8: 762: 10–11, AN 9: 43: 10–11).

[40] Intended to allow unions – not permitted under the 1972 law – to participate in criminal law suits.

Contrary to popular belief, the Communist bills were not the source of another highly contested point of the 1990 Gayssot law. The proposed ban on revisionism emanated not from "Stalinist" Communists (as implied by the right in Parliamentary debates),[41] but rather from the governing Socialists themselves. The Socialists' 1989 antiracist bill was quietly appended to that of the Communists when the rapporteur drafted the official National Assembly bill in 1990.[42] The Socialist Party (PS) argued that outlawing revisionist history was essential given the burgeoning of such theses and cited in particular National Front leader Jean-Marie Le Pen's 1987 statement that the Holocaust was a mere "detail" of history.[43] According to the Socialists, the 1987 law banning *apologies* of crimes against humanity was insufficient to punish historical revisionism; moreover, they pointed out, this new form of expressive racism had already been banned in the Federal Republic of Germany as of 1985.[44]

What is striking in this era of anti-immigrant politics was the extent to which political leaders focused their legislative energies on concerns over expressive racism and anti-Semitism. It is true that Le Pen's verbal barbs were directed not just at immigrants, but also at Jews. Nevertheless, the hot politics of these years centered squarely on immigrants' rights, with thousands of people marching and rallying for French-born North African youth (the *beurs*) and against racism and restrictive immigration policies. Although antiracist concerns were shifting in some quarters, prevailing frames linking race and racism to anti-Semitism and to speech acts still prevailed in elite policymaking circles.

This did not imply, however, that politicians were anxious to jump on a legislation bandwagon. The Parliamentary Socialist Party expressed an interest in a new round of antiracism legislation in the late 1980s, yet the Socialist government undertook no action to bring their bills to light. The 1988 Rocard government was not completely passive, however, when it came to antiracism. Following in the footsteps of the 1986–1988 conservative government, the Socialist Minister of Justice issued a circular

[41] See JODP AN, May 2, 1990, esp. 931.

[42] See AN 9: 1296. The Socialist Party bill was first submitted in 1988 (with Georges Sarre as first signatory), and then resubmitted unaltered under the first signature of Louis Mermaz in 1989 (AN 8: 1247, AN 9: 1004).

[43] AN 9: 1004: 5.

[44] AN 9: 1004: 6. The Socialists proposed that revisionism (denying or minimizing the Holocaust) be punished by imprisonment of up to a year and/or a maximum fine of 300,000 francs. Their bill also called for the guilty party to cover the cost of a public declaration of the judgment (a publication in the press) and for expanding the right to be a "civil party" to associations of war resisters or deportees.

enjoining the judiciary to be "particularly vigilant" with respect to racist crimes.[45] Moreover, in response to a December 1988 bombing of an immigrant housing project (a Sonacotra foyer), the Prime Minister established a working group on racism in his office (Rocard 1990).[46] Creation of this working group, however, did not presage any major reforms. Instead it reflected the Prime Minister's desire to apply the current legislation more fully and rapidly, "rather than the elaboration of new legislation."[47] Even with the Communist and Socialist bills available in Parliament, the Socialist government had no plans to enact antiracist legislation at the onset of the 1990s.

Legislation on the Agenda

Unlike many pieces of legislation that are long in the planning and drafting stages, the Gayssot law arrived on the agenda suddenly and almost by accident. A series of events that unfolded in the early spring of 1990 catapulted the Communist Party bill onto the National Assembly by way of a Parliamentary initiative. Although the 1990 law followed in the footsteps of the 1972 antiracism provisions in this sense, such a path is uncommon in a political system that allocates the power to advance legislative bills primarily to the government. The distinctiveness of the process reflects the conjuncture of problems of racism with French institutional machinations of early 1990; together, these factors generated the unforeseen arrival of the Gayssot bill on the official agenda.

Problems of racism played a role in moving race onto the front burner, yet legislative action did not arise due to particularly pressing race crises. Although the election of a National Front deputy to the Assembly in a December 1989 by-election – the first and only FN representative in the 1988 legislative session – and the headscarf affair involving the tensions between Islamic symbols and *laïque* public schools[48] kept issues of immigration, racism, and integration in the headlines, there was no identifiable race crime that spurred politicians to act in early 1990.[49] Contrary to what

[45] July 6, 1989 (NOR: JUSD8930049C): 43–7.

[46] See also *Libération*, December 21, 1988.

[47] *Le Monde*, December 22, 1988.

[48] *Laïque* can be translated as "lay," although in France it is an historically loaded term which approximates America's "separation of church and state." On the headscarf affair, see Beriss (1990), Kepel (1997), and Thomas (1998).

[49] There were indeed incidents around this time, but they were not the driving force behind the legal action (*Le Monde*, March 28, 1990).

some observers have implied (Fysh and Wolfreys 1998: 179), the desecration of the Jewish cemetery in the town of Carpentras took place *after* the Gayssot bill was officially under consideration and thus was not itself a spur to getting antiracism on the agenda.[50] Moreover, to the extent that antiracist organizations were involved in highlighting problems of racism and pressing for government action, there was no turning point in their activities at this time. Progressive associations had been making suggestions for legal changes since at least 1987. This pressure was neither forceful nor sustained, and there were no strong campaigns or well-organized lobbies for new legislation in early 1990.[51]

Rather, the catalyst for the new law was Prime Minister Rocard's late March speech, following publication of a report on the state of racism in France.[52] The National Advisory Commission on Human Rights' (CNCDH)[53] report provided statistics on the progression of racist attacks and racist acts, discussed actions undertaken by various ministries, and advanced suggestions for policy or legislative changes (Commission Nationale Consultative des Droits de l'Homme 1990). Although Rocard used the publication of this report to jump-start discussions on antiracism, he did not sign on to its recommendations for action.[54] Instead, during his March 27, 1990, press conference, he called for an early April multiparty roundtable to discuss the report's findings.[55] The Prime Minister also suggested creating regional antiracism structures and advanced his own proposals for legislative changes.[56] Among these included creation

[50] The Carpentras desecration took place on the night of May 9–10, 1990; the Gayssot bill was first debated in the National Assembly on May 2, 1990.

[51] Arguments for legal changes were raised during a colloquium on "the law and discrimination" in 1987 (LICRA/MRAP 1987) and were then reproduced periodically by groups such as the LICRA. Groups such as France Plus and SOS Racisme also suggested changes, but in a less focused manner than the proposals formulated by the LICRA (Commission Nationale Consultative des Droits de l'Homme 1990). See also *Libération*, May 4, 1990, Haut Conseil à l'Intégration (1998).

[52] Rocard was of course privy to the information in the report well before it was published. One of his technical advisors (Mr. Louis Joinet) co-chaired the meetings that led to the report.

[53] The Commission Nationale Consultative des Droits de l'Homme is a government advisory group which comments and prepares reports on government projects in all areas of human rights.

[54] Rather than emanating from the CNCDH as a body, the proposals were lists of suggestions from associations such as LICRA and SOS Racisme.

[55] The talks were to take place on April 3, 1990 and excluded the National Front.

[56] His principal proposal was to remove the sanctioning of certain racist acts from the 1881 press law, thereby giving them a more "normal" criminal status. One of the

of a penalty for denying crimes against humanity.[57] All of these actions demonstrated the Prime Minister's support for revising antiracist legislation; yet his office had not submitted – nor even drafted – an official government bill. If Rocard backed legislative change, he clearly favored all-party, consensual reform.

The right reacted to the events of early 1990 by attempting to refocus political debate on immigration. The leaders of the RPR and UDF (Jacques Chirac and Valéry Giscard d'Estaing) elected not to attend the Prime Minister's April roundtable on racism, which was denounced as a "media coup."[58] The rightist parties did send representatives, however, who after securing the Prime Minister's commitment to a Parliamentary debate on immigration, emerged from the meeting seemingly content. There was no all-party announcement of forthcoming antiracist legislation. As a newspaper headline summarized the state of affairs following the parley, "if all the participants at the round table at Matignon agree on fighting xenophobia, they diverge over the methods to use."[59]

Given the lack of consensus over legislative reforms and the absence of a government antiracism bill, any momentum toward passing new laws was certainly undercut. The window of opportunity for action that opened briefly with publication of the CNCDH report appeared to be closing. But concurrent to the heightened attention to antiracism was an unrelated initiative for institutional reform of the National Assembly. Under the rules of the Fifth Republic, the Parliament had little or no power to bring its bills into public debate since the government controlled the official agenda. The President of the National Assembly (and former Prime Minister) Laurent Fabius had just convinced Prime Minister Rocard to return a modicum of power to the Parliament by devoting time to bills originating in the National Assembly.[60] This institutional innovation generated another opening for advocates of antiracism legislation.

The Communist Party dusted off and formally submitted for consideration its 1988 Gayssot bill in light of the recent public deliberations over antiracist initiatives. The bill was accepted by the National Assembly

perceived drawbacks of using the press law was that the statute of limitations for crimes was a mere three months – often insufficient time to bring charges of racist pamphleteering.

57 *Le Monde*, March 29, 1990.

58 *Figaro-Magazine*, April 7, 1990: 72–5, *Le Monde*, April 4, 1990; *La Croix*, April 4, 1990, *Le Figaro*, April 3, 1990.

59 *Libération*, April 5, 1990.

60 *Nouvel Observateur*, May 10/16, 1990, interview with Gayssot, July 4, 1997.

leadership on April 17, 1990.[61] Fabius was favorable to this proposal for personal as well as party reasons. In addition to the Socialist Party's reliance on Communist votes given the government's lack of an absolute majority, Fabius had judged Rocard's "round table" approach to antiracism too soft, and wanted to engage the National Front more directly.[62] Moreover, according to inside observers, the text of the Gayssot bill was seen at the time as "harmless and inoffensive," and neither of the mainstream right parties nor the government raised any objection to it.[63]

It was perhaps only a matter of time before the government put forward its own antiracism project in response to the problems highlighted by the CNCDH's report. Yet given the Prime Minister's desire for consensual reforms and the right's ambivalence, the government may never have launched potentially controversial, publicity-prone legislation. The combination of institutional tinkering in the National Assembly, the lack of a Socialist Parliamentary majority, and the existence of a preexisting Communist bill combined to return antiracist legislation to the Parliamentary agenda. The Gayssot proposition arrived through the back door, without much government reflection, and through the chance timing of Parliamentary institutional reforms.

From the Agenda to the Law: Three Key Issues

When the National Assembly leadership assigned a rapporteur to the Gayssot bill, it included the 1989 Socialist bill in its legislative plans. The official bill – which emerged from committee deliberations and was debated in the two houses of Parliament – thus contained a package of ideas originating in the two left parties. But many of these proposals had at one time or another found support among leaders on the right, and all were presumed to be palatable across the political spectrum.[64] When they were discussed in committee and especially in the National Assembly, however, three key elements of the proposals were intensely contested, substantially amended, or simply excised. These included concerns over publicity, civil rights, and revisionism.

If debates over civil rights and revisionism generated much heat during the 1990 law's passage, changes to the publicity provisions were little

[61] *Libération*, 4 May 1990, *Humanité*, March 30, 1990.
[62] *Quotidien de Paris*, May 3, 1990.
[63] *Libération*, May 4, 1990, *Nouvel Observateur*, May 10/16, 1990.
[64] *Nouvel Observateur*, May 10/16, 1990.

noticed. The Gayssot law successfully created institutional provisions to publicize the problem of racism, a necessary element to keep the issue prominent on the national agenda. It provided antiracist associations with a public "right of response" in the wake of a conviction for expressive racism in the press and allowed judges to require that racist convictions be announced in a newspaper.[65] Most importantly, it mandated an annual report to the Prime Minister on the fight against racism, which has served as a focal point for media coverage of racism and the state's response. The original Gayssot bill, as noted above, included many more provisions, such as a "public holiday" of antiracism, during which the government would be responsible for coordinating a "day of antiracist information and action," designed to reaffirm the nation's refusal of racism. In addition, the original bill demanded that the government submit a yearly report to Parliament outlining the progress made in the fight against racism to be followed by a televised debate.[66]

These provisions seemed over-ambitious to politicians on both sides of the aisle, and were chipped away gradually and without much fanfare at all stages of the Parliamentary process. The changes were not highly contested political battles; indeed, the motions to temper the original provisions originated within the left.[67] Nonetheless, the stakes in this debate were greater than the corresponding press coverage reflected.[68] The government successfully opposed almost all high-profile and publicity-generating elements in the original Gayssot bill. Although a page or two of press coverage typically follows the Prime Minister's response to the annual CNCDH report, there is no required government or Parliamentary debate or action. The final version of the law thus built in a level of "duckability" on race issues, reflecting the logic that it is wise to avoid

[65] JOLD, 14 July 1990: 8333–4.

[66] AN 8: 762; AN 9: 43. The report was to be made on March 21, the UN's International Day Against Racism.

[67] François Asensi, the Communist rapporteur, took the first step by eliminating the government's responsibility for organizing the annual day against racism (AN 9: 1296). In committee, a Socialist deputy's amendment (François Massot's) excised the requirement of a televised antiracism debate in Parliament. On the floor of the National Assembly, the government further weakened the publicity provisions of the bill. It eliminated the national day of antiracist action and information as well as the mandatory Parliamentary discussion of the annual report. Moreover, the government refused to support attempts by the Communist Party to reinstate the Parliamentary and public debate and the national day of information and action (JODP AN, May 2, 1990: 901–62).

[68] Gayssot himself strongly regretted that March 21 did not become a national day against racism (interview with Gayssot, April 7, 1997).

unearthing the potential land mine of racism on a fixed and almost certainly politically inauspicious schedule.

Although the publicity provisions were weakened outside of the public eye, the proposals to deprive convicted racists of civil rights stirred up passionate debate.[69] The Parliamentary bill proposed to enable judges – at their discretion – to penalize those found guilty of racist crimes[70] with deprivation of civil rights,[71] including the right to vote and the right to be elected to public office. This was argued to be an inordinate burden on the media and an insufferable attack on freedom of the press. Under French law, newspaper editors are banned from practicing their profession if they have been deprived of their civil rights through a conviction. Moreover, because editors are responsible for their newspaper's articles, in theory they could lose their professional rights if their journalists quoted racist statements made by third parties. Although certainly not a probable outcome, this possibility prompted an outcry from media organizations.[72] The right carried this refrain into the Parliamentary debate, hammering the government with claims that it was trying to "muzzle the press."[73] The government responded by passing an amendment eliminating the application of civil rights penalty to editors (therefore eliminating the risk that they would be banned from their jobs) and by accepting an amendment of the right that granted equivalent protection to journalists.[74]

The right also challenged the left by arguing in the National Assembly that the plan to deprive convicted racists of their civil rights was a thinly

[69] A failed proposal to amend the 1881 press law also deserves mention. The rapporteur, in line with the public suggestions made in March by Prime Minister Rocard, proposed to extend the statute of limitations on crimes of expressive racism from three months to one year. This would have edged such race crimes out of the context of the 1881 press law and into the domain of common law, an area which many experts feel provides a more effective institutional remedy. Asensi's suggestion was voted down in committee, however; the law on expressive racism therefore remained fully in the domain of the 1881 press law.

[70] The rapporteur's original proposals called for the civil rights penalty to apply in all cases of racist crimes; the committee limited application to what it considered the worst racist crimes (AN 9: 1296: 20).

[71] As determined by Article 42 of the French penal code.

[72] Such as the Fédération Nationale de la Presse Française, the Syndicat des Quotidiens Régionaux, as well as journalist organizations (see *Quotidien de Paris*, 3 May, 1990; *Le Monde*, May 3, 1990, *Le Figaro*, May 3, 1990).

[73] JODP AN, May 2, 1990: 902.

[74] JODP AN, May 2, 1990: 952–4. Note that journalists would not have been banned from practicing their profession in case of deprivation of civil rights. This amendment was therefore designed to appease the media lobby in the face of its mobilization.

veiled ad hominem attack on Jean-Marie Le Pen.[75] Le Pen himself claimed that the law as a whole targeted the FN.[76] The Socialists responded simply by stating that those who made racist statements were not worthy of being elected to office.[77] Nevertheless, it is clear that the law was crafted in the context of the rise of the National Front; to plead ignorance or disinterestedness in its effects on the FN rang disingenuous to many on the right. After considering the criticisms, the government excised the ban on the right to vote. Yet, by permitting courts to deny convicted racists the right to be elected and to hold office, the left clearly sought to box in Le Pen and his associates. Future RPR Minister of Justice Jacques Toubon interjected during the debate "I understand that the Government does not want to go as far as civic death, that it prefers political death. I understand that is in fact the entire goal of the maneuver."[78]

If the Gayssot law is most frequently associated with one element, it is undoubtedly the provision banning revisionism.[79] The revisionism article of the 1990 law rendered it illegal to *contest* crimes against humanity, going beyond the 1987 penalties against the *apology* of such crimes.[80] This step raised the hackles of some historians, fearful of a measure that smacked of establishing an "official history."[81] In earlier years, the right had divided over the merits of such a legal provision. Although the progressive Hannoun report had recommended against

[75] Francis Delattre, Philippe de Villiers, and Louis de Broissia disapproved of the law in part for this reason. Marie-France Stirbois, the sole FN deputy at the time, also used this argument as one of many for opposing the law (JODP AN, May 2, 1990: 906–7, 909).

[76] *Quotidien de Paris*, May 3, 1990.

[77] JODP AN, May 2, 1990: 928–9.

[78] JODP AN, May 2, 1990: 946.

[79] The law punished those who contested the existence of crimes against humanity committed during World War II (namely, the Holocaust), which some at the time referred to as revisionism and others as negationism. Negationism has since become the term of choice in France for these crimes, since revisionism has also been applied to valid academic work which "revised" the understanding of history. I use revisionism instead of the French term negationism to reflect popular English language usage of the term and to avoid introduction of a neologism.

[80] The crimes that cannot be legally denied in France are those defined by Article 6 of the international military tribunal statute annexed to the London accord of August 8, 1945, and that were committed by members of an organization declared to be criminal (such as the Gestapo or SS), or by a person recognized as guilty of such crimes by a French or international court. The effect of this formula is to capture only those who deny the Holocaust. See JOLD, July 14, 1990: 8333–4, Ministry of Justice Circular CRIM 90-09 F1/08-27-90.

[81] See the interview with Rébérioux in *Libération*, May 4, 1990.

outlawing revisionism (Hannoun 1987), journalists had attributed support for banning revisionism at various times to heavyweights Philippe Séguin and Jacques Chirac,[82] and the hard-nosed and earthy former Interior Minister Charles Pasqua had reportedly warmed to the proposal as recently as the Prime Minister's April 1990 roundtable on racism.[83] Nevertheless, when it came to the public National Assembly debate, future RPR Minister of Justice Jacques Toubon argued that a revisionism provision would undermine freedom of academic research and might even give credibility to revisionist theses simply by outlawing them. Although the right voted against the antiracism bill as a whole at the end of a very long night of debate, it did not vote against the government's formulation of the revisionism article, suggesting limits to its hostility to this provision which it dubbed "one of the principal innovations of this bill."[84]

The mainstream right expended tremendous energy opposing the 1990 Gayssot law, in spite of a clear commitment among party leaders to the cause of antiracism. The National Assembly debate was rife with acrimony and procedural delaying techniques and dragged on until dawn.[85] Deputies repeatedly drew on anti-Communist rhetoric to condemn a bill which they argued originated in a Stalinist party,[86] seemingly unaware that the law of 1972 – passed by a rightist government – also had its origins in Communist Party proposals.[87] Once the bill moved to the upper house, the predominantly rightist Senate refused to assent the project, repeatedly voting measures in committee precluding discussion on the floor. This served to retard passage of the law (while concurrently preempting any Senate influence over its ultimate form) and sent a clear signal of the upper house's overwhelming disapproval of the legislation.

[82] *Quotidien de Paris*, May 3, 1990.

[83] *Nouvel Observateur*, May 10–16, 1990.

[84] JODP AN, May 2, 1990: 954, 954–7.

[85] Many of the procedural roadblocks were erected by the National Front deputy (Marie-France Stirbois), though the mainstream right was also responsible for significant delays.

[86] JODP AN, May 2, 1990: 901–07; *Le Monde*, May 4, 1990.

[87] Right parties also complained (1) that a Communist bill (and not a RPR or UDF bill) was being considered by the Socialist Parliamentary leadership; (2) that after a grueling night's debate in late April, all of their representatives were absent when the bill was discussed in committee; and (3) that the National Assembly debate of May 2, was being held between the holidays of May 1 and May 8.

Why did the right so vehemently oppose the Gayssot law? In part, leaders on the right objected to the specific provisions embodied in the legislation. There were legitimate concerns over freedom of speech that motivated objections to the civil rights sanctions (particularly where the media was concerned) and to the revisionism provisions. Moreover, as noted above, outlawing revisionism had been examined in detail and rejected by RPR progressives merely three years earlier (Hannoun 1987: 113–15). Yet the right had been sending neutral or even positive signals about the law in the weeks prior to the National Assembly debate in early May. The left aimed at a consensus on antiracism and the right had not objected in mid-April to the topic being placed on the Parliamentary agenda.[88] In fact, several mainstream right leaders had come out in favor of Gayssot-type proposals.[89]

The right's aversion to this bill seems to have been determined by its electoral tango with the National Front. During the FN's annual May 1, rally, Le Pen shone the media spotlight at the Parliamentary process by decrying its forthcoming debate of a "wicked law" that aimed to "vote the political death of patriots."[90] The following day the mainstream right mounted its hearty opposition to the bill, ultimately voting with the lone National Front deputy against the antiracism bill. While the right fired volleys at the Communists and at the bill, the left accused the right of sympathy with the National Front. Minister of Justice Pierre Arpaillange proclaimed that "it was enough for Mr. Le Pen to say yesterday that it [the law] was bad for you to follow suit."[91] Whether or not the right reacted directly to the statements of the previous day, the FN undoubtedly influenced the mainstream right's tactical position, given that it was tacitly competing with the far right for anti-immigrant votes. Moreover, the entire process was scrutinized by intense media coverage, with Le Pen himself casting a shadow over the debate by his physical presence in the balcony of the National Assembly on the night of May 2.

Although the mobilization of the right affected the outcome of the law by eliminating the application of civil rights penalties to the media, it changed little else. The 1990 Gayssot law[92] permitted judges, at

[88] *Nouvel Observateur*, May 10–16, 1990, *Libération*, May 4, 1990.
[89] *Nouvel Observateur*, May 10–16, 1990, *Libération*, May 4, 1990.
[90] *Nouvel Observateur*, May 10–16, 1990, *Le Monde*, May 4, 1990.
[91] JODP AN, May 2, 1990: 903.
[92] Law 90-615 of July 13, 1990 against racism, anti-Semitism and xenophobia (JOLD, July 14, 1990: 8333–4).

their discretion, to deprive individuals convicted of racism of certain civil rights – most notably the right to be elected to public office.[93] The law also created a new crime of revisionism, rendering it illegal in France to contest the historical existence of the Holocaust. Although most of the publicity measures were chipped away during the Parliamentary process, the final version of the Gayssot law mandated an annual report on racism,[94] submitted to the Prime Minister each March by the National Advisory Commission on Human Rights. Finally, the 1990 law expanded the scope of associations' participation in the legal process, allowing a broader range of associations access to the civil party status in cases of racism,[95] and permitting antiracist associations a "right of response" in the written press in cases of expressive racism.

Conclusion

The law of 1972 remains the fundamental point of orientation for the French state in the field of race policies. Nevertheless, the country's antiracism institutions have not stood still. Several low-profile but influential changes to the law were made in the 1970s and 1980s. Notable among them was the 1978 provision that all-but-banned collecting data on race or ethnicity. Without such statistics, it is exceedingly difficult to measure and to prove systematic or large-scale discrimination. France's refusal to collect data on race remains one of the most significant differences between its policies and those of countries such as Britain and the United States, and reflects the widely held frame that ethnic data is likely to be more harmful than helpful.

Twentieth-century developments in French race policies culminated in the 1990 Gayssot law. Without altering the underpinnings of the French model, this legislation added substantial new elements to the national institutional repertoire. The CNCDH report on racism submitted to the Prime Minister in late March 1990 served as the catalyst for getting race

[93] Also the right to sit on a jury, and the right to be a public servant (*accès à la fonction publique et exercice de ces fonctions*). The law also increased penalties for guilty parties.

[94] Technically, a report on the struggle against racism (JOLD, July 14, 1990: 8333).

[95] Along with associations designed to fight racism, associations designed to help victims of discrimination (based on national origin, ethnicity, race, or religion) and associations designed to "defend the moral interests and honor of the Resistance or of those deported" acquired the right to become "civil parties" in certain categories of antiracism legal proceedings (JOLD, July 14, 1990: 8334).

back on the national agenda. Yet it was the political parties, abetted by an institutional change in the National Assembly, that provided the initial impetus to action that resulted in the legislation. The Communists and Socialists furnished the proposals that were to become the law, not an association such as the MRAP (as was the case in 1972), or the government (as is the case with most laws in the French Fifth Republic). In contrast to passage of the 1972 law, however, the Gayssot law generated heated debates and resulted in a far from unanimous backing of the project.

Of tremendous importance to race policies in recent decades has been the immigration context. If the 1972 legislation and many of the changes leading up to the Gayssot law were enacted independent of National Front influence, few debates over race since the mid-1980s have escaped the far right's scrutiny. Several of the legal initiatives of the 1980s and 1990s have been designed to respond to racism generated by the FN. Socialist antirevisionism bills of 1988 and 1989, for example, were inspired by Le Pen's 1987 comments that the Holocaust was a mere "detail" of history. Although the right formally opposed the 1990 law and vilified the left for perceived ad hominem attacks on Le Pen, six years later it responded to the FN leader's rhetoric in a similar fashion. Under the initiative of Minister of Justice Jacques Toubon – the point man for the RPR in challenging the Gayssot law – the Juppé government submitted a 1996 bill designed to punish those who made statements that impugned the dignity or honor of minorities.[96] The government argued that a new law was necessary because the current one failed to cover generalized racist statements that proclaimed, for example, the "inequality of the races" – a direct reference to a remark by Le Pen.[97]

The shift in context between 1972 and the 1990s did not, however, change the overall structure of French antiracist institutions. They remained primarily focused on expressive racism, relying on nongovernmental groups and on the criminal law (rather than administrative agencies and the civil law) to undertake and to enforce the fight against racism.

[96] AN 10: 3045. The precise formula of the expressions to be punished were those that "endanger the dignity, honor or consideration of a person or of a group or many groups of persons because of their real or supposed origin or membership or nonmembership in an ethnic group, a nation, a race or a religion, whether determined or undetermined" (AN 10: 3045: 9–10). The complex formulation is designed to cover any possible verbal attack on minorities.

[97] AN 10: 3045: 5. The bill did not become law because the chair of the Law Committee (Pierre Mazeaud) used his institutional position to block it from advancing through Parliament.

If British race relations provisions share similarities with those of North America, the same has not been as true of French antiracism structures. French actors did not seek lessons from countries to the west, preferring instead to concentrate on domestic issues, or to look to Germany for institutional inspiration. Throughout the 1990s, France maintained colorblind policies, downplayed direct comparisons of substantive equality between groups, and minimized the attention paid to issues of access racism. France's antiracism model has remained distinct in significant ways from the race relations approach of its cross-Channel neighbor.

7

Race Frames and Race Policymaking in Britain and France

British and French race policies have evolved from their fragmentary postwar form into relatively well-developed institutions today. They have not, however, proceeded smoothly, nor have they followed identical paths. Multiple subplots and unexpected twists and turns have marked the history of race policies in these two countries, from Labour's about-face on immigration policies in the 1960s to France's shifting rules that let Parliament place antiracism on the official agenda in 1990. Moreover, in spite of similarities in numbers and percentages of ethnic minorities, each country struck out in a substantially different race policy direction. Closely examining the historical record has unveiled details about how and why leaders in each country chose their race relations and antiracism structures.

Tracking the evolution of race policies in Britain and France also makes it possible to examine and to assess theoretical approaches to the study of comparative public policymaking. Chapter 1 outlined the power-interest, problem-solving, and institutional perspectives on policymaking, and suggested that each served to illuminate the policymaking process. It also focused on frames, arguing that mainstream views of policymaking downplayed the role of such ideational variables in accounts of policy choices. Chapters 2 through 6 drew on these theoretical schools of thought to help analyze the construction of race institutions in Britain and France. This chapter, in turn, uses the empirical material to evaluate the theoretical perspectives themselves, with special emphasis placed on the role of frames in policy analysis.

Assessing whether and how frames are useful in studies of comparative public policymaking requires answering a series of questions. Is it possible to identify frames within a country? Can we demonstrate that they have independent causal influence and therefore that policy outcomes cannot be accounted for without them? How do frames interact with other variables such as power, interests, and institutions, and how can frames be systematically integrated into perspectives on comparative public policymaking? Under what circumstances are frames likely to be especially central to policy analysis? Finally, what factors account for the origins of frames and for the circumstances under which they change?

In order to address these questions, the opening section of this chapter begins by identifying each country's race frames. In keeping with the criteria set out in Chapter 1, frames are relatively coherent and durable across time in Britain and France, without being uniform or immune to change. Section two assesses frames' impact on the policymaking process, demonstrating their significant influence in pointing experts and politicians toward policy choices. Naturally, frames are not the only important variables affecting outcomes. The power-interest, problem-solving, and institutional approaches each help to explain race policy development in the two countries. However, juxtaposing frames with other schools of thought demonstrates that frames play a larger role at some stages of policymaking than at others and that, on the whole, race frames remain the key to understanding each country's domestic policy choices and to explaining many important race policy differences across countries.

Comparing theoretical schools of thought also helps to clarify how frames interact with other variables, building bridges between perspectives and better integrating ideational variables into the mainstream of policy analysis; this is the goal of section three. To further develop an understanding of the role of ideas in policymaking, section four teases out hypotheses about the conditions under which frames have the most impact. Finally, section five offers a template for understanding the sources of frames in general as well as an argument about the origins of British and French race frames in particular. Although the bulk of this book deploys frames as variables to explain race policies, the final section of this chapter shifts the object of inquiry by asking what factors explain the race frames themselves.

Identifying British and French Race Frames

Frames are sets of cognitive and moral maps that orient actors within a policy sphere. They are how people conceptualize and evaluate key terms – such as race and racism – associated with an issue area, and include metaphors or analogies that provide a context for understanding real world events. Three dimensions of each country's race frames are especially important in these cases: whether "race" and "ethnicity" are viewed as meaningful, valid, and acceptable terms; the acts that are viewed as prototypical racist acts; and the geographical or historical context used to orient one's understanding of racism.

For frames to be a useful tool in explanations of policymaking, they must be identifiable within a policy sphere. In pinning them down, however, it is necessary to remember that frames are rarely uniform within a country and they are seldom fixed. It is less important to find that everyone has always shared precisely the same frame than to be able to identify which actors hold which frames and to chart their evolution over time. With this in mind, is it possible to identify British and French race frames from the postwar years to the turn of the century?

Several important threads have been woven into British race frames over the past half-century. British politicians and policymakers have largely *accepted race and ethnicity* as valid categories of analysis and have emphasized skin color as a critical factor in understanding race. It has also been common for British actors to think in terms of racial groups (later, ethnic groups), either fearing conflict between them or trying to promote equality across them. The form of racism that most often captures public and elite attention and that has been the subject of most policy debates is *access racism*. Although other forms of racism are not ignored, discrimination in employment, housing, and access to goods and services has dominated British concern since the 1960s. Finally, key actors have consistently interpreted Britain's problems of racism in the context of the *North American analogy*. Many members of the British elite have paid ongoing attention to policies and developments emanating from across the Atlantic. Together, these elements have formed the core of British race frames.

Color discrimination has been a prominent concern of progressives in Britain since the early days of postwar immigration. Although it may seem natural for most English speakers to conceptualize racism in terms of skin color, in the aftermath of the Holocaust such a frame was not universal. By the mid-1950s, however, the Labour Party had established a small subcommittee to field complaints of color discrimination against immigrants.[1]

[1] The members of this subcommittee, even at this early date, began limited correspondence with associations in the United States such as the NAACP (see, for example, LPA File Box: "Race Relations and Immigration / Racial Discrimination Debate

When riots broke out in Nottingham and Notting Hill in 1958, what was in fact anti-immigrant violence was widely interpreted as an instance of racial conflict pitting black West Indians against white residents (Miles 1984).[2] Two other high-profile events, the 1962 Commonwealth Immigrants Act (CIA) and the 1964 election result in the constituency of Smethwick gave further credence to the interpretation of British problems as based in color racism. The 1962 CIA limited the number of ethnic minority immigrants entering Britain without restricting Irish immigration; and the Conservative victory in Smethwick (despite a national swing to Labour) was widely attributed to race baiting given the use of the slogan "if you want a nigger neighbor, vote Liberal or Labour" (Hansen 2000: 132). The view that Britain was plagued by discrimination based on color was cemented by the influential 1967 Political and Economic Planning study persuasively demonstrating preference given to white foreigners over nonwhite Commonwealth immigrants (Political and Economic Planning 1967). In more recent years, studies making use of ethnic data have evoked the theme of "racial disadvantage" (Brown 1984, Modood and Berthoud 1997, Smith 1974, Smith and Whalley 1975), reinforcing the conception of racism in Britain as linked to group belonging and nonwhite skin color.[3]

Beginning in the early 1960s, some politicians and liberal experts began to interpret Britain's "race problems" in North American terms. In 1962, the Institute of Race Relations commissioned a landmark study on race in Britain, modeled on Swedish social scientist Gunnar Myrdal's (1944a, 1944b) *An American Dilemma* (Rose 1969: xix–xxiii).[4] Believing that British racism was analogous to that of the United States, Canada, and even South Africa (interviews with Jowell, Lord Lester, July 8, and July 23, 1997), a small group of Labour Party lawyers sent one of its members to study North American provisions against discrimination in 1964. Examining and drawing on the North American analogy culminated in the mid-1970s with Home Secretary Jenkins' trip to the United States just prior to submitting antidiscrimination legislation in Parliament.

1958 / Notes and Memoranda 1958 / Press Cuttings 1960–1 / Memoranda etc. 1962–3, 1965").

[2] It was interpreted as many things, including as a threat to public order (Miles 1984). The point remains, however, that color rose to the fore as a salient key for many observers to understanding what was taking place.

[3] These reports also cite other factors (such as immigrants' language problems) that contribute to racial disadvantage.

[4] The IRR sought "A Myrdal for Britain while there was still time" (Rose 1969: xix).

Although throughout the 1960s many British political leaders had conceptualized British ethnic pluralism in terms of "race relations," progressives had been reluctant to argue that racial (or ethnic) groups existed, especially given some conservatives' use of racial categories as a tool for limiting minority participation in certain industries.[5] By the mid-1970s, however, drawing on lessons learned through comparison with North American policies, progressives came to accept the definition and even tabulation of racial or ethnic groups as a means to promote racial equality. Only by knowing exactly how unequal society was, they reasoned, could the country devise policies to overcome racial inequalities. One aspect of progressives' race frames – the North American analogy – therefore served to reshape another aspect – their views on racial categories. Over time, the belief in the counting and aiding of ethnic or racial minorities has spread throughout British society, with ethnic monitoring codified at the national level in the 1991 British census.

If Britain's frames focused attention primarily on access racism and interpreted problems largely in terms of conflict and inequalities between racial groups, France's race frames have differed substantially. Most French actors *refuse racial or ethnic categorization*, arguing that these types of distinctions are inherently socially divisive and therefore pernicious. Conceptualizations of prototypical racist acts have typically concentrated more on *expressive racism* and (especially early on) *anti-Semitism* than on discrimination against people because of their skin color. In addition, French policymakers and interest groups first ignored and subsequently *rejected the North American analogy* as relevant for their domestic situation. France's race frames are thus clearly distinguishable from those that prevail in Britain.

In contrast to the relatively noncontroversial use of the concepts race and ethnicity in many countries, most French activists, scholars, and politicians deliberately eschew such terms. For the Parliamentarian who drafted the final version of the 1972 law, "speaking of races is always a delicate matter, for we run the risk of giving credibility to the idea that there are different distinctions [*qualitatives*] within the human species."[6] Just such an accusation was launched at the scholar that used the term "ethnicity" in her mid-1990s study of French integration (Le Bras 1998,

[5] The 1968 Race Relations Act contained a provision allowing limits on immigrant workers in certain industries in the interest of preserving "racial balance" in the workplace (Lester and Bindman 1972: 140–1).

[6] Communication with Terrenoire, October 24, 1999.

Tribalat 1995), and skepticism about recognizing racial and ethnic groups also animates those who branded early 1980s proposals for a "right to difference" for minoritites as the first step down a slippery slope to a "difference of rights" (Taguieff 1987: 328–9). In short, race and ethnicity are terms that the French prefer to avoid rather than to embrace.

From the years following World War II through passage of the 1990 antiracism law, French policy experts and politicians have been most concerned about expressive racism. The MRAP's initial inspiration for forming an association and for pressing for the 1972 law was what it perceived to be resurgent anti-Semitism in films and in the press (MRAP 1984: 9–15). As a leading member of the MRAP recalls, during the decades immediately following the war, the predominant concerns of the group were "neonazism, the revival of anti-Semitism and the Cold War" (Lévy 1993: 3). The major portion of the antiracism bills submitted to Parliament in the second half of the twentieth century has sought to root out and to punish expressive racism, often making explicit reference to anti-Semitic speech.

French frames have focused relatively more on what is sometimes termed "Hitler" racism,[7] but it is important to note that France has not ignored other types of racism.[8] With increasing frequency, Parliamentarians and human rights groups cite anti-immigrant racism as a common French problem (see AN 9: 1296, and Lévy 1993). Even in earlier years, both the MRAP and antiracist policy entrepreneurs in the National Assembly made reference to this topic, although they argued that despite the presence of access racism in French society, it was not as prevalent as in other countries (AN 1: 38, Lyon-Caen 1959, Paraf 1964: 166–7). When the government briefly took up the cause of legislation in the early 1960s, however, it focused more attention on access than expressive racism, perhaps due to the historical context of decolonization.[9] When the antiracism law was finally passed in 1972, provisions against access racism were included and formed part of the core of French institutions. Yet, antiminority

[7] Submitting the MRAP's bills to Parliament in 1959, the Communist Party echoed this theme by regretting that "Hitlerism" had proven a school for perfecting propaganda for too many French citizens (AN 1: 37).

[8] In contrast to the situation in Britain, however, it is interesting to note that anti-immigrant racism in France is not necessarily seen as racism based on skin color; discrimination by color is not included in the list of offenses criminalized by the 1972 law.

[9] France was in the thick of the Algerian war. As noted in Chapter 5, the government eventually backed down from passing such a law in the early 1960s.

discrimination has remained the recessive theme of French race policies, and until recently attention to these issues has been sparse in academic and public debates.[10]

In passing the 1972 and 1990 laws, France did not identify its problems of racism with those in North America or Britain, even though they were in many ways identical. French race experts have rarely drawn on the context of the English-speaking world as a source of policy learning, routinely downplaying or denying parallels between the French and the American or British problems of racism.[11] Although the foreign service branch of the French government reportedly commissioned a study of British antidiscrimination laws in the 1960s,[12] it was almost certainly never read by the MRAP legal group nor by the Parliamentarians or Justice Ministry officials responsible for the 1972 law, as it was not present in any of the three groups' archives and there was no reference to it in public documents from the era. Moreover, the MRAP newsletter, which reported on racism issues around the globe, gave scant coverage to the major U.S. civil rights laws of the 1960s and to the British Race Relations Acts (see *Droit et Liberté*, 1963–76). When it scanned the international horizon in the late 1950s for information about race policies, the MRAP did not follow the approach of the British who turned first to North America. Rather, the MRAP focused more attention on Soviet bloc exemplars, arguing that antiracist legislation would bring France in line with laws or legal proposals in Germany, Poland, the USSR, Albania, Bulgaria, Romania, Czechoslovakia, and Yugoslavia, which had not hesitated to "reinforce the criminal fight against the after-effects of Hitler racism" (Lyon-Caen 1959).[13]

French race frames thus have an internal consistency and a distinctiveness from their British counterparts. Actors in the two countries have tended to think and talk about race and racism in different ways, and they have drawn on different analogies and contexts in analyzing their domestic situation. Of course, not everyone in Britain or France has held precisely the same frames. In some cases – especially the skeptical populists in Britain – actors have had diametrically opposed frame elements from

[10] Since the publication of a recent report on discrimination (Haut Conseil à l'Intégration 1998), attention to these issues has risen substantially in France.

[11] Interviews with Palant, Lévy, March 10, and March 19, 1997.

[12] Interviews with Lord Lester, July 23, 1997, De La Presle, July 28, 1997.

[13] The MRAP examined foreign countries primarily to buttress its case for a French law. They used such examples to get political attention, without necessarily drawing on foreign lessons in crafting their own proposals.

others in their country. Frames have also evolved over time. Progressives in Britain only gradually came to embrace the identification of individuals by race as a way to promote equality across divergent minority groups. Nevertheless, there remains a coherence to the prevailing frames in each country, and a continuity of these frames across time.

The Influence of Frames

Gauging frames' concrete impact on race policies can only be done in the context of evaluating the influence of the theoretical perspectives outlined in Chapter 2. What light do power-interest, problem-solving, institutional, and framing schools of thought shed on policy outcomes in Britain and France? Power-interest perspectives offer a useful starting point for understanding domestic policy choices and cross-national policy variation. As we have seen, bargaining among political actors within each country had an important impact on the contours of race legislation in several cases. This was particularly true during negotiations over the British Race Relations Act of 1965, when the government's proposals were radically overhauled mid-way through the legislative process in response to pressures from left and right. In 1968, British progressives and skeptics squared off in Parliament and hammered out compromises that were barely acceptable to each side. Power struggles also affected the final form of the 1990 French law, with the right succeeding in excising the penalty of civil rights losses for the journalism industry.

Nevertheless, these kinds of compromises were not always central to shaping policy outcomes, nor were the policy aspects they affected always central to the laws. Recall that the 1972 French law passed both the National Assembly and the Senate with unanimous support and with very few changes from the original MRAP proposals that dated back to the late 1950s. The British Race Relations Act of 1976 did not necessarily incorporate every item on the progressives' wish list, but there were many fewer compromises struck with the right than in previous rounds of legislation.

Power-interest variables are also not very useful in explaining cross-national race policy differences. In theory, different power resources of similar actors may account for different outcomes across countries. A strong versus a weak political left, for example, has been argued to influence policies on labor laws and the welfare state (Korpi 1983, Stephens 1979, Swenson 1991). In fact, the power resources of comparable actors in Britain and France – such as political parties and race bureaucracies – did vary during the formulation of each country's race policies. The French

1972 foundational law (and the 1978 and 1987 amendments) was passed under the aegis of a rightist government, in contrast to the sponsorship of all three British laws by the leftist Labour Party. Moreover, whereas in Britain the quasigovernmental bureaucracy (and to a lesser extent minorities themselves) weighed in during two of the three rounds of legislation, France's much weaker and much more recent advisory body has had little effect on the shape of policy outcomes.

Yet, the evidence suggests that the different power resources of the left, of minorities, and of race bureaucracies cannot explain cross-national policy differences. Simply stated, analogous actors in Britain and France advocated different policy outcomes. For the power-resource arguments to persuade, we would expect that had a leftist government been in power in 1970s France, the outcome of the law would have resembled the British laws passed by Labour governments. This is not so. The proposals for the French law of 1972 originated in the Communist Party. Moreover, the Communists and the Socialists unanimously supported the rightist government's final version. Had the French left been in power, therefore, the law would not have mirrored Britain's Labour-sponsored initiatives, but would in all likelihood have looked identical to the final version passed by the French right in 1972.

In addition, liberal, human rights interest groups in each country differed over their preferred policies. Once progressives came to dominate the British race bureaucracy, they supported policies such as positive action, ethnic monitoring, and civil law sanctions for access racism. Their counterparts in France, by contrast, have rarely if ever supported such policies. Had French progressives been installed in an official race bureaucracy, therefore, it is unlikely that the two countries' policies would have converged. It has been analogous actors' different goals, rather than their different power resources, that better account for cross-national policy variation.[14]

Assessing the problem-solving school of thought, it is important to recognize that several elements of British and French institutions came about as a direct result of perceived problems with preexisting institutions. Notably, when British policy experts shifted access racism enforcement in 1976 toward civil courts, they did so as a response to the weaknesses of the administrative conciliation approach. Allowing victims of racism to take their cases directly to court was viewed as a way to encourage quicker

[14] There is no evidence of behind-the-scenes similarities in underlying goals between British and French experts or politicians.

and more effective resolutions to complaints. French law's establishment of criminal penalties for access racism and of the right for antiracist associations to participate in the legal process was a reaction to the perceived ineffectiveness of preexisting civil law measures and state enforcement of the laws. Moreover, passage of the 1990 French law and the submission of a 1996 government bill were in part a response to statements made by far right leader Jean-Marie Le Pen about the Holocaust being merely a "detail of history" and about the "inequality of the races."

Stating that policy outcomes responded to societal and political problems is not sufficient to explain race policies in the two countries, however, because it does not clarify why a particular problem was perceived to require a particular solution. For example, why did the rise of Le Pen and his rhetoric generate the passage (and, later, the proposed passage) of expressive racism legislation when the rise of Enoch Powell in Britain in the 1960s and 1970s did not provoke a similar response? Throughout their histories, Britain and France have each faced problems of access, expressive, and physical racism. Each legislated against access and expressive racism (leaving physical racism largely aside[15]); yet each passed laws that diverged substantially from those of its neighbor. In other words, similar problems in the two countries led to very different policy solutions. This is not to dispute that there were differences in the level or kind of problems faced in particular instances. But it suggests that policy choices and cross-national policy differences cannot all be chalked up to material differences in problems of racism.

How well do institutional perspectives explain the race policy outcomes in these two countries? As with the power-interest and problem-solving approaches, institutional variables do account for some elements of race policies in the two countries. When establishing expressive racism bans, for example, each country drew on fledgling extant laws as points of reference. Britain integrated its incitement provisions within the 1936 Public Order Act in 1976.[16] French policy experts constructed their expressive racism proposals to be compatible with the language of the 1939 Marchandeau decree (which referred to the 1881 press law), explicitly calculating that this formulation would win Parliamentary allies. Moreover, the 1990 French law banning denial of Nazi war crimes leaned heavily

[15] France allows antiracist associations to participate in court cases involving violent crime motivated by racism and Britain passed a Crime and Disorder Act in 1998 to address the issue of racially aggravated offences. The primary path for punishing physical racism, however, remains laws targeted at race-neutral crimes.

[16] Eleven years after it created them in the 1965 Race Relations Act.

on international treaties and court decisions for definitions of the crimes that it became illegal to contest. In each of these cases, however, the desire to pass a law banning expressive racism or revisionism preceded the search for an appropriate institutional formula. Therefore, although the preexisting institutions influenced the final wording of the laws, they did not determine the presence or absence of expressive racism or revisionism clauses in either country.

Institutions appear to have assumed a more influential explanatory role for two elements of the French structures. The 1972 law allowed antiracist associations to become civil parties in cases of racism, providing them with the power to initiate court proceedings even when the public prosecutor declined to do so. In 1990, the state delegated power to judges to deprive convicted racists of certain civil rights, notably the right to stand for election. These particular elements were greatly facilitated by institutional rules that grated civil party status to other types of groups and permitted deprivation of civil rights for other types of offenses. Although it is possible to imagine these elements in British law, they are more plausibly seen as instruments viable only in the pre-existing French institutional context.

If institutional factors succeed in illuminating some outcomes, however, they cannot explain many of the differences between British and French policies. One might hypothesize that the similar British and American common law legal systems account for the facility with which Britain adopted an administrative-civil approach to policymaking whereas the Romano-Germanic legal tradition in France favored the establishment of criminal procedures.[17] Yet, this is not the case. The United States' common law institutions have proven fully compatible with criminal sanctions for racist crimes. Criminal procedures predominated in the early years of antidiscrimination law in North America; only later did administrative procedures develop slowly at the state level (Jowell 1965: 164–8). Moreover, during the early stages of British institutionalization, political leaders and legal experts such as Home Secretary Frank Soskice felt that the criminal law approach was "more in line with [British] legal tradition" (Hindell 1965: 398). There was therefore no natural fit between the administrative–civil approach and common law systems.

Moreover, France's institutions were as adaptable to the administrative and civil law model as British ones. Civil (employment) laws barring

[17] On comparative legal systems, see David and Brierley (1985).

discrimination in the workplace currently exist in France. Although they have rarely been invoked (Vourc'h, de Rudder, and Tripier 1996: 160), there is no institutional reason why they could not become the principal mechanism for sanctioning job-related forms of access racism.[18] France also has precedents for British-style administrative commissions.[19] The French government's human rights advisory group (the CNCDH) could itself have been adapted into an equivalent to Britain's Commission for Racial Equality, given adequate political will. In 2000, the French government set up the Group for the Study of and Struggle Against Discriminations (Groupe d'Etude et de Lutte contre les Discriminations, or GELD) designed to undertake certain antidiscrimination initiatives (Commission Nationale Consultative des Droits de l'Homme 2001: 109–34). Although this organization is not equivalent in strength to Britain's CRE, it – or some other organization – may eventually become a comparable administrative body. Furthermore, race-conscious policies such as positive action and ethnic monitoring had no domestic precedent in either country, yet they were adopted in Britain but not in France. They, like antirevisionist policies (adopted in France but not in Britain), were wholly new concoctions. It is therefore difficult to argue that such divergent policy outcomes were deeply influenced by preexisting institutional configurations.

How well do frames succeed in illuminating race policy choices in the two countries? In several key instances, race experts and politicians in Britain developed their policy proposals based explicitly upon the study of North American provisions against access racism based on color. During deliberations over the 1965 Race Relations Act, the Society of Labour Lawyers working group – and later CARD – advocated a conciliation-based administrative apparatus (backed by civil courts) rather than criminal sanctions for countering access racism.[20] Having visited North America on a fact-finding tour, Jeffrey Jowell (1965: 168) argued that "discrimination, as American and Canadian experience has shown, can be successfully diminished by a law; more particularly by its administrative enforcement." Although policy experts were beginning to draw on

[18] In fact, in 2001, the French Parliament passed a law making it easier to prove discrimination in employment courts.

[19] Such as the Commission Nationale Informatique et Libertés (CNIL). While its strength and effectiveness may be debatable, it is not radically different in form or relative power from Britain's Commission for Racial Equality.

[20] They also demonstrated the feasibility of sanctions against employment and housing discrimination; these provisions were not enacted until 1968.

it heavily, the North American analogy was not universally accepted in Britain by the mid-1960s. The Labour government itself ignored overseas lessons when it introduced its 1964 bill proposing criminal penalties for access racism. Labour's own backbenchers and the Conservative opposition countered by calling for an "American solution" (Lester and Bindman 1972: 112–15, Hansard 711: 926–1060). As the Conservative shadow Home Secretary stated:

> This attempt to import the taint of criminality into this aspect of our affairs will not work.... [The Home Secretary] must have studied, as I and my right hon. Friends have studied, the practice in the United States of America. Everyone will tell him, if he will ask, or if his officials will ask, that it will not work in the United States of America. We have rather a good test case there, because some of the States have applied the criminal solution and others have adopted the conciliation method. Where they have adopted conciliation, it has, on the whole, worked not too badly; where they have tried the criminal approach, it has not worked at all, or practically not at all. (Hansard 711: 948)

In the end, North American policy solutions prevailed and helped cement the perception that lessons from overseas were indeed germane to British race policy choices.

During the build-up to the 1968 Race Relations Act, concerned parties focused their attention on the problem of access racism in employment and housing, two areas not covered by the 1965 law (Lester and Bindman 1972: 122–9, Race Relations Board 1967: 15).[21] Once again attention turned to the North American exemplar. When the newly-established Race Relations Board commissioned a report on the state of international legislation against such discrimination, it focused the vast majority of its attention on North American laws and policies (Street, Howe, and Bindman 1967). Although not all of the report's specific recommendations were enacted by Parliament, the 1968 Race Relations Act extended coverage to access racism in employment, housing, and provision of a wider range of goods and services. These solutions were viewed as legitimate and effective means of tackling problems of color discrimination given lessons learned from the North American context.

The 1976 Race Relations Act continued to respond to problems of color racism, with an even stronger emphasis on minority rights and group-based inequalities. Drawing on the North American analogy, the Home Secretary and his expert advisor learned of the practical value of indirect

[21] With the minor exception of a ban on discriminatory housing covenants (Lester and Bindman 1972: 423).

discrimination and positive action provisions during a 1974 trip to the United States (Lester 1994: 227). Returning to Britain, they redrafted the government bills to include these elements in British antidiscrimination law (interview with Lord Lester, July 23, 1997). British leaders' focus on access racism as the most important dimension of the problem (even in an era punctuated by Enoch Powell's public appeal to nativist sentiment), their evolving views on equality among minority groups, and their learning from the American context were therefore as central to producing Britain's race-conscious policies as the country's race frames were in shaping earlier policy decisions.[22]

French race frames differed from their British counterparts in their focus on anti-Semitism and expressive racism, by valuing color-blindness and race neutrality, and by largely ignoring or rejecting the North American analogy. In contrast to British debates, French debates over their first antiracism law contained virtually no references to North American or even to British laws against racism, even though these Anglo-Saxon countries each had an extensive repertoire of provisions by 1972. In particular, French policy experts did not examine the possibility of establishing a state structure to lead the fight against racism, nor did they consider developing civil law remedies for punishing access racism. Instead, they focused on their domestic context to assess their societal problems and to generate policy ideas.

Because the MRAP and its Parliamentary allies deemed France's pre-1972 expressive racism laws weakly enforced by a virtually uninterested state (see AN 4: 2357 and MRAP 1984), they (along with other human rights interest groups) shied away from advocating an administrative solution and lobbied for legal powers for antiracist associations. According to one lawyer working in the field, an antiracist commission would be weak and ineffectual, masking powerlessness and inactivity with rhetoric and reports (interview with Sellami, January 28, 1997). Moreover, because they viewed the limited civil and administrative procedures relevant to access racism as "complicated and expensive," they proposed criminal sanctions, "the mere threat of which will be more effective than the provisions currently in place" (Lyon-Caen 1959).

The French aversion to race consciousness manifests itself in the widespread rejection of affirmative action policies, which have been

[22] Britain has by no means adopted all of the North American provisions on discrimination, nor has it taken on board policies without adapting them to its national needs, institutions and situations.

deemed dangerous and counter-productive in the fight against racism.[23] The tendency to take race out of antiracism also appears clearly in the 1978 law on information storage and freedom (*informatique et liberté*),[24] which outlawed computerized storage of data on racial origins without the express consent of the individual or (in cases of public interest) of the state. When asked about this aspect of the French law with regard to immigrant groups in the 1990s, one influential French administrator reflected:

> What would we have to have? Legislation which says that one is recognized as being an immigrant, in order to have special rights, if one has parents of foreign origin or has at least two grand-parents of foreign origin. That would be an acceptable definition. Do you know what that is? That is the ordinance of 18 November 1940 which defines the Jew according to the Vichy regime, which says that one is a Jew if one has one Jewish parent or two Jewish grand-parents. It is impossible to imagine a French law which uses this formulation. It would have a frightening effect. It is absolute evil.[25]

Throughout the 1980s and 1990s, French policies continued to respond primarily to the twin concerns of perceived domestic institutional inefficiencies and "Hitler" racism. Parliamentary groups of all stripes have hammered on themes of Nazism, proposing and passing laws to ban the apology of Nazism, the apology of crimes against humanity, and eventually challenges to the historical existence of the Holocaust. By comparison, these efforts and laws have been wholly absent in Britain. Moreover, the brunt of French policymakers' and interest groups' attention through the late 1990s has been on expressive racism, particularly prominent given the success of Jean-Marie Le Pen's National Front and his less than amiable statements about immigrants and Jews.

Acts of expressive, "Hitler" racism have therefore been the predominant concern of most institutional initiatives in France, with access and "anti-immigrant" racism relegated to the political and policy back burners for the majority of the postwar era. French antiracist entrepreneurs have learned primarily from their existing domestic structures rather than identifying with the American or British analogies, and have focused more on formal equality before the law than on substantive equalities between

[23] As in the United States, affirmative action policies are often tarred with the "quota" brush to further delegitimize them (interview with Fellous, March 17, 1997). For an elaboration on traditional French attitudes toward affirmative action, see Bleich (2001).

[24] Law number 78-17.

[25] Confidential interview, Paris, June 30, 1997.

racial or ethnic groups. British policies were simply not viewed as effective or appropriate solutions to France's concerns over racism, given French interpretations and value judgments about race and racism and the context in which leaders assessed their problems. France's race frames have influenced its policy choices, leading the country down a significantly different path from that of Great Britain.

Integrating Frames into Models of Comparative Public Policymaking

As influential as frames were in shaping the course of policymaking in Britain and France, they were not the only factors that determined race policies. Systematically integrating frames into studies of comparative public policymaking necessitates moving beyond a head-to-head comparison of theoretical perspectives and the underlying implication that any one perspective can offer a comprehensive explanation of policy outcomes. In order to judge the respective roles of frames and other variables, it is helpful to ask a series of questions relevant to every study of the policymaking process. Who are the actors responsible for initiatives? What are those actors' goals? And what factors constrain or enable their actions? In short, to understand the direction policies take, we need to know which individuals or groups are involved in the process, what they hope to accomplish, and what influences on their interactions help to funnel outcomes in a particular direction.

No single perspective on policymaking has cornered the market on explaining these issues. It is possible, however, to use the ensemble of these perspectives as a tool kit to generate hypotheses about actors, goals, and influences that can be tested against instances of policymaking that interest us. In any individual case, one type of explanation may trump another, or one type of variable may be particularly significant or uninteresting. When examining a variety of cases, by contrast, it is more important to grasp how the theoretical perspectives address the three key questions in order to estimate which tools are most appropriate for which tasks.

When searching for the actors most responsible for policy initiatives, for example, the power-interest and problem-solving perspectives draw our attention to the impact of a variety of specific groups ranging from political party leaderships to lobbyists to coalitions or "middlemen" that cut across traditional boundaries. These perspectives provide a useful point of departure for identifying actors undertaking policy initiatives. Institutional and ideational perspectives often help round out our understanding of why some groups are involved in certain policy spheres – because they are required to be by a constitution, for example, or because they have special legitimacy in a particular domain – yet they rarely identify groups outside the universe of those considered by the first two schools of thought. Power-interest and problem-solving perspectives are thus typically a more fruitful point of departure for comprehending the actors most responsible for policy initiatives.

Power-interest perspectives also highlight common motives in policymaking episodes, such as gaining votes, enhancing political influence, expanding bureaucratic turf, or maximizing economic benefits. Problem-solving perspectives highlight an additional range of goals. Public officials may puzzle over the best solutions to societal concerns such as equality and prosperity, seeking to achieve outcomes that benefit a wide variety of people. Knowing that practitioners set their sights on eliminating racism or even on "growing" the economy, however, only helps if we know their conceptions of those terms. Frames are well-placed to reveal just this, and thus provide crucial insight into actors' goals. Institutional perspectives, while they sometimes highlight the impact of standard operating procedures or bureaucratic motives ("where you stand depends on where you sit"), are on the whole not crafted to account for actors' motives.

Institutional accounts blossom when it comes to understanding the constraints and the enabling factors that influence policy outcomes. Written and unwritten laws, preexisting policies, conventions, and norms all shape interactions among actors, encouraging certain policy trajectories and discouraging others. In addition, power distributions constitute central influences on the policymaking process. The number of voters mobilized, rocks thrown, or guns in the hands of supporters can have an obvious impact on policy outcomes. For their part, frames can also constrain and enable policymaking. Beliefs about what race and racism are, for example, shape the range of policy options considered, ruling out options in one country that seem natural and effective in another. This may tilt the balance of probable action in a particular direction.

Ideas can help analysts of comparative public policymaking to understand which actors are involved in policymaking, what their goals are, and what influences constrain or enable their action, thereby contributing to explanations of policy outcomes. In the cases of race policymaking presented here, they most clearly influence cross-national policy differences because distributions of frames were, on average, quite different across countries. Within each country, frames helped to propel policy in a particular direction. But the range of policy choices within each country was not determined solely or rigidly by frames. Domestic policy outcomes depended on the internal distribution of frames as well as on the distribution of power resources, the constellation and salience of material or power interests, concrete manifestations of racism, and the constraints of pre-existing institutions.[26]

Frames are tools in our analytical belt, and just as with other variables, they are more helpful at some points and in some cases than in others. In general, frames are more likely to speak to actors' goals and the constraints and enabling factors influencing their actions than they are to identify the key actors in play. Both in the cases examined here and in general, however, it is necessary not only to contrast frames to other factors, but also to examine how they work side-by-side and even interact with variables highlighted by other schools of thought. Much takes place at the overlap and interstices of the various perspectives.

When Do Frames Matter Most?

Understanding how frames matter and how they fit into general approaches to policymaking is essential, yet it is equally vital to assess the conditions under which frames are likely to influence policy outcomes. In other words, when do frames matter most? Although this study was not explicitly designed to answer this question, it does provide evidence that speaks to this issue.[27] To grasp the conditions under which frames affect policy outcomes, it is first necessary to examine how frames are distributed within a polity.

If frames are distributed unimodally – that is, shared by a wide variety of actors – they are likely to be quite important to policymaking. Sometimes, the fundamental underlying agreements over frames within a polity and how they shape domestic policy outcomes are only apparent once we contrast them with frames that prevail outside of that political unit. In the cases of British and French race policies, for example, no matter how deep the internal divisions in each country, there was often a set of common assumptions about the meaning of race, prototypical racist acts, and the relevance of foreign models to domestic debates. That each country's policymaking participants may have been unaware of this does not mean that the frames were unimportant. It is only possible to observe and judge

[26] I thank Ira Katznelson for a conversation that helped clarify this point.

[27] Scholarship that addresses this question directly (although not necessarily exclusively) includes Goldstein (1988), Hall (1989), Hall (1993b), Berman (1998), and especially Walsh (2000) and Hansen and King (2001).

the influence of domestic frames by contrasting them to prevailing frames elsewhere.

Simply because frames are unimodally distributed, however, does not automatically mean that they are stable or influential. Frames gain influence when they attain a taken-for-granted quality that closes off potential challenges to them. As was evident in the debates over the British Race Relations Act of 1965, the North American analogy was not yet taken for granted by all; in fact, for the Conservatives, it was more of a tool to advance party interests. The North American analogy was therefore important in part because of its perceived "fit" with political interests of powerful actors (see Hall 1989, Hall 1993b). Nevertheless, because there is a tendency for actors to maintain their frames over time rather than to radically overhaul them, there may be a "first mover advantage" to a particular framing of a policy issue, such that if a frame becomes dominant early in the history of a policy sphere, it tends to perdure,[28] especially if it is inscribed in written institutions (see Berman 1998, Goldstein 1988). Students of American policymaking, spin doctors, and lobbyists know that being the first to frame an issue can have a substantial impact on others' interpretations of events and therefore on the future path of policy. In both Britain and France, the early efforts of Labour lawyers, the MRAP, and other associations structured debates about race and have had a lasting influence on each country's policy choices.

Although frames are likely to be influential when distributed unimodally, they were not always uniform within Britain and France, nor are they likely to be in other cases. Policymaking rarely takes place without some level of conflict over frames. When frames are distributed in a multimodal fashion – where there is disagreement over fundamental cognitive or moral maps within a policy sphere – there are several conditions under which they are likely to matter. They can strongly influence outcomes if they are dominant in a subsection of the population that has control over the levers of power. If frames differ across party lines and one party controls the national Parliament, it may impose on its opponents policy solutions influenced by its frames. In a similar vein, even if frames are widely distributed, they may have a substantial impact if political institutions confine decisionmaking power to a small group of individuals who themselves share policy frames. Institutions (such as independent central banks, for example) may serve to narrow the range of actors in a

[28] Another way to phrase this is that there is a "first consolidator advantage," a term inspired by Thelen's (2000) critique of "first mover advantage" arguments.

policy sphere, allocating power to bureaucrats and insulating them from outside pressures.[29]

Finally, even if frames are widely dispersed, the perceived salience of the issue at hand can affect which frames (and therefore which policies) are considered. The more salient an issue, the longer it is considered and the more seriously alternative frames may be examined. Low salience may circumscribe the range of participants interested in involving themselves in the decisionmaking process, thereby limiting the emergence of a variety of possible frames and rendering disproportionately significant those that remain. A case in point is the French law of 1972, enacted at a time when racism was not considered a particularly vital issue by the government. The legislature therefore passed the Parliamentary proposals on the table without rigorously examining policy alternatives. The frames that marked those proposals thus had a tremendous impact on the policies established.

The Origins of Race Frames

Beyond understanding the conditions under which frames have the greatest impact, it is also important to consider where frames come from and why they may change. If frames are truly significant causal variables that account for policy outcomes, it is worth exploring their own causes. Yet there is a dispute among scholars over the value of analyzing the origins of ideas. Berman (2001) argues that without attention to ideas as dependent variables, ideational arguments are weakened. Kingdon (1995), in contrast, warns against the dangers of infinite regress in tracing the wellspring of ideas. It is possible to strike a balance in this debate by peeling back one layer of the ideational onion – in other words, by explaining policy outcomes with reference to frames, and then by exploring the most significant and proximate causes of those frames. This strategy provides a stronger base for an ideational argument without succumbing to the problematic seductions of infinite regress. It serves to unveil the origins of ideas without getting lost in their history.

What forces serve to generate frames in a policy sphere?[30] Scholars have developed at least five perspectives on the origins of ideas that can

[29] On how the number of actors can affect policymaking, see Schattschneider (1960); with applications to immigration politics, see Guiraudon (2000); with reference to the impact of ideas, see Walsh (2000) and Hansen and King (2001).

[30] Note that this is different from understanding the conditions under which new ideas are likely to take hold in a polity (see Berman 2001).

shed light on this question. Structuralists point to objective differences in social structures, such as class or geography, as the sources of ideas that influence views on issues such as capitalism or nationhood.[31] Instrumentalists argue that ideas are chosen and rise to the fore because they correspond to the interests of influential actors. In a world replete with competing and contrasting views, this perspective asserts, actors pick and choose ideas that serve their interests.[32] Institutional approaches highlight the wholesale transfer of ideas from one institutional sphere to another, the power of ideas that are embedded in important institutions, or the role that institutions can play in filtering new ideas.[33] Scholars working in an informational vein typically stress the influence of objective, environmental stimuli on individuals' and groups' actions. Learning theories emphasize the role of such stimuli in altering frames of reference and, ultimately, action.[34] Finally, interpretive analysts suggest that individual policymakers and society as a whole come to acquire their frames principally through socialization, a process through which "norms and ideals are transmitted from one party to another" (Checkel 1999: 4).

These perspectives have each proved enlightening in numerous spheres of policymaking, and indeed, offer important insights into the origin of

[31] Classic structuralists like Marx or Pareto advance these arguments (see Hall 1993a). In a more contemporary vein, Inglehart (1977; 1990; 1997) draws on similar premises when discussing the causes of value change and the rise of post-materialist ideas in Western societies since World War II; Brubaker (1992) has argued that variation in European political geography best accounts for France's political and territorial versus Germany's ethno-cultural idioms of citizenship; and Todd claims that differences in nations' integration of immigrants can be explained by legacies of family structures. According to Todd, universalist ideas of inclusion are found in societies in which inheritance was divided equally among brothers, whereas societies which favored the eldest brother developed differentialist modes of viewing new immigrant populations (Todd 1994: 13).

[32] The bulk of the U.S. policymaking literature, for example, views framing as a conscious process of manipulating ideas in order to advance private interests. For Stone (1989: 282), "political actors *deliberately portray* [conditions, difficulties or issues] in ways calculated to gain support for their side." See also Baumgartner and Jones (1993: 23), for whom policy domains are characterized by "the strategic struggle over the definition of issues."

[33] For a variety of perspectives on the interaction between institutions and ideas see Dobbin (1994), Goldstein (1988, 1993), March and Olsen (1989), Hall (1989), Weir (1992), and Bleich (1998).

[34] For Shrivastava (1983: 17), learning "involves a reorientation of worldviews of important decision-makers, as well as structural and procedural changes, to incorporate the newly acquired knowledge." Bayesian theory operates from a similar starting point, typically stressing that "the acquisition of new evidence impacts on previous degrees of belief to produce new degrees of belief" (Earman 1992: 34).

race frames in Britain and France. Nevertheless, it is the interpretive school of thought that provides the most compelling key to understanding the two countries' race frames. Socialization through formative experiences and discourse has had a tremendous impact on the way race frames were molded and forged.[35] Lived experiences – either individual or shared with a cohort – can form the building blocks of an actor's frames. This appears to be particularly true if the experiences constitute "formative moments" of youth.[36] Discourses such as those that dominate the political culture or those that are prominent in schools and in conversations with family, friends, and colleagues also serve to convey frame elements. They help actors work out their beliefs through interactions with others (Finnemore 1996, Wildavsky 1987).[37]

Lived experiences and discourses are central sources of race frames in Britain and France. Formative personal experiences played a particularly visible role in accounting for British policy experts' attentions to color-based access racism and the North American analogy. Many of the original group of the Society of Labour Lawyers who were influential in introducing these themes in the 1965 and 1968 rounds of race relations legislation had studied at Harvard Law School, gaining exposure to the American race and legal context.[38] Moreover, a key proponent and advocate of antidiscrimination legislation throughout all three Race Relations Acts (Anthony Lester) had served as a civil rights observer in the American South in the early 1960s (Lester 1996). These personal experiences helped reinforce the connections between Britain and North America and led to visits by actors who subsequently penned influential reports about the value of North American lessons to British race concerns (Jowell 1965; Street, Howe, and Bindman 1967). In addition, the prevailing discourse in 1960s and 1970s Britain encouraged high-level politicians such as Home

[35] I omit the path of socialization Checkel (1999: 4–6) calls "social mobilization." I do so because social mobilization arguments focus in the first instance on the effect of norm-motivated groups' restructuring of the instrumental choices of elites, without describing either how groups get imbued with the norm and without specifying how elites themselves come to embrace new identities.

[36] For parallel arguments in the fields of political parties and American foreign policy see Duverger (1954: xxiii) and May (1973: 18).

[37] Deviating from the "accepted" norms prompts social sanctions of disapproval. While these socialization mechanisms are rarely strong enough to *determine* any one person's attitudes or actions, interpretivists argue that they influence broad, societal distributions of prevailing ideas.

[38] Other important advocates of North American style policies in Britain over the years – such as Shirley Williams and Roderick MacFarquar – also had long-standing ties with North America.

Secretary Roy Jenkins to travel overseas and to attend to developments in U.S. and Canadian race policies.

If the personal experiences of policy experts were critical catalysts to the development of British race frames, these factors cannot necessarily account for broader acceptance of frame elements among politicians, the media and the public. Longstanding contacts with the United States and with the Commonwealth and colonies also helped pave the way to 1960s British race frames. The arrival of black American soldiers and West Indian immigrants in the 1940s and the contemporaneous concern with racial problems in the colonies facilitated the adoption of the race relations paradigm on British soil (King 1995: 133–6; Rich 1986: 169–2). Although this paradigm was transmitted in Britain partly through institutionalized colonial contacts,[39] it was also fostered by the Edinburgh school of anthropology which spawned authors such as Kenneth Little and Michael Banton, whose seminal studies of blacks in Britain helped to shape postwar conceptions of the issues at stake. These authors, in turn, were influenced by the development of race relations as an object of study in the 1920s by Robert Park and the Chicago school of sociology (Rich 1986: 170).[40]

The shift to more widespread public acceptance of color as a central element of British race frames came with the politicization of immigrant tensions in a racialized manner. Although the 1958 riots in Nottingham and Notting Hill involved fights between immigrants and native-born British, populist politicians and the media soon characterized the conflict as race-based and advocated race-based solutions of halting immigration (Miles 1984). Immigration was indeed significantly restricted by the 1962 Commonwealth Immigrants Act as the Conservatives (and soon after, Labour) followed the wishes of the public, quite willing to see the solution to their problems in racialized terms given prevailing cultural beliefs about "dark strangers."[41] Finally, the instrumentalist use of race by Peter Griffiths during the 1964 campaign in the borough of Smethwick and later statements by Enoch Powell cemented the elite vision of color

[39] Rich (1986: 174) states that "at the 1949 Commonwealth Relations Conference held at Bigwin Inn, Ontario, there was more discussion on 'racial problems' than on 'colonial policies.' "

[40] Although cross-fertilization took place, Rich (1986: 192) notes that the British researchers did not simply accept American race relations theories as developed by the Chicago school.

[41] To quote the title of Sheila Patterson's (1965) book. See Paul (1997) for an alternative view of the relationship between elites, masses, and race.

and race as potentially explosive lines of social conflict and as meriting attention on those terms.

To help understand why anti-Semitism became a fundamental part of the French race frame that influenced the 1972 law, it is essential to identify the coterie of policy experts engaged with the issue of racism. The groups that were the principal carriers of the antiracism project were human rights organizations, such as the Human Rights League, the LICA and the MRAP, founded respectively during the Dreyfus Affair of the 1890s, in the 1920s in response to anti-Semitic East European pogroms, and during the Vichy regime of the 1940s. Members of these associations – and especially members of the MRAP – were therefore particularly sensitized to racism of the Vichy type. Although the state repeatedly denied that anti-Semitism was resurgent in the 1950s and 1960s, and although the majority of the country avoided reflecting on Vichy by accepting the myth of "resistancialism" (Rousso 1994: 10), members of the MRAP and other groups continued to compile a catalogue of racism during these years. At the top of their list were anti-Semitic acts that recalled the 1930s and 1940s, the fall of the Third Republic, and the rise of the Vichy regime. Several MRAP members were in the Resistance (some were Jewish) and had survived deportation to Nazi camps. They were therefore indelibly marked by their war experiences and clung to the antiracist project even when it was an issue of low salience for the rest of the nation. When the political class legislated in 1972, as we saw in Chapter 5, it adopted the long-standing MRAP-inspired proposals originally influenced by a definition of the problems of racism that focused primarily on anti-Semitism.[42]

Close attention to expressive racism flowed not only from antiracist association members' personal experiences, but also from more widespread societal memories of the 1930s and the Vichy era. Although there was undoubtedly access racism prior to 1945, the Third Republic had shown itself relatively open to the socioeconomic and political rise of Jews.[43] In spite of many Jews' passionate dedication to the Republic, there remained

[42] According to Rousso's (1994: 10) timeline, by 1972, the "Vichy syndrome" had entered its third phase: the myth of resistancialism was broken and there was a "return of the repressed." It is not clear, however, that this had any direct impact on the antiracism law of 1972. The fourth phase of the syndrome – which included a reawakening of Jewish memory – did not begin until 1974 (Rousso 1994: 10).

[43] Birnbaum (1992: 488–90) recounts that in spite of the fact that there were domains that were closed to Jews (such as the *Inspection de Finances*, the *Cour des Comptes* and the *Quai d'Orsay*), there were many "state Jews" (*Juifs d'Etat*) who were highly successful in the Republic and who were therefore faithful servants of France.

openly anti-Semitic newspapers and groups that engaged in expressive racism throughout the first decades of the twentieth century. These actions prompted the 1939 Marchandeau decree, which subsequently formed the focal point for postwar antiracist actions. The rebirth of anti-Semitic publications and films in the 1940s and 1950s, however marginal they may have been, triggered MRAP and other human rights groups' memories of the 1930s and of the disastrous path to Vichy, just as later statements by Le Pen and others on the far right have done for the public at large in recent decades.

France's penchant for equality before the law as opposed to substantive equality – a corollary of its race frames – is grounded to a large extent on a shared discourse about the lessons of the French Revolution and of Vichy.[44] Most French citizens agree that the Republican tradition does not permit groups such as races or ethnicities to make identitarian claims on the state. Moreover, because ethnic marking was used for the nefarious purpose of isolating and deporting Jews during World War II, it is difficult to convince anyone in France that categorizing individuals in this way is acceptable practice. Historical memories therefore help to create an especially strong stigma against unequal treatment by race or ethnicity.

A broad skepticism about the potential for the United States to serve as a positive model tilts the balance even further away from the possibility of recognizing race and ethnicity. Centuries-old competition over visions of universalism (Hoffmann 2000) underpins the running rhetorical snipings of the French elite vis-à-vis America, which, if not constant or uniform, continue to mark relations between the two countries into the new millennium.[45] Whereas from the 1920s through the 1970s, anti-American sentiment in France focused primarily on modes of production and consumption (Mathy 1993: 2), in the waning decades of the century, strategies for organizing ethnic pluralism, immigration, and integration have been elevated to code red status among influential intellectuals.[46] As Fassin (1999: 226) writes, describing a much cited 1989 article by the high-profile Régis Debray, "when discussing the politics of multiculturalism, 'America' is the Other – a radically different culture of cultural difference."

[44] For an extended discussion of the factors influencing the "color-blind" model in France, see Bleich (2001).

[45] See Mathy (1993) for an excellent overview of elite French writings about America, both negative and positive.

[46] See reviews by Granjon (1994) and Fassin (1999), as well as the writings of authors such as Todd (1994).

As important as political culture and historical memory are, one must avoid the conclusion that any and all elements of discourse or experience shape frames. It is often thought that differences between British and French modes of managing issues of integration are in some way related to their imperial pasts. Favell (1998: 3–4), for example, states:

> The responses of France and Britain [to the problematic of immigration], as befits their respective colonial reputations, appear to be almost reversed mirror images of one [an]other: France emphasizing the universalist idea of integration, of transforming immigrants into full French *citoyens*; Britain seeing integration as a question of managing public order and relations between majority and minority populations, and allowing ethnic cultures and practices to mediate the process.

However, there is little evidence tying either race policies or race frames directly to modes of colonization or decolonization in either country. Given that there were many more similarities than dissimilarities in the management of the two countries' imperial holdings,[47] it is difficult to argue that divergent race frames correlate with divergent colonial pasts. Moreover, and most tellingly, few policymakers or practitioners in postwar Britain or France referred to colonial lessons when discussing how to fight domestic racism. Contrary to what may be assumed, the memories and experiences of empire do not appear to have been central influences on each country's domestic race frames.

Unlike some models of political culture or national traditions perspectives that view ideas as fixed and immutable, framing arguments hold that ideas are subject to change and that they are no less significant because they evolve over time. When analyzing frame change as opposed to the origins of frames, informational models of learning seem more appropriate explanatory tools than interpretive models of socialization. British progressives' qualified acceptance of the concepts of race and ethnicity in policymaking, for example, came about because of their learning from the North American model that monitoring ethnic groups could serve to promote racial integration. Shifting contexts and new information available through exposure to international arenas such as the European Union or the United Nations can also alter conceptions about race and racism. Exposure to new ideas, information, and discourse is never sufficient to

[47] By this I mean that the thumbnail sketch of British colonial policies as encompassing indirect rule and management of races versus French strategies of direct rule and assimilation is too simple a characterization since each country used a similarly wide variety of approaches in its colonies (see Fieldhouse 1981, Heussler 1971, von Albertini 1982, von Albertini and Wirz 1982).

guarantee a transition, but it can open a window of opportunity for individuals to reconsider their policy frames.

It is clear that no single variable or explanatory framework can account for British and French race frames. Structural, instrumental, institutional, informational, and interpretive elements all played a role in molding frames at various stages of each country's history. Nevertheless, because frame elements in both countries are so closely associated with specific groups of actors, we must look first to the factors that directed their attention to color racism versus anti-Semitism, that impelled them to draw on the North American analogy or not, and that encouraged them to embrace forms of group equality thinking or to adhere to formal equality before the law. Doing so demonstrates that personal experiences of core actors, discourses found in political cultures, and memories of national historical experiences explain the lion's share of leading actors' thought processes. Socialization variables thus prove essential to understanding British and French race frames and are likely to provide a useful starting point for analyzing the origins of frames in a variety of policy spheres.

Conclusion

The trajectories of British and French race policies and the significant differences between them cannot be accounted for without closely examining each country's history. Careful process tracing reveals that multiple factors have hammered policy outcomes into their current form. Yet, among all forces, frames stand out as being highly influential. They are not blunt instruments that are timeless and immutable, nor do they crowd out the effect of other variables. They are, however, identifiable and durable. Moreover, their effect can be established through their presence before and during cycles of policymaking and through the explicit connection decisionmakers draw between their ideas and their policy choices.

Drawing on an ideational perspective to account for policy outcomes does not necessitate setting aside nonideational factors. Nor does striving to integrate ideas into models of policymaking imply that they are secondary variables, to be considered only when and if others do not suffice. Frames must be examined in every instance of policymaking, as must power, interests, institutions, and problems. Frames may prove more or less influential in any particular case, as may other variables. Arriving at a more complete and compelling account of policymaking requires analyzing the ways in which ideas such as frames are likely to affect the process, and understanding the ways in which frames interact with other important variables. To round out the picture of what frames are, how they matter, and where they come from, we must also develop a sense of the conditions under which frames are likely to be especially influential, and be able to trace the origins of those frames. Only by assembling all of these elements can we effectively model the role of ideas in comparative public policymaking.

8

Race, Racism, and Integration in Europe

Recent Developments, Options, and Trade-offs

Western Europe has welcomed millions of ethnic minority immigrants in the decades since World War II. These individuals have made important contributions to the productivity and dynamism of their new homelands. Moreover, they have become an integral part of unions, churches, and community organizations; they have borne children who have grown up attending the nation's schools; and in many cases they and their descendants have become full-fledged citizens of their new countries. The positive influence of immigrants and their children on national life has not, however, served as a shield against the effects of racism. Ethnic minorities often bear the brunt of economic disadvantages, venomous harassment, or physical violence because of the color of their skin, their accent, or their faith.[1]

States have been relatively slow to respond to these negative side effects of diversity. When the first postwar wave of ethnic minorities began arriving in Europe in the 1950s and early 1960s, it was legal for pub owners to refuse them a drink because they were not white, for employers to fling racial insults at them, and for landlords to write advertisements for prospective tenants that plainly stated "no coloureds." In 1963, the owner of a Bristol bus company claimed that he would not employ non-whites as bus drivers for fear that whites would then refuse to drive (*The Times*, May 7, 1963). Although this prompted a boycott from the city's nonwhite population, no legal action was possible: under the law, employers had the full authority to select workers based on racial or ethnic criteria. Race

[1] Although it is not often discussed, ethnic majority members may also suffer from discrimination, harassment and violence on racial or ethnic grounds.

policies emerged only in the mid-1960s and afterward in Britain, France, and elsewhere in Western Europe.

In contrast to the first two decades after the war when most political leaders and average citizens ignored or denied evidence of racism, there is now a greater consciousness among Europeans about these issues. In the 1980s, the European Union[2] began to turn its attention to the topic of racism, commissioning surveys in member states, holding hearings, and issuing reports.[3] Individual countries have also increasingly recognized and acted on this issue. From the 1960s through the 1990s, virtually every country in the region enacted legislation to combat racism. Britain and France have themselves reopened policy debates about racism in the past few years, and are in the process of updating their institutions. Racism is on the agenda in Western Europe as a pressing problem, a public concern, and a political issue.

In order to discern how best to handle issues of race and racism, it is vital to understand the range of policy options available and the pros and cons of different choices. This book began mapping the topology of European race policies with its discussion of the central differences between the British and French approaches in the Introduction. It is important, however, to look beyond this set of policies and to examine the developments of the past few years in Britain and France that have introduced new elements to each country's race institutions. Moreover, it is useful to scrutinize policy tools used elsewhere in Europe to know whether there are radically different approaches available on the continent, or, conversely, if European countries tend gravitate toward either the British or the French model of race policies.[4] Such a review of recent developments and continental policy alternatives helps to establish a baseline for assessing the trade-offs inherent in different approaches.

Contemporary Race Policies

In the past half decade, Britain has augmented its race relations legislation through two substantial laws. In 1998, the Crime and Disorder Act

[2] Then called the European Community.

[3] See, for example, European Parliament Committee of Inquiry into the Rise of Fascism and Racism in Europe (1985), European Parliament Committee of Inquiry on Racism and Xenophobia (1991), and Commission of the European Communities (1992).

[4] In other words, can European countries be classified as having one of a limited number of policy sets in the way that Esping-Andersen (1990) identifies three "worlds" of welfare capitalism?

created new offenses in the realm of expressive racism (such as racially aggravated harassment) as well in the domain of physical racism (such as racially aggravated assault and racially aggravated criminal damage).[5] This law enables prosecutors and courts to impose stiffer penalties for crimes motivated by racial animus. Whereas the maximum sentence for the crime of common assault is six months imprisonment and a £5,000 fine, a guilty verdict for racially aggravated common assault can result in up to two years in jail and an unlimited fine. As well as increasing penalties for racism, the 1998 law explicitly embeds crimes of physical racism into the country's institutional repertoire, a step that Britain and many other countries have long been reluctant to take.

The British Parliament also passed the Race Relations (Amendment) Act in 2000. This law arrived in the wake of an official inquiry into the police mishandling of a highly publicized murder. Stephen Lawrence and a friend were attacked as they waited for a bus in southeast London in April 1993. After shouting racial abuse, a group of white youths stabbed Lawrence twice, severing an artery before leaving him to bleed to death (*The Independent*, April 24, 1993). The government-commissioned MacPherson Report discussed the influence of "institutional racism" on the subsequently bungled police investigation, defining the term (after reviewing prevailing definitions in British society) as: "The collective failure of an organisation to provide an appropriate and professional service to people because of their colour, culture, or ethnic origin. It can be seen or detected in processes, attitudes and behaviour which amount to discrimination through unwitting prejudice, ignorance, thoughtlessness and racist stereotyping which disadvantage minority ethnic people."[6]

In keeping with the recommendations of the report, and at least partly in an effort to contravene the effects of institutional racism, the 2000 Race Relations Act extends coverage of the 1976 act to the police and other public officials previously exempt from the laws against discrimination.

[5] Beyond creating new offenses, the law also enables courts to take evidence of racism into account at the sentencing stage of all crimes. See the British Home Office's memo on the 1998 law, located at http://www.homeoffice.gov.uk/cdact/racagoff.htm

[6] Section 6.34 of The Stephen Lawrence Inquiry; Report of an Inquiry by Sir William MacPherson of Cluny; Presented to Parliament by the Secretary of State for the Home Department by Command of Her Majesty, February 1999 (http://www.official-documents.co.uk/document/cm42/4262/4262.htm). It is interesting to note that the first definition of institutional racism offered in the report (section 6.22) is that of Stokely Carmichael and Charles V. Hamilton in their 1967 book *Black Power: The Politics of Liberation in America.*

It holds chief officers liable for acts of racism by policemen and women under their supervision, thereby creating a strong incentive for them to enact internal policies that root out racism. The 2000 act also places a "general duty" on public authorities as diverse as the army, governing bodies of schools, and sewage authorities to eliminate discrimination and to promote equality of opportunity and positive relations between individuals of different racial groups.[7] How these legislative changes translate into actions remains to be seen. Whether they are sufficient to tackle the institutional racism identified by the MacPherson Report is also an open question. However, it is clear that the 2000 Race Relations (Amendment) Act and the 1998 Crime and Disorder Act have introduced new powers, duties, and requirements into the British system that significantly extend the 1976 act and that offer food for thought for other European countries seeking insights into antiracist policy options.

Over the past few years, France has also revisited its antiracism institutions, altering them less through legislation than through executive branch policy changes. In particular, French government officials have begun to turn their attention to the problems of discrimination that for decades registered only dimly on the national radar screen. In 1999, the government launched its plan for departmental-level commissions on citizenship (CODAC), which it defined as "a space for listening, reflection, impetus, and putting into place actions designed to fight discrimination" (Commission Nationale Consultative des Droits de l'Homme 2001: 111).[8] The CODAC are designed to bring together local bureaucrats, politicians, and members of civil society to discuss problems of racism and their potential solutions.

The French government has also established a national hotline for reporting acts of discrimination, overseen by a recently created national Group for the Study of and Struggle against Discrimination (GELD).[9] Unlike the UK's Commission for Racial Equality, the GELD has no power in the legal domain, nor can it engage in audits of industries, nor is it

[7] The Commission for Racial Equality and the Home Secretary are responsible for a degree of oversight of this duty.

[8] CODAC stands for Commissions Départementales d'Accès à la Citoyenneté. They replace and subsume departmental structures designed to fight racism established in 1993 by the government (Commission Nationale Consultative des Droits de l'Homme 2001: 111).

[9] The Groupe d'Etude et de Lutte contre les Discriminations (GELD) was created in 2000 and took over the work of the Groupe d'Etude sur les Discriminations (GED), itself founded in 1999 (Commission Nationale Consultative des Droits de l'Homme 2001: 118, 122).

responsible for national media campaigns against racism. Its bailiwick thus far is limited to undertaking studies of the extent of discrimination and the means for better countering its effects. As with the CODAC, the GELD serves primarily as an institution that produces information – and therefore increases communication – about racism with an eye toward better policy development and implementation. As one astute observer has noted, it is not clear that these steps will resolve the frustration felt among victims of discrimination, since the bodies do not have enormous power to change race policies (Hargreaves 2000).[10]

In keeping with the new national focus on discrimination, the French legislature has also taken up the baton in the form of efforts to lower the threshold of proof necessary to obtain a conviction for discrimination in civil courts. Although civil courts are rarely invoked in France to fight racism, there have been moves to encourage complainants to use them more actively by reversing the burden of proof in discrimination cases. New legal language makes the employer responsible for proving that his or her decision to hire, promote, train, or fire a worker was not motivated by an effort to discriminate, given at least a modicum of evidence implying discriminatory behavior.[11] Parallel language has also been introduced in the domain of housing.[12] Protections against indirect discrimination and victimization have also recently come to Parliamentary attention.[13] In short, the French institutions may be in the process of a significant shift by encoding into law greater protections in the domain of access racism. It is unclear how transformative such developments will be. They have not gone so far as to ensure that civil law becomes the weapon of choice in the fight against access racism, nor do they overturn the role given to associations (as opposed to a national administrative body) in countering racism, nor do they recognize race as an acceptable social category for the purposes of ethnic monitoring or affirmative action.[14] While the French

[10] In 2001, France also renamed its Fonds d'Action Sociale (FAS) the Fonds d'Action et de Soutien pour l'Intégration et la Lutte contre les Discriminations (FASILD). The mandate of the organization, however, does not appear to differ dramatically from that of the FAS.

[11] Law 2001-1066 of November 16, 2001.

[12] Law 2002-73 of January 17, 2002.

[13] Law 2001-1066.

[14] It is worth noting, however, that some scholars have begun examining more closely the pros as well as the cons of affirmative action (De Rudder, Poiret, and Vourc'h 2000, Noblet 2001), and some researchers have even begun decrying what they see as covert forms of affirmative action creeping into French public policy by the administrative back door (Calvès 2000).

model may be evolving, it has not become (and will not soon become) the same as the British approach to fighting racism.

Looking beyond the borders of Britain and France reveals that other European states have also enacted legislation against various forms of racism. Germany, for example, has laws that permit the banning of racist groups as well as punishment of incitement to racial hatred. To the extent possible, however, the term race is absent from German structures, as it remains taboo in light of the Nazi experience (Thränhardt 2000: 166). Postwar legislation thus took the form of a constitutional mechanism for limiting freedom of association of groups whose purpose or activities "are directed against the constitutional order or the concept of international understanding," as well as a section in the criminal code that prohibited "attacks on human dignity which are likely to breach the public peace, committed in the form of acts of particular gravity against parts of the population" (cited in Fennema 2000: 120). Much like France, Germany has concentrated its energies on expressive racism rather than on access racism, and has strictly avoided any policies that hint at race consciousness.

The Netherlands has been among the most active European countries in experimenting with antiracist institutions. Through the mid-1990s, its structures evolved along lines parallel to those in Britain. It focused much attention on issues of access racism, rewriting its constitution to incorporate an article against discrimination in 1983, establishing a National Institute against Racial Discrimination (LBR) in 1985, classifying certain residents by ethnic minority group status, and initiating affirmative action policies in the early 1980s (Fennema 2000, Rodrigues 1994). However, the Dutch structures also have several elements in common with French institutions. For a long time, the criminal law was favored over the civil law for punishing discrimination (Rodrigues 1994: 385–86). Moreover, in recent years, the Netherlands has placed diminished emphasis on ethnically-targeted policies and has shifted instead to a politics that emphasizes individual integration or assimilation (Ireland 2000: 243–50, Thränhardt 2000: 172). Reflecting this trend, the positive discrimination elements embedded in a mid-1990s law on employment equity were toned down in 1998 (Fennema 2000: 131). In keeping with a French sensibility, expressive racism in Holland has consistently formed a part of the national agenda: several leaders of political parties have been convicted of incitement to racial discrimination and hatred and one party (CP'86) was declared illegal and disbanded by an Amsterdam court (Fennema 2000: 130).

The European Union has been a relative newcomer to debates and policymaking in the field of racism. Nevertheless, it has produced a substantial number of documents and initiatives over the past few years. Balancing the interests of its fifteen members, it has taken actions that have a wide base of support, such as sponsoring the European Year Against Racism and founding the European Monitoring Center on Racism and Xenophobia.[15] Although most of its initiatives have aimed to increase awareness about the problems of racism through information gathering and dissemination, it also supports a number of antiracist advocacy networks at both the national and international levels.

On the legislative front, the Council of the European Union adopted a joint action in 1996 (96/443/JHA), enjoining member states to ensure judicial cooperation in pursuing expressive racist crimes, such as incitement to racial hatred and the condoning of crimes against humanity, as well as in pursuing parties that participate in racist organizations. As for countering access racism, the EU waited until the Treaty of Amsterdam provided the constitutional means to "take appropriate action to combat discrimination" based on "racial or ethnic origin."[16] The council subsequently issued a directive to all member states in 2000 on equal treatment between persons irrespective of racial or ethnic origin (2000/43/EC). This EU legislation, which nations must enable by 2003, mandates equal access for all persons in the realms of employment, training, union and professional membership, healthcare and other welfare state benefits, education, housing, and supply of goods and services available to the public.

Interestingly, the directive requires both that states permit associations with a legitimate interest (such as antiracist groups) to engage in judicial and administrative procedures, and that they designate a body for the promotion of equal treatment along racial and ethnic grounds, thereby taking on board the procedures most common in France *and* Britain rather than deciding between them or leaving the method unspecified. The legislation

[15] Both in 1997.

[16] Prior to 1997 there had been debate over whether it was legally permissible for the EU to act on issues of discrimination, or whether such decisions were to be taken exclusively at the national level. Article 13 of the revised treaty establishing the European Community reads: "Without prejudice to the other provision of this Treaty and within the limits of the powers conferred by it upon the Community, the Council, acting unanimously on a proposal from the Commission and after consulting the European Parliament, may take appropriate action to combat discrimination based on sex, racial or ethnic origin, religion or belief, disability, age or sexual orientation."

requires protections against both direct and indirect discrimination, and permits (but does not require) positive action and exceptions to race neutrality for "genuine and determining occupational requirements."[17] It remains to be seen how the members of the EU will implement this directive, yet it is noteworthy that the EU is seeking to require certain minimum protections across countries, while leaving a large amount of leeway for each state to decide for itself just how far – and in which direction – to proceed in banning access racism.

Race Policies: Assessing Trade-offs

With such a plethora of race policy options and approaches available, where might countries go from here in their attempts to integrate immigrants and ethnic groups in a diverse Europe? Answering this question would be easy if it could be concluded that the British, French, or another system served as a model for others to emulate. Unfortunately, such a conclusion is not possible. The effect of national institutions on levels of racism is uncertain. Countries like Britain and France have enacted a variety of different race policies, yet it is not clear that racism has diminished more in one country than another.[18] The continued support of millions of French voters for the National Front despite its infighting and disarray, and the rash of violence pitting ethnic groups against each other in British cities during the summer of 2001 suggest that each country still has miles to go in the fight against racism. Instead of singing the praises of any particular system, it is therefore more productive to highlight the types of choices that European countries face, and the trade-offs between policy options.

There are three questions that states must ask when it comes to issues of race and racism: Is it better to have more or fewer race policies? Are some policies better or worse for countering racism? And, is it preferable to be nearer to the race-conscious or color-blind end of the

[17] It also defines harassment as a form of discrimination (as well as instructions to discriminate), shifts the burden of proof to the defendant once a prima facie case for discrimination has been made (except in criminal court proceedings), establishes protections against victimization, and enjoins states to encourage unions and employers within each country to coordinate antiracist strategies. The full text of Council Directive 2000/43/EC of June 29, 2000 can be found in the EU Official Journal L 180, 19/07/2000: 0022–0026.

[18] Or even that it has diminished at all.

spectrum in managing ethnic diversity? These can be summarized as the "more or fewer," "better or worse," and "race-conscious or color-blind" questions.

Reviewing the past few decades, it is possible to discern a trend toward increasing the number of legally-defined racist crimes as well as toward multiplying the tools made available to counter various forms of racism. Each round of race legislation in Britain and France has added many more facets to its race policy repertoire than it has subtracted. Over time, Europe has moved from a continent virtually without protections, to one where incitement to racial hatred and employment discrimination have been widely outlawed. Beyond these commonly prohibited forms of racism, offenses such as Holocaust denial, racially aggravated assault, and institutional racism have become actionable in some states. In addition, countries have typically supplied more policy instruments for fighting racism. National bureaucracies have been created where none existed before and they have attained greater influence. Some countries have multiplied the procedures available for complainants seeking justice, allowing them the choice of turning to associations or the bureaucracy for help with conciliation or going it alone with either a criminal or a civil law suit. While such a trend has not been without exception nor has it been fast-paced, it is noteworthy that when choices have been made, states have typically opted for more rather than fewer race policies.

How far should states go? At one extreme, we might envision a country scanning the horizon for all current laws and policies in Europe and erecting parallel structures within its borders. This state could then ban all forms of access, expressive, and physical racism presently penalized by law, and could enable a wide variety of bureaucracies and associations to pursue the struggle against racism through a diversity of legal and administrative means. This or any other expansive strategy has two principal advantages. To the extent that societies abhor racism and seek to curtail its tangible forms, strict and wide-ranging legislation may deter racists from acting upon their beliefs and may punish those that do. Aside from such a practical consideration, race laws also fulfill a symbolic function. They act as signals to targeted ethnic groups and to society as a whole that racism is unacceptable, and they invoke sentiments of equality and fair play within the country. Passing a law demonstrates that the government is not afraid to confront the public problems of its day.

Yet states have shown themselves to be cautious when it comes to enacting race policies. They do not roll out evermore provisions willy-nilly.

In fact, there are significant downsides to multiplying the types of infractions that are punishable, to raising the penalties for existing infractions, and to increasing the number of legal avenues and organizations available for countering racism. More antiracist policies are not necessarily better than fewer. Racists have proven adept at skirting existing laws, calling their effectiveness into question. Even successful prosecutions may ultimately backfire if the perpetrator is viewed as a martyr. Such outcomes can cause widespread disillusionment. If expectations are raised through high-profile legislation, and yet racism continues as a prominent and seemingly unchecked social problem, the public's confidence in the state may be significantly undermined. Moreover, in spite of the equal protection they offer to all victims of racism, race laws are frequently viewed as sops to minorities. Although the perception that too much has been given to ethnic minorities has occasionally generated protests, it more commonly simmers below the surface as general resentment. When asked, one British interviewee – a barrister in training – complained bitterly that minorities merely had to cry racism following a failed job interview to force a company to settle out of court for large sums of money. In her opinion (not supported by any data), the system was strongly biased in favor of nonwhites. Majority backlash thus constitutes another potential drawback to multiplying race laws.

States must also ask if among all of the possible actions they can take to fight racism it is true that some are better and some are worse. In most cases it is not possible to draw definitive conclusions, because too many other variables need to be accounted for in the calculations. Whether administrative agencies or non-governmental associations are more effective in countering racism depends on a host of factors ranging from the formal powers granted to each by the state, to the legitimacy and leadership role particular organizations are able to establish within the polity. Nonetheless, scrutinizing the implementation of British and French institutions does permit at least one lesson about better or worse policies. All else equal, using the civil law to punish access racism produces more complaints, more court cases, and more settlements than using the criminal law. Because of differential standards of proof, it is markedly easier for victims to establish that discrimination has occurred before civil courts than before criminal courts. This will become even more true once European countries enact EU-mandated laws that shift the onus to defendants to prove nondiscrimination. If the goal is to provide legal means to obtain compensation for victims of racism and to encourage them to seek justice, the civil law approach seems clearly superior to the criminal law for punishing access racism.[19]

The third important concern of states involves the choice between race-conscious and color-blind policy approaches. Whereas it is possible for a state to avoid selecting either administrative agencies or powerful associations as leaders in the domain of race by having both, it is not possible for a country to be at the same time race-conscious and color-blind. Of course, states are not faced with a stark, all-or-nothing decision. Rather, they must judge the extent to which they will recognize race, and in what domains. This is an issue that many countries struggle with, and is often reflected in tensions over affirmative action and the census.[20] As we have seen, Britain and France have parted ways on this point. Without going as far down the path as the United States or Canada, Britain has followed in North American footsteps by adopting certain race-conscious policies. France, by contrast, has strictly avoided policies directed at ethnic communities.

Recognizing race has the advantage of allowing a state to collect potentially significant data. Ethnic monitoring provides information about where different ethnic groups stand in the fields of employment, housing, education, health care, and so on. It permits the nation to pinpoint discrepancies between groups in areas such as school expulsions, representation in industries or government bureaucracies, and relative wealth. Without such statistics, it is easy to underestimate the significance of racial disparities within the country. In addition to gathering information, official race-consciousness permits the state to craft policies that correct for uneven distributions of goods, benefits, wealth, and skills. Forms of positive action aim to attain a greater measure of substantive equality by racial or ethnic group. They are, however, only one type of race-conscious policy at the disposal of the state. Governments may choose to fund ethnic minority organizations in order to cultivate skills in different communities. They can also draw ethnic leaders into formal or informal discussions, recognizing

[19] This conclusion has also been reached by Michael Banton (unpublished manuscript), one of the world's foremost experts on race policies. Naturally, the goal of society may not be to provide encouragement and compensation to victims of discrimination; it may instead be to make a national statement that discrimination is wrong or even to avoid lawsuits altogether, in which case the criminal law may be a more appropriate mechanism, no matter how few cases arrive on the docket.

[20] For overviews of the debate over affirmative action in the US and elsewhere, see Skrentny (1996, 2001), and Weiner and Katzenstein (1981). Recent work that addresses the role of the census in defining ethnic groups includes Nobles (2000), Skerry (2000), and Kertzer and Arel (2002).

that their experiences may provide new insights and new ideas about how to manage public problems.

While openly recognizing race through ethnic monitoring can produce benefits for society, it can also cause confusion and give rise to misdirected actions. Racial and ethnic data that reveal group-based differences do not by themselves demonstrate the significance of race or the existence of racism. Such differences may be explained by a host of other factors, ranging from incomplete language acquisition by immigrants, to socioeconomic disparities that happen to overlap with ethnicity (but are not caused by racism), or even to statistical anomalies. If nonwhite immigrants originating from a country with few educational opportunities and a different mother tongue have a higher rate of unemployment and earn less than whites, it is not easy to conclude that such disparities are due to racial factors. Ethnic data may be seized upon as evidence of racism without adequate digging into the meaning of the statistics.

In addition to being concerned about misinterpreting the results of ethnic monitoring, race-conscious societies must ask themselves whether they are willing to reinforce racial and ethnic group identities through their policies. Britain does not go very far in this direction, especially when compared to countries such as India (Parikh 2001, Weiner 1989a, Weiner 1989b) or even the United States (Omi and Winant 1994). But it does go much further than France, where most people believe that the state should ignore racial and ethnic identities rather than reinforce them. The color-blind model – at least in France – seems to correlate with a reduced sense of importance of groups defined by color, if not by culture (Lamont 2001). By invoking equality among citizens and national indifference to race and ethnicity, color-blind states appeal to a sense of sameness that parallels the public disapproval of racism embodied in laws against racism. France's color-blind approach may appear to be less capable of dealing with the meaningful disadvantages that accrue to some people because of their race or ethnicity. Yet, accepting the common terrain of Frenchness may help efface internal lines of difference that often seem to divide countries like the United States into ethnic camps.

In sum, citizens, politicians, and policymakers are facing an increased number of race policy options in an era when racism is rising on the European agenda. The new actions undertaken by Britain, France, and the EU, and the structures in place in other European countries, highlight the range of available choices. Even though it is not possible to offer one-size-fits-all recommendations for countering racism and for managing ethnic relations, it is not too soon to examine the trade-offs associated with a variety of policy approaches. Discussing the more or fewer, better or worse, and race-conscious or color-blind questions clarifies the debates about race and racism that European countries must pursue. Ensuring successful integration in a diverse world is too important for the consequences of race policies to be misunderstood.

References

Ageron, Charles-Robert. 1991. *La Décolonisation Française*. Paris: Arman Colin.

Ahumada, Carmen. 1991. La Loi et le Racisme. *Revue Pratique de Droit Social* 549:25–30.

Almond, Gabriel A., and Sidney Verba. 1989 (1963). *The Civic Culture: Political Attitudes and Democracy in Five Nations*. Newbury Park, CA: Sage.

Ball, Wendy, and John Solomos, eds. 1990. *Race and Local Politics*. London: MacMillan.

Banton, Michael. 1955. *The Coloured Quarter: Negro Immigrants in an English City*. London: Jonathan Cape.

1994. Effective Implementation of the UN Racial Convention. *New Community* 20 (3):475–487.

1996. *International Action Against Racial Discrimination*. Oxford: Clarendon Press.

unpublished manuscript. *National Variations in Conceptions of Racism*.

Barker, Martin. 1981. *The New Racism*. London: Junction Books.

Baumgartner, Frank R., and Bryan D. Jones. 1993. *Agendas and Instability in American Politics*. Chicago: University of Chicago Press.

Beishon, Sharon, Satnam Virdee, and Ann Hagell. 1995. *Nursing in a Multi-Ethnic NHS*. London: Policy Studies Institute.

Bennett, Colin J., and Michael Howlett. 1992. The Lessons of Learning: Reconciling Theories of Policy Learning and Policy Change. *Policy Sciences* 25:275–294.

Benoît, Jean. 1980. *Dossier E . . . comme Esclaves*. Paris: Editions Alain Moreau.

Ben-Tovim, Gideon, John Gabriel, Ian Law, and Kathleen Stredder. 1986. *The Local Politics of Race*. London: MacMillan.

Berezin, Mabel. 1997. Politics and Culture: A Less Fissured Terrain. *Annual Review of Sociology* 23:361–383.

Beriss, David. 1990. Scarves, Schools, and Segregation: The Foulard Affair. *French Politics and Society* 8 (no. 1, Winter):1–13.

Berman, Sheri. 1998. *The Social Democratic Moment: Ideas and Politics in the Making of Interwar Europe*. Cambridge, MA: Harvard University Press.

2001. Ideas, Norms and Culture in Political Analysis. *Comparative Politics* 33 (no. 2, January):231–250.

Betz, Hans-Georg. 1994. *Radical Right-Wing Populism in Western Europe*. New York: St. Martin's Press.

Betz, Hans-Georg, and Stefan Immerfall, eds. 1998. *The New Politics of the Right: Neo-Populist Parties and Movements in Established Democracies*. New York: St. Martin's Press.

Birnbaum, Pierre. 1992. *Les Fous de la République: Histoire Politique des Juifs d'Etat de Gambetta à Vichy*. Paris: Fayard.

Blatt, David Stuart. 1996. Immigration Politics and Immigrant Collective Action in France, 1968–1993. Ph.D. dissertation, Government Department, Cornell University, Ithaca, NY.

Bleich, Erik. 1998. From International Ideas to Domestic Policies: Educational Multiculturalism in England and France. *Comparative Politics* 31 (no. 1, October):81–100.

2001. The French Model: Color-Blind Integration. In *Color Lines: Affirmative Action, Immigration, and Civil Rights Options for America*, edited by J. D. Skrentny. Chicago: University of Chicago Press.

Blum, Alain. 2002. Resistance to Identity Categorization in France. In *Census and Identity: The Politics of Race, Ethnicity, and Language in National Censuses*, edited by D. I. Kertzer and D. Arel. Cambridge: Cambridge University Press.

Blyth, Mark M. 1997. "Any More Bright Ideas?" The Ideational Turn of Comparative Political Economy. *Comparative Politics* 29 (no. 2, January):229–250.

Bonham Carter, Mark. 1987. The Liberal Hour and Race Relations Law. *New Community* 14 (1/2):1–8.

Bourdieu, Pierre. 1990. *The Logic of Practice*. Translated by Richard Nice. Stanford, CA: Stanford University Press.

Brown, C. 1984. *Black and White Britain: The Third PSI Survey*. London: Heinemann.

Brubaker, Rogers. 1992. *Citizenship and Nationhood in France and Germany*. Cambridge, MA: Harvard University Press.

Bulmer, Martin. 1996. The Ethnic Group Question in the 1991 Census of Population. In *Ethnicity in the 1991 Census: Volume One – Demographic Characteristics of the Ethnic Minority Populations*, edited by D. Coleman and J. Salt. London: HMSO.

Callaghan, James. 1987. *Time and Chance*. London: Collins.

Calvès, Gwënaèle. 2000. Les Politiques Françaises de Lutte contre le Racisme, des Politiques en Mutation. *French Politics, Culture and Society* 18 (no. 3, Fall): 75–82.

Camus, Jean-Yves. 1996. *Le Front National: Histoire et Analyses*. Paris: Editions Oliviers Laurens.

Cappella, Joseph N., and Kathleen Hall Jamieson. 1997. *Spiral of Cynicism: The Press and the Public Good*. New York: Oxford University Press.

Carter, Bob, Marci Green, and Rick Halpern. 1996. Immigration Policy and the Racialization of Migrant Labour: The Construction of National Identities in the USA and Britain. *Ethnic and Racial Studies* 19 (1):135–157.

Carter, B., C. Harris, and S. Joshi. 1987. The 1951–1955 Conservative Government and the Racialisation of Black Immigration. *Immigrants and Minorities* 6:335–347.

Chapsal, Jacques. 1981. *La Vie Politique sous la Ve République*. Paris: Presses Universitaires de France.

Checkel, Jeffrey T. 1998. The Constructivist Turn in International Relations Theory. *World Politics* 50 (no. 2, January):324–348.

1999. International Institutions and Socialization. *ARENA Working Papers* (WP 99/5):http://www.sv.uio.no/arena/publications/wp99_5.htm.

Cohen, Michael, James March, and Johan Olsen. 1972. A Garbage Can Model of Organizational Choice. *Administrative Science Quarterly* 17 (March 1972): 1–25.

Cohen, William B. 1980. Legacy of Empire: The Algerian Connection. *Journal of Contemporary History* 15 (no. 1, January):97–123.

Coleman, David, and John Salt. 1996a. The Ethnic Group Question in the 1991 Census: A New Landmark in British Social Statistics. In *Ethnicity in the 1991 Census: Volume One – Demographic Characteristics of the Ethnic Minority Populations*, edited by D. Coleman and J. Salt. London: HMSO.

eds. 1996b. *Ethnicity in the 1991 Census: Volume One – Demographic Characteristics of the Ethnic Minority Populations*. 4 vols. Vol. 1. London: HMSO.

Commission de la Nationalité. 1988. *Etre Français Aujourd'hui et Demain*. Paris: La Documentation Française.

Commission for Racial Equality. 1985. *Positive Action & Equal Opportunity in Employment*. London: Commission for Racial Equality.

1992. *Second Review of the Race Relations Act 1976*. London: CRE.

1996. Annual Report of the Commission for Racial Equality: January to December 1995. London: Commission for Racial Equality.

Commission Nationale Consultative des Droits de l'Homme. 1990. Rapport au Premier Ministre sur la Lutte Contre le Racisme et la Xénophobie. 1989. Paris: Commission Nationale Consultative des Droits de l'Homme.

2001. *2000. La Lutte contre le Racisme et la Xénophobie: Rapport d'Activité*. Paris: La Documentation Française.

Commission of the European Communities. 1992. *Legal Instruments to Combat Racism and Xenophobia*. Brussels: Directorate General, Employment, Industrial Relations and Social Affairs.

Community Relations Commission. 1975a. Community Relations 1974–5: The Annual Report of the Community Relations Commission. London: HMSO.

1975b. Review of the Race Relations Act. London: HMSO.

Cosgrave, Patrick. 1990. *The Lives of Enoch Powell*. London: Pan Books.

Costa-Lascoux, Jacqueline. 1991. Des Lois Contre le Racisme. In *Face au Racisme: Analyses, Hypothèses, Perspectives*, edited by P.-A. Taguieff. Paris: Éditions La Découverte.

1994. French Legislation Against Racism and Discrimination. *New Community* 20 (3):371–379.

Craig, F. W. S., ed. 1975. *British General Election Manifestos: 1900–1974*. London: MacMillan.

Crewe, Ivor. 1979. The Black, Brown and Green Votes. *New Society* (April 12):76–78.

Cross, Colin. 1961. *The Fascists in Britain*. London: Barrie and Rockliff.

Crossman, Richard. 1975. *The Diaries of a Cabinet Minister, Minister of Housing 1964–66*. 2 vols. Vol. 1. London: Hamish Hamilton and Jonathan Cape.

1976. *The Diaries of a Cabinet Minister, Lord President of the Council and Leader of the House of Commons 1966–68*. 2 vols. Vol. 2. London: Hamish Hamilton and Jonathan Cape.

Crowley, John. 1993. Paradoxes in the Politicisation of Race: A Comparison of the UK and France. *New Community* 19 (4):627–643.

Cruz, Consuelo. 2000. Identity and Persuasion: How Nations Remember Their Pasts and Make Their Futures. *World Politics* 52 (3):275–312.

David, René, and John E. E. Brierley. 1985. *Major Legal Systems in the World Today*. 3rd ed. London: Stevens & Son.

De Rudder, Véronique, Christian Poiret, and François Vourc'h. 2000. *L'Inégalité Raciste: L'Universalité Républicaine à l'Epreuve*. Paris: Presses Universitaires de France.

Deakin, Nicholas. 1965. *Colour and the British Electorate, 1964: Six Case Studies*. London: Pall Mall Press for the Institute for Race Relations.

Dean, Dennis. 1993. The Conservative Government and the 1961 Commonwealth Immigration Act: The Inside Story. *Race & Class* 35 (no. 2, October-December):57–74.

Dean, D. W. 1992. Conservative Governments and the Restriction of Commonwealth Immigration in the 1950s: The Problem of Constraint. *The Historical Journal* 35 (no. 1, March):171–194.

Dobbin, Frank. 1994. *Forging Industrial Policy*. Cambridge: Cambridge University Press.

Du Bois, W. E. B. 1989 (1903). *The Souls of Black Folk*. New York: Bantam Books.

Durkheim, Emile. 1997. *The Division of Labor in Society*. Translated by Lewis A. Coser. New York: The Free Press.

Duverger, Maurice. 1954. *Political Parties*. New York: Wiley.

Earman, John. 1992. *Bayes or Bust? A Critical Examination of Bayesian Confirmation Theory*. Cambridge, MA: The MIT Press.

Entman, Robert M. 1993. Framing: Toward Clarification of a Fractured Paradigm. *Journal of Communication* 43 (no. 4, Autumn):51–58.

Esping-Andersen, Gøsta. 1990. *The Three Worlds of Welfare Capitalism*. Princeton: Princeton University Press.

European Parliament Committee of Inquiry into the Rise of Fascism and Racism in Europe. 1985. *Report of the Committee of Inquiry into the Rise of Fascism and Racism in Europe*. Strasbourg: Commission of the European Communities.

European Parliament Committee of Inquiry on Racism and Xenophobia. 1991. *Report on the Findings of the Inquiry*. Luxembourg: Office for Official Publication of the European Communities.

Fanon, Frantz. 1966 (1961). *The Wretched of the Earth*. Translated by Constance Farrington. New York: Grove Press.

Fassin, Eric. 1999. "Good to Think": The American Reference in French Discourses of Immigration and Ethnicity. In *Multicultural Questions*, edited by C. Joppke and S. Lukes. Oxford: Oxford University Press.

Favell, Adrian. 1998. *Philosophies of Integration: Immigration and the Idea of Citizenship in France and Britain*. London: MacMillan.

Feldblum, Miriam. 1999. *Reconstructing Citizenship: The Politics of Nationality Reform and Immigration in Contemporary France*. Albany: State University of New York Press.

Fennema, Meindert. 2000. Legal Repression of Extreme-Right Parties and Racial Discrimination. In *Challenging Immigration and Ethnic Relations Politics: Comparative European Perspectives*, edited by R. Koopmans and P. Statham. Oxford: Oxford University Press.

Fieldhouse, David K. 1981. *Colonialism: 1870–1945*. London: Weidenfeld and Nicolson.

Finnemore, Martha. 1996a. *National Interests in International Society*. Ithaca, NY: Cornell University Press.

1996b. Norms, Culture and World Politics: Insights from Sociology's Institutionalism. *International Organization* 50 (2):325–347.

Finnemore, Martha, and Kathryn Sikkink. 2001. Taking Stock: The Constructivist Research Program in International Relations and Comparative Politics. *Annual Review of Political Science* 4:391–416.

FitzGerald, Marian. 1987. *Black People and Party Politics in Britain*. London: The Runnymede Trust.

Foot, P. 1965. *Immigration and Race in British Politics*. Harmondsworth: Penguin.

Formisano, Ronald P. 2001. The Concept of Political Culture. *Journal of Interdisciplinary History* XXXI (no. 3, Winter):393–426.

Foulon-Piganiol, Jacques. 1975. La Lutte contre le Racisme: Esquise d'un Bilan de Trois Années de Jurisprudence. *Recueil Dalloz* 26 (juillet):159–160.

Freeman, Gary P. 1979. *Immigrant Labor and Racial Conflict in Industrial Societies: The French and British Experience 1945–1975*. Princeton: Princeton University Press.

1995. Modes of Immigration Politics in Liberal Democratic States. *International Migration Review* 29 (4) 881–902.

Frieden, Jeffry A. 1991. Invested Interests: The Politics of National Economic Policies in a World of Global Finance. *International Organization* 45 (no. 4, Autumn):425–451.

Fysh, Peter, and Jim Wolfreys. 1998. *The Politics of Racism in France*. New York: St. Martin's Press.

Gamson, William A. 1992. *Talking Politics*. Cambridge: Cambridge University Press.

Garrett, Geoffrey, and Barry Weingast. 1993. Ideas, Interests, and Institutions: Constructing the European Community's Internal Market. In *Ideas and Foreign Policy: Beliefs, Institutions and Political Change*, edited by J. Goldstein and R. O. Keohane, Ithaca, NY: Cornell University Press.

Geertz, Clifford. 1973. The Integrative Revolution: Primordial Sentiments and Civil Politics in the New States. In *The Interpretation of Cultures*, edited by C. Geertz. New York: Basic Books.

Geiger, Shelly Leanne. 1989. Labour Party Politics and Race in Britain, 1948–1987: The Relative Importances of National Political Party Initiatives and Mobilization from Below in Securing the Political Advancement of Blacks in Britain. B.A. Thesis, Department of Government, Harvard University, Cambridge, MA.

Giddens, Anthony. 1979. *Central Problems in Social Theory: Action, Structure and Contradiction in Social Analysis*. Berkeley: University of California Press.

Glazer, Nathan, and Ken Young, eds. 1983. *Ethnic Pluralism and Public Policy: Achieving Equality in the United States and Britain*. Lexington, MA: D. C. Heath and Company.

Goffman, Erving. 1974. *Frame Analysis: An Essay on the Organization of Experience*. Cambridge, MA: Harvard University Press.

Goldstein, Judith. 1988. Ideas, Institutions, and American Trade Policy. *International Organization* 42 (no. 1, Winter):179–217.

1993. *Ideas, Interests, and American Trade Policy*. Ithaca, NY: Cornell University Press.

Goldstein, Judith, and Robert O. Keohane, eds. 1993. *Ideas and Foreign Policy: Beliefs, Institutions and Political Change*. Ithaca, NY: Cornell University Press.

Gordon, Paul. 1990. A Dirty War: The New Right and Local Authority Anti-Racism. In *Race and Local Politics*, edited by W. Ball and J. Solomos. London: MacMillan.

Granjon, Marie-Christine. 1994. Le Regard en Biais. Attitudes Françaises et Multiculturalisme Américain (1990–1993). *Vingtième Siècle* 43 (July-September):18–29.

Great Britain: Cabinet Office. 1995. Civil Service Data Summary 1995: Women, Race, Disability. London: Equal Opportunities Division, Cabinet Office.

Great Britain: Department for Education. 1995. Ethnic Monitoring of School Pupils. London: Department for Education.

Great Britain: Home Office. 1965. Immigration from the Commonwealth. London: HMSO.

1974. Equality for Women. London: HMSO.

1975. Racial Discrimination. London: HMSO.

1994. Race and the Criminal Justice System: 1994. London: Home Office.

1996a. Race and the Criminal Justice System: 1995. London: Home Office.

1996b. United Kingdom Policy on Ethnic Minorities: A Summary. London: Community Relations Unit.

undated. *Racial Discrimination: A Guide to the Race Relations Act 1976*. London: Home Office.

Great Britain: Royal Commission on Population. 1949. Report. London: HMSO.

Great Britain: Select Committee on Race Relations and Immigration. 1975a. *The Organisation of Race Relations Administration*. Vol. 1. London: HMSO.

1975b. *The Organisation of Race Relations Administration*. Vol. 2. London: HMSO.

1975c. *The Organisation of Race Relations Administration*. Vol. 3. London: HMSO.

Gregory, Jeanne. 1987. *Sex, Race and the Law: Legislating for Equality*. London: Sage.

Guiraudon, Virginie. 2000. *Les Politiques d'Immigration en Europe: Allemagne France Pays-Bas*. Paris: L'Harmattan.

Haas, Peter M. 1989. Do Regimes Matter? Epistemic Communities and Mediterranean Pollution Control. *International Organization* 43 (no. 3, Summer): 377–403.

Hall, John A. 1993. Ideas and the Social Sciences. In *Ideas and Foreign Policy: Beliefs, Institutions, and Political Change*, edited by J. Goldstein and R. O. Keohane. Ithaca, NY: Cornell University Press.

Hall, Peter A. 1986. *Governing the Economy*. Oxford: Oxford University Press.

ed. 1989. *The Political Power of Economic Ideas: Keynesianism across Nations*. Princeton: Princeton University Press.

1993. Policy Paradigms, Social Learning, and the State: The Case of Economic Policymaking in Britain. *Comparative Politics* 25 (no. 3, April):275–296.

Hall, Peter A., and Rosemary C. R. Taylor. 1996. Political Science and the Three New Institutionalisms. *Political Studies* XLIV:936–957.

Hannoun, Michel. 1987. *L'Homme est l'Espérance de l'Homme*. Paris: La Documentation Française.

Hansen, Randall. 1997. The Institution of Citizenship: Immigration Policy and Nationality Law in Post-War Britain. D.Phil, Faculty of Social Studies, Oxford University, Oxford.

1999. The Kenyan Asians, British Politics, and the Commonwealth Immigrants Act, 1968. *Historical Journal* 42 (3):809–834.

2000. *Citizenship and Immigration in Postwar Britain*. Oxford: Oxford University Press.

Hansen, Randall, and Desmond King. 2001. Eugenic Ideas, Political Interests, and Policy Variance: Immigration and Sterilization Policy in Britain and the U.S. *World Politics* 53 (no. 2, January):237–263.

Hargreaves, Alec G. 1995. *Immigration, 'Race' and Ethnicity in Contemporary France*. London: Routledge.

2000. Half-Measures: Antidiscrimination Policy in France. *French Politics, Culture and Society* 18 (no. 3, Fall):83–101.

Haut Conseil à l'Intégration. 1991. *Pour un Modèle Français d'Intégration*. Paris: La Documentation Française.

1992. *Conditions Juridiques et Culturelles de l'Intégration*. Paris: La Documentation Française.

1993. *L'Intégration à la Française*. Paris: La Documentation Française.

1995. *Liens Culturels et Intégration*. Paris: La Documentation Française.

1998. *Lutte Contre les Discriminations : Faire Respecter le Principe d'Egalité : Rapport au Premier Ministre*. Paris: La Documentation Française.

Heclo, Hugh. 1974. *Modern Social Politics in Britain and Sweden*. New Haven: Yale University Press.

Heineman, Benjamin W. 1972. *The Politics of the Powerless: A Study of the Campaign Against Racial Discrimination*. London: Oxford University Press for the Institute of Race Relations.

Hepple, Bob. 1968. *Race, Jobs and the Law in Britain*. London: Allen Lane, The Penguin Press.

Heussler, Robert. 1971. British Rule in Africa. In *France and Britain in Africa*, edited by P. Gifford and W. R. Louis. New Haven: Yale University Press.

Hindell, K. 1965. The Genesis of the Race Relations Bill. *Political Quarterly* 36 (4): 390–406.

Hoffmann, Stanley. 2000. Deux Universalismes en Conflit. *The Tocqueville Review* XXI (1):65–71.

Hollifield, James F. 1992. *Immigrants, Markets, and States: The Political Economy of Postwar Europe*. Cambridge, MA: Harvard University Press.

Howard, Anthony. 1963. The Skin Game. *New Statesman* LXVI (1706, November 22):726.

Huntington, Samuel P. 1993. The Clash of Civilizations? *Foreign Affairs* 72 (no. 3, Summer):22–49.

Immergut, Ellen M. 1998. The Theoretical Core of the New Institutionalism. *Politics & Society* 26 (no. 1, March):5–34.

Inglehart, Ronald. 1977. *The Silent Revolution: Changing Values and Political Styles among Western Publics*. Princeton: Princeton University Press.

1990. *Culture Shift in Advanced Industrial Society*. Princeton: Princeton University Press.

1997. *Modernization and Postmodernization: Cultural, Economic, and Political Change in 43 Societies*. Princeton: Princeton University Press.

Ireland, Patrick. 2000. Reaping What They Sow: Institutions and Immigrant Political Participation in Western Europe. In *Challenging Immigration and Ethnic Relations Politics: Comparative European Perspectives*, edited by R. Koopmans and P. Statham. Oxford: Oxford University Press.

1994. *The Policy Challenge of Ethnic Diversity: Immigrant Politics in France and Switzerland*. Cambridge, MA: Harvard University Press.

Iyengar, Shanto. 1991. *Is Anyone Responsible? How Television Frames Political Issues*. Chicago: University of Chicago Press.

Jacobsen, John Kurt. 1995. Much Ado about Ideas: The Cognitive Factor in Economic Policy. *World Politics* 47 (January):283–310.

Jenkins, Roy. 1991. *A Life at the Centre*. London: MacMillan.

Jewson, Nick, David Mason, Alison Drewett, and Will Rossiter. 1995. Formal Equal Opportunities Policies and Employment Best Practice. London: Department for Education and Employment.

Jobert, Bruno, and Pierre Muller. 1987. *L'Etat en Action: Politiques Publiques et Corporatismes*. Paris: Presses Universitaires de France.

Jones, Bryan D. 1994. *Reconceiving Decision-Making in Democratic Politics: Attention, Choice, and Public Policy*. Chicago: University of Chicago Press.

Jones, Thomas David. 1995. Human Rights: Freedom of Expression and Group Defamation under British, Canadian, Indian, Nigerian and United States Law: A Comparative Analysis. *Suffolk Transnational Law Review* 18 (no. 2, Summer):427–588.

Joppke, Christian. 1999. *Immigration and the Nation-State: The United States, Germany, and Great Britain*. Oxford: Oxford University Press.

Jowell, Jeffrey. 1965. The Administrative Enforcement of Laws against Discrimination. *Public Law* (Summer):119–186.

Kastoryano, Riva. 1996. *La France, l'Allemagne et Leurs Immigrés: Négotier l'Identité*. Paris: Armand Colin.

Kato, Junko. 1996. Review Article: Institutions and Rationality in Politics – Three varieties of Neo-Institutionalists. *British Journal of Political Science* 26 (no. 4, October):553–582.

Katzenstein, Peter J., ed. 1978. *Between Power and Plenty*. Madison: University of Wisconsin Press.

ed. 1996. *The Culture of National Security: Norms and Identity in World Politics*. New York: Columbia University Press.

Katznelson, Ira. 1976. *Black Men, White Cities: Race Relations and Migration in the United States 1900–30 and Britain 1948–68*. Chicago: University of Chicago Press.

Kepel, Gilles. 1997. *Allah in the West*. Translated by Susan Milner. Cambridge: Polity Press.

Kertzer, David I., and Dominique Arel, eds. 2002. *Census and Identity: The Politics of Race, Ethnicity, and Language in National Censuses*. Cambridge: Cambridge University Press.

Khong, Yuen Foong. 1992. *Analogies at War*. Princeton: Princeton University Press.

King, Desmond. 1995. *Separate and Unequal: Black Americans and the US Federal Government*. Oxford: Oxford University Press.

King, Gary, Robert O. Keohane, and Sidney Verba. 1994. *Designing Social Inquiry: Scientific Inference in Qualitative Research*. Princeton: Princeton University Press.

Kingdon, John W. 1995. *Agendas, Alternatives, and Public Policies*. 2nd ed. New York: HarperCollins.

Kitschelt, Herbert. 1995. *The Radical Right in Western Europe: A Comparative Analysis*. Ann Arbor: University of Michigan.

Knight, Jack. 1992. *Institutions and Social Conflict*. Cambridge: Cambridge University Press.

Koelble, Thomas A. 1995. The New Institutionalism in Political Science and Sociology. *Comparative Politics* 27 (no. 2, January):231–243.

Korpi, Walter. 1983. *The Democratic Class Struggle*. London: Routledge & Kegan Paul.

Korpi, Walter, and Michael Shalev. 1979. Strikes, Industrial Relations and Class Conflict in Capitalist Societies. *British Journal of Sociology* 30 (June):164–187.

Krasner, Stephen D. 1984. Approaches to the State: Alternative Conceptions and Historical Dynamics. *Comparative Politics* 16 (2):223–246.

Kuhn, Thomas S. 1996 (1962). *The Structure of Scientific Revolutions*. 3rd ed. Chicago: University of Chicago Press.

Kushnick, Louis. 1971. British Anti-Discrimination Legislation. In *The Prevention of Racial Discrimination in Britain*, edited by S. Abbott. London: Oxford University Press, for the UN Institute for Training and Research and the Institute of Race Relations.

Labour Party. 1970. Report of the 69th Annual Conference of the Labour Party. London: The Labour Party.

1974. Report of the 73rd Annual Conference of the Labour Party. London: The Labour Party.
Lamont, Michèle. 2000. *The Dignity of Working Men: Morality and the Boundaries of Race, Class, and Immigration.* New York: Russell Sage Foundation.
2001. Immigration and the Salience of Racial Boundaries among French Workers. *French Politics, Culture and Society* 19 (no. 1, Spring):1–21.
L'Année Politique, Economique, Sociale et Diplomatique en France: 1972. 1973. Paris: Presses Universitaires de France.
Lapeyronnie, Didier. 1993. *L'Individu et les Minorités: la France et la Grande-Bretagne Face à Leurs Immigrés.* Paris: Presses Universitaires de France.
Layton-Henry, Zig. 1992. *The Politics of Immigration: Immigration, 'Race' and 'Race' Relations in Post-war Britain.* Oxford: Blackwell.
1984. *The Politics of Race in Britain.* London: George Allen & Unwin.
Le Bras, Hervé. 1998. *Le Démon des Origines: Démographie et Extrême Droite.* Paris: Editions de l'Aube.
Lester, Anthony. 1987. Anti-Discrimination Legislation in Great Britain. *New Community* XIV (1/2):21–31.
1994. Discrimination: What Can Lawyers Learn From History? *Public Law* (Summer):224–237.
1996. *The Politics of the Race Relations Act 1976*: unpublished manuscript.
Lester, Anthony, and Geoffrey Bindman. 1972. *Race and Law.* London: Longman.
Lester, Lord, of Herne Hill QC. 1997. Making Discrimination Law Effective: Old Barriers and New Frontiers. *International Journal of Discrimination and the Law* 2:167–181.
Levine, Michel. 1985. *Les Ratonnades d'Octobre: Un Meurtre Collectif à Paris en 1961.* Paris: Editions Ramsay.
Lévy, Albert. 1993. *Mémoire du MRAP*: unpublished manuscript.
LICRA/MRAP. 1987. *Les Actes du Colloque à la Cour de Cassation.* Paris: Proceedings from conference: Droit et Discrimination: 15 Ans d'Application de la Loi contre le Racisme.
Lieberman, Robert C. 2001. A Tale of Two Countries: The Politics of Color Blindness in France and the United States. *French Politics, Culture and Society* 19 (no. 3, Fall):32–59.
Lindblom, Charles E. 1959. The Science of "Muddling Through." *Public Administration Review* XIX (no. 2, Spring):79–88.
Little, K. L. 1948. *Negroes in Britain: A Study of Racial Relations in English Society.* London: Kegan Paul, Trench, Trubner & Co.
Lloyd, Cathie. 1991. Concepts, Models and Anti-Racist Strategies in Britain and France. *New Community* 18 (1):63–73.
Lloyd, Cathie. 1998. *Discourses of Antiracism in France.* Aldershot: Ashgate.
Lomas, G. B. Gillian. 1973. *Census 1971: The Coloured Population of Great Britain: Preliminary Report.* London: The Runnymede Trust.
Lyon-Caen, Léon. 1959. Le MRAP Soumet au Parlement Deux Propositions de Loi. *Droit et Liberté* (180 [284]).
Macridis, Roy C. 1986. Groups and Group Theory. In *Comparative Politics: Notes and Readings*, edited by R. C. Macridis and B. E. Brown. Chicago: Dorsey Press.

Mahoney, James. 2000. Path Dependence in Historical Sociology. *Theory and Society* 29 (no. 4, August):507–548.
Majone, Giandomenico. 1989. *Evidence, Argument and Persuasion in the Policy Process.* New Haven: Yale University Press.
Mankes, Michael. 1994. Combating Individual Employment Discrimination in the United States and Great Britain: A Novel Remedial Approach. *Comparative Labor Law Journal* 16 (no. 1, Fall):67–116.
March, James, and Johan P. Olsen. 1989. *Rediscovering Institutions: The Organizational Basis of Politics.* New York: Free Press.
Marx, Anthony W. 1998. *Making Race and Nation: A Comparison of the United States, South Africa and Brazil.* Cambridge: Cambridge University Press.
Mathy, Jean-Philippe. 1993. *Extrême-Occident: French Intellectuals and America.* Chicago: University of Chicago Press.
May, Ernest R. 1973. *"Lessons" of the Past: The Use and Misuse of History in American Foreign Policy.* New York: Oxford University Press.
McAdam, Doug. 1988. *Political Process and the Development of Black Insurgency, 1930–1970.* Chicago: University of Chicago Press.
McCrudden, Christopher. 1983. Anti-Discrimination Goals and the Legal Process. In *Ethnic Pluralism and Public Policy: Achieving Equality in the United States and Britain*, edited by N. Glazer and K. Young. Lexington, MA: D. C. Heath and Company.
McIntosh, Neil, and David J. Smith. 1974. The Extent of Racial Discrimination. London: Political and Economic Planning.
McNamara, Kathleen R. 1998. *The Currency of Ideas: Monetary Politics in the European Union.* Ithaca, NY: Cornell University Press.
Meehan, Elizabeth M. 1985. *Women's Rights at Work: Campaigns and Policy in Britain and the United States.* London: MacMillan.
Messina, Anthony M. 1989. *Race and Party Competition in Britain.* Oxford: Oxford University Press.
Miles, Robert. 1984. The Riots of 1958: Notes on the Ideological Construction of 'Race Relations' as a Political Issue in Britain. *Immigrants and Minorities* 3 (3):252–275.
1990. The Racialization of British Politics. *Political Studies* 38 (2):277–285.
1993. *Racism after "Race Relations"*. London: Routledge.
Modood, Tariq, and Richard Berthoud, eds. 1997. *Ethnic Minorities in Britain: Diversity and Disadvantage.* London: Policy Studies Institute.
Money, Jeannette. 1999. *Fences and Neighbors: The Political Geography of Immigration Control.* Ithaca, NY: Cornell University Press.
MRAP. 1984. *Chronique du Flagrant Racisme*. Paris: Editions La Découverte.
Muller, Pierre. 1997. Les Politiques Publiques comme Construction d'un Rapport au Monde. In *La Construction du Sens dans les Politiques Publiques: Débats autour de la Notion de Référentiel*, edited by A. Faure, G. Pollet and P. Warin. Paris: l'Harmattan.
Myrdal, Gunnar. 1944a. *An American Dilemma: The Negro Problem and Modern Democracy.* Vol. 1. New York: Harper & Brothers Publishers.
1944b. *An American Dilemma: The Negro Problem and Modern Democracy.* Vol. 2. New York: Harper & Brothers Publishers.

Nagel, Joane. 1986. The Political Construction of Ethnicity. In *Competitive Ethnic Relations*, edited by S. Olzak. Orlando: Academic Press.

NCCL: National Council for Civil Liberties. 1960. Conference on Anti-Semitism and Racial Incitement. London: NCCL.

Nobles, Melissa. 2000. *Shades of Citizenship: Race and the Census in Modern Politics*. Stanford, CA: Stanford University Press.

Noblet, Pascal. 2001. "Affirmative Action" aux Etats-Unis et Discrimination Positive en France. In *De l'Egalité Formelle à l'Egalité Réelle*, edited by M. Boucher. Paris: L'Harmattan.

North, Douglass C. 1990. *Institutions, Institutional Change and Economic Performance*. Cambridge: Cambridge University Press.

Ollerearnshaw, Susan. 1983. The Promotion of Employment Equality in Britain. In *Ethnic Pluralism and Public Policy: Achieving Equality in the United States and Britain*, edited by N. Glazer and K. Young. Lexington, MA: D. C. Heath and Company.

Omi, Michael, and Howard Winant. 1994. *Racial Formation in the United States: From the 1960s to the 1990s*. 2nd ed. New York: Routledge.

Paraf, Pierre. 1964. *Le Racism dans le Monde*. Paris: Payot.

Parikh, Sunita. 2001. Affirmative Action, Caste, and Party Politics in Contemporary India. In *Color Lines: Affirmative Action, Immigration, and Civil Rights Options for America*, edited by J. D. Skrentny. Chicago: University of Chicago Press.

Patterson, Sheila. 1965. *Dark Strangers*. Harmondsworth, Middlesex: Penguin.

1969. *Immigration and Race Relations in Britain, 1960–1967*. London: Oxford University Press for the Institute of Race Relations.

Paul, Kathleen. 1997. *Whitewashing Britain: Race and Citizenship in the Postwar Era*. Ithaca, NY: Cornell University Press.

Payne, Rodger A. 2001. Persuasion, Frames and Norm Construction. *European Journal of International Relations* 7 (1):37–61.

Peach, Ceri, ed. 1996. *Ethnicity in the 1991 Census: Volume Two – The Ethnic Minority Populations of Great Britain*. London: HMSO.

Pervillé, Guy. 1991. *De l'Empire Français à la Décolonisation*. Paris: Hachette.

Pierson, Paul. 1993. When Effect Becomes Cause: Policy Feedback and Political Change. *World Politics* 45 (July):595–628.

2000. Increasing Returns, Path Dependence, and the Study of Politics. *American Political Science Review* 94 (no. 2, June):251–267.

Pinder, John, ed. 1981. *Fifty Years of Political and Economic Planning*. London: Heinemann.

Political and Economic Planning. 1967. *A PEP Report on Racial Discrimination*. London: Political and Economic Planning.

Powell, Walter W., and Paul J. DiMaggio, eds. 1991. *The New Institutionalism in Organizational Analysis*. Chicago: University of Chicago Press.

Putnam, Robert. 1993. *Making Democracy Work: Civic Traditions in Modern Italy*. Princeton: Princeton University Press.

Race Relations Board. 1967. Report of the Race Relations Board for 1966–67. London: HMSO.

1972. Report of the Race Relations Board for 1971–72. London: HMSO.

1973. Report of the Race Relations Board for 1972. London: HMSO.
1974. Report of the Race Relations Board for 1973. London: HMSO.
1975. Report of the Race Relations Board for 1974. London: HMSO.

Race Relations Employment Advisory Service. 1994. *Positive Action: Promoting Racial Equality in Employment.* London: Employment Department Group.

Ratcliffe, Peter, ed. 1996. *Ethnicity in the 1991 Census: Volume Three – Social Geography and Ethnicity in Britain: Geographical Spread, Spatial Concentration and Internal Migration.* London: HMSO.

Raufer, Xavier. 1991. Front National: Sur les Motifs d'une Ascension. *Le Débat* (no. 63, January-February):91–108.

Rein, Martin, and Donald Schön. 1993. Reframing Policy Discourse. In *The Argumentative Turn in Policy Analysis and Planning*, edited by F. Fischer and J. Forester. Durham: Duke University Press.

Rendel, Margherita, and Geoffrey Bindman. 1975. *The Sex Discrimination Bill, Race and the Law.* London: Runnymede Trust.

Rex, John, and Beatrice Drury, eds. 1994. *Ethnic Mobilisation in a Multicultural Europe.* Aldershot: Avebury.

Rex, John, and Robert Moore. 1967. *Race, Community and Conflict: A Study of Sparkbrook.* London: Oxford University Press for the Institute of Race Relations.

Rich, Paul B. 1986. *Race and Empire in British Politics.* Cambridge: Cambridge University Press.

Risse-Kappen, Thomas. 1994. Ideas Do Not Float Freely: Transnational Coalitions, Domestic Structures, and the End of the Cold War. *International Organization* 48 (no. 2, Spring):185–214.

Rocard, Michel. 1990. Ensemble contre le Racisme. Paris: Service d'Information et de Diffusion du Premier Ministre.

Rodrigues, Peter R. 1994. Racial Discrimination and the Law in the Netherlands. *New Community* 20 (no. 3, April):381–391.

Rogowski, Ronald. 1989. *Commerce and Coalitions: How Trade Affects Domestic Political Alignments.* Princeton: Princeton University Press.

Rose, E. J. B. 1969. *Colour and Citizenship.* London: Oxford University Press for the Institute of Race Relations.

Rose, Richard. 1993. *Lesson-Drawing in Public Policy: A Guide to Learning in Time and Space.* Chatham, NJ: Chatham House Publishers, Inc.

Rousso, Henry. 1994. *The Vichy Syndrome: History and Memory in France since 1944.* Translated by Arthur Goldhammer. Cambridge, MA: Harvard University Press.

Roy, Olivier. 1994. Islam in France: Religion, Ethnic Community or Social Ghetto? In *Muslims in Europe*, edited by B. Lewis and D. Schnapper. London: Pinter Publishers.

Russel, Trevor. 1978. *The Tory Party: Its Policies, Divisions and Future.* Harmondsworth: Penguin.

Sabatier, Paul A. 1987. Knowledge, Policy-Oriented Learning, and Policy Change: An Advocacy Coalition Framework. *Knowledge: Creation, Diffusion, Utilization* 8 (no. 4, June):649–692.

Safran, William. 1989. The French State and Ethnic Minority Cultures: Policy Dimensions and Problems. In *Ethnoterritorial Politics, Policy and the Western World*, edited by J. R. Rudolph and R. J. Thompson. Boulder: Lynne Rienner.

Saggar, Shamit. 1991. *Race and Public Policy: A Study of Local Politics and Government*. Aldershot, U.K.: Avebury.

1993. Re-examining the 1964–70 Labour Government's Race Relations Strategy. *Contemporary Record* 7 (2):253–281.

Saguy, Abigail. in press. *What is Sexual Harassment?: From Capitol Hill to the Sorbonne*. Berkeley and Los Angeles: University of California Press.

Salt, John. 1996. Immigration and Ethnic Group. In *Ethnicity in the 1991 Census: Volume One – Demographic Characteristics of the Ethnic Minority Populations*, edited by D. Coleman and J. Salt. London: HMSO.

Sanders, Peter. 1983. Anti-Discrimination Law Enforcement in Britain. In *Ethnic Pluralism and Public Policy: Achieving Equality in the United States and Britain*, edited by N. Glazer and K. Young. Lexington, MA: D. C. Heath and Company.

Schain, Martin. 1996. The Immigration Debate and the National Front. In *Chirac's Challenge*, edited by J. Keeler and M. Schain. New York: St. Martin's Press.

Schain, Martin A., Aristide Zolberg, and Patrick Hossay, eds. in press. *Shadows Over Europe: The Development and Impact of the Extreme Right in Western Europe*. New York: Palgrave.

Schattschneider, E. E. 1960. *The Semi-Sovereign People*. New York: Holt, Rinehart and Winston.

Schelling, Thomas C. 1980. *The Strategy of Conflict*. 2nd ed. Cambridge, MA: Harvard University Press.

Schnapper, Dominique. 1992. *L'Europe des Immigrés*. Paris: François Bourin.

Schön, Donald A., and Martin Rein. 1994. *Frame Reflection: Toward the Resolution of Intractable Policy Controversies*. New York: Basic Books.

Sewell Jr., William H. 1992. A Theory of Structure: Duality, Agency, and Transformation. *American Journal of Sociology* 98 (no. 1, July):1–29.

Shepherd, Robert. 1996. *Enoch Powell*. London: Hutchinson.

Shklar, Judith. 1964. Decisionism. In *Nomos VII: Rational Decision*, edited by C. J. Friedrich. New York: Atherton Press.

Shrivastava, Paul. 1983. A Typology of Organizational Learning Systems. *Journal of Management Studies* 20 (no. 1, January):7–28.

Silverman, Maxim, ed. 1991. *Race, Discourse and Power in France*. Aldershot U.K.: Avebury.

1992. *Deconstructing the Nation: Immigration, Racism and Citizenship in Modern France*. London: Routledge.

Sirinelli, Jean-François, ed. 1995. *Dictionnaire Historique de la Vie Politique Française au XXe Siècle*. Paris: Presses Universitaires de France.

Sked, Alan, and Chris Cook. 1990. *Post-War Britain: A Political History*. 3rd ed. London: Penguin.

Skerry, Peter. 2000. *Counting on the Census? Race, Group Identity, and the Evasion of Politics*. Washington, D. C.: Brookings Institution Press.

Skrentny, John David. 1996. *The Ironies of Affirmative Action: Politics, Culture, and Justice in America*. Chicago: University of Chicago Press.

ed. 2001. *Color Lines: Affirmative Action, Immigration, and Civil Rights Options for America*. Chicago: University of Chicago Press.

Smith, Anna Marie. 1994. *New Right Discourse on Race and Sexuality: Britain, 1968–1990*. Cambridge: Cambridge University Press.

Smith, David J. 1974. *Racial Disadvantage in Employment*. London: Political and Economic Planning.

1976. *The Facts of Racial Disadvantage: A National Survey*. London: Political and Economic Planning.

1977. *Racial Disadvantage in Britain: The PEP Report*. Harmondsworth, U.K.: Penguin Books.

Smith, David J., and Anne Whalley. 1975. *Racial Minorities and Public Housing*. London: Political and Economic Planning.

Solomos, John. 1986. *Riots, Urban Protest and Social Policy: The Interplay of Reform and Social Control*. Coventry: Centre for Research in Ethnic Relations.

Solomos, John, and Wendy Ball. 1990. New Initiatives and the Possibilities of Reform. In *Race and Local Politics*, edited by W. Ball and J. Solomos. London: MacMillan.

Sooben, Philip N. 1990. *The Origins of the Race Relations Act*. Coventry: Centre for Research in Ethnic Relations, University of Warwick.

SORA. 2001. Attitudes Towards Minority Groups in the European Union. Vienna: European Monitoring Centre on Racism and Xenophobia.

Soysal, Yasemin Nuhoglu. 1994. *Limits of Citizenship: Migrants and Postnational Membership in Europe*. Chicago: University of Chicago Press.

Stephens, John. 1979. *The Transition from Capitalism to Socialism*. London: Macmillan.

Stone, Deborah A. 1989. Causal Stories and the Formation of Policy Agendas. *Political Science Quarterly* 104 (2):281–300.

Street, Harry, Geoffrey Howe, and Geoffrey Bindman. 1967. *Anti-Discrimination Legislation: The Street Report*. London: Political and Economic Planning.

Surel, Yves. 2000. The Role of Cognitive and Normative Frames in Policy-Making. *Journal of European Public Policy* 7 (no. 4, October):495–512.

Swenson, Peter. 1991. Bringing Capital Back In, or Social Democracy Reconsidered: Employer Power, Cross-Class Alliances, and Centralization of Industrial Relations in Denmark and Sweden. *World Politics* 43 (no. 3, July):513–544.

Taguieff, Pierre-André. 1987. *La Force du Préjugé: Essai sur le Racisme et ses Doubles*. Paris: Éditions La Découverte.

Tarrow, Sidney. 1998. *Power in Movement: Social Movements and Contentious Politics*. 2nd ed. Cambridge: Cambridge University Press.

Taylor, Paul. 2000. Positive Action in the United Kingdom. In *Combating Racial Discrimination: Affirmative Action as a Model for Europe*, edited by E. Appelt and M. Jarosch. New York: Oxford University Press.

Teles, Steven M. 1998. Why Is There No Affirmative Action in Britain? *American Behavioral Scientist* 41 (no. 7, April):1004–1026.

Thelen, Kathleen. 2000. Timing and Temporality in the Analysis of Institutional Evolution and Change. *Studies in American Political Development* 14 (no. 1, Spring):101–108.

Thomas, Elaine Renee. 1998. Nation After Empire: The Political Logic and Intellectual Limits of Citizenship and Immigration Controversies in France and Britain, 1981–1989. Ph.D. dissertation, Political Science, University of California, Berkeley, Berkeley, CA.

Thränhardt, Dietrich. 2000. Conflict, Consensus, and Policy Outcomes: Immigration and Integration in Germany and The Netherlands. In *Challenging Immigration and Ethnic Relations Politics: Comparative European Perspectives*, edited by R. Koopmans and P. Statham. Oxford: Oxford University Press.

Todd, Emmanuel. 1994. *Le Destin des Immigrés: Assimilation et Ségrégation dans les Démocraties Occidentales*. Paris: Seuil.

Tomlinson, Sally. 1990. *Multicultural Education in White Schools*. London: Batsford.

Trades Union Congress. 1967. Trades Union Congress Report. London.

Tribalat, Michèle. 1995. *Faire France: Une Grande Enquête sur les Immigrés et Leurs Enfants*. Paris: La Découverte.

Tversky, Amos, and Daniel Kahneman. 1986. The Framing of Decisions and the Psychology of Choice. In *Rational Choice*, edited by J. Elster. New York: New York University Press.

von Albertini, Rudolf. 1982. *Decolonization*. New York: Africana Publishing Company.

von Albertini, Rudolf, and Albert Wirz. 1982. *European Colonial Rule: 1880–1940*. Westport, CT: Greenwood Press.

Vourc'h, François, Véronique de Rudder, and Maryse Tripier. 1996. Racisme et Discrimination dans le Travail: une Réalité Occultée. *L'Homme et la Société* (no. 121–122, July-December):145–160.

Walsh, James I. 2000. When do Ideas Matter? Explaining the Successes and Failures of Thatcherite Ideas. *Comparative Political Studies* 33 (no. 4, May):483–516.

Weil, Patrick. 1991. *La France et ses Etrangers: l'Aventure d'une Politique de l'Immigration 1938–1991*. Paris: Calmann-Lévy.

1995a. *La France et ses Étrangers: L'Aventure d'une Politique de l'Immigration de 1938 à Nos Jours*. 2nd ed. Paris: Gallimard.

1995b. Racisme et Discrimination dans la Politique Française de l'Immigration: 1938–45/1974–95. *Vingtième Siècle* 47 (July-September):77–102.

Weil, Patrick, and John Crowley. 1994. Integration in Theory and Practice: A Comparison of France and Britain. *West European Politics* 17 (no. 2, April):110–126.

Weiner, Myron. 1989a. India's Minorities: Who Are They? What Do They Want? In *The Indian Paradox: Essays in Indian Politics*, edited by A. Varshney. New Delhi: Sage.

1989b. The Political Consequences of Preferential Policies. In *The Indian Paradox: Essays in Indian Politics*, edited by A. Varshney. New Delhi: Sage.

Weiner, Myron, and Mary Fainsod Katzenstein. 1981. *India's Preferential Policies: Migrants, the Middle Classes, and Ethnic Equality*. Chicago: University of Chicago Press.

Weir, Margaret. 1992. Ideas and the Politics of Bounded Innovation. In *Structuring Politics: Historical Institutionalism in Comparative Analysis*, edited by

S. Steinmo, K. Thelen and F. Longstreth. Cambridge: Cambridge University Press.

1995. The Politics of Racial Isolation in Europe and America. In *Classifying by Race*, edited by P. E. Peterson. Princeton: Princeton University Press.

Weir, Margaret, and Theda Skocpol. 1985. State Structures and the Possibilities for "Keynesian" Responses to the Great Depression in Sweden, Britain, and the United States. In *Bringing the State Back In*, edited by P. B. Evans, D. Rueschemeyer and T. Skocpol. Cambridge: Cambridge University Press.

Weisbrot, Robert. 1990. *Freedom Bound: A History of America's Civil Rights Movement.* New York: W. W. Norton & Company.

Welsh, Colin, James Knox, and Mark Brett. 1994. *Acting Positively: Positive Action under the Race Relations Act 1976.* London: Employment Department.

Wendt, Alexander. 1987. The Agent-Structure Problem in International Relations Theory. *International Organization* 41:335–370.

1999. *Social Theory of International Politics.* Cambridge: Cambridge University Press.

Wihtol de Wenden, Catherine. 1988. *Les Immigrés et la Politique: Cent Cinquante Ans d'Evolution.* Paris: Presses de la Fondation Nationale des Sciences Politiques.

Wildavsky, Aaron. 1987. Choosing Preferences by Constructing Institutions: A Cultural Theory of Preference Formation. *American Political Science Review* 81 (no. 1, March):3–21.

Wilson, Richard W. 2000. The Many Voices of Political Culture: Assessing Different Approaches. *World Politics* 52 (2):246–273.

Young, Ken. 1983. Ethnic Pluralism and the Policy Agenda in Britain. In *Ethnic Pluralism and Public Policy: Achieving Equality in the United States and Britain*, edited by N. Glazer and K. Young. Lexington, MA: D. C. Heath and Company.

Ziegler, Philip. 1993. *Wilson: The Authorized Life of Lord Wilson of Reivaulx.* London: Weidenfeld & Nicolson.

Index

For EU product safety concerns, contact us at Calle de José Abascal, 56–1°, 28003 Madrid, Spain or eugpsr@cambridge.org.

www.ingramcontent.com/pod-product-compliance
Ingram Content Group UK Ltd.
Pitfield, Milton Keynes, MK11 3LW, UK
UKHW010041140625
459647UK00012BA/1531